Christmas

From Doug, 1974

THE GREAT GREEN

Books by Calvin Kentfield

The Alchemist's Voyage
The Angel and the Sailor
All Men Are Mariners
The Great Wandering Goony Bird
Three: 1971 **(The Last One)**
The Pacific Coast
The Great Green

A Loose Memoir
of Merchant Marine Life
in the Middle
of the Twentieth Century
with Examples
of True Experience
Being Turned into Fiction

The Dial Press · New York · 1974

THE GREAT GREEN

Calvin Kentfield

Grateful acknowledgement is made to the following for permission to reprint from copyrighted material:

Encyclopaedia Britannica for material from its eleventh edition, 1910–1911.

Harcourt Brace Jovanovich, Inc., for material from *The Alchemist's Voyage* copyright © 1955 by Calvin Kentfield.

McGraw-Hill Book Company, for material from *All Men Are Mariners*, copyright © 1962 by Calvin Kentfield, and *The Angel and the Sailor*, copyright © 1957 by Calvin Kentfield.

Random House, Inc., for material from *The Great Wandering Goony Bird* copyright © 1957, 1958, 1959, 1960, 1963 by Calvin Kentfield.

Stackpole Books for material from *Memoirs of George Sherston* by Siegfried Sassoon.

Library of Congress Cataloging in Publication Data

Kentfield, Calvin, 1924–
The great green.

1. Kentfield, Calvin, 1924– I. Title.
PS3561.E534Z515 813'.5'4 [B] 73-10245

This book is for Jim Hamilton, Ken Lamott, Steve and Billie Ramsey—and for Mary Lindsay, God love her

Foreword

No one knows for certain how the world began, whether it was made or whether it made itself from energy or love, if it was a piece of the sun or the Word of God, if it rose from χάος or $E = mc^2$.

In the beginning, say some early Polynesians, there was Po. Po was a nothing without light, heat, sound, form, or motion; a nothingness like modern sophisticated Space which is defined, metaphysically, by the *Oxford English Dictionary* as a continuous, unbounded, or unlimited extension in every direction, void of matter. The late C. Day-Lewis said it was Heaven. Astronomically, the OED refers to Space rather poetically as "the stellar depths," those depths through which, according to Albert Einstein, a ray of light might travel for 500 billion years only to return to its beginning. Boundless, perhaps, but not infinite; Space—the boundless inane.

In the beginning, then, was Po, or, saith John the Evangelist: In the beginning was the Word, λοχος. Or, for the pastoral Hebrews by the salty shores of Lake Asphaltites, God, in the Beginning, created Heaven and Earth and the Earth was without form, and void, and darkness was upon the face of the deep.

The Deep.

In the beginning, whether the beginning be conceived by a first cataract Egyptian or a feathered native of the Mesoamerican jungle, there was always a Deep, an abyss of water.

The human mind conceives nothingness with great strain, if

at all; nothingness boggles the mind, but create some limits, a naked form, clothe the form in symbol, give it a name—call it Po—give it a number or a substance—water—then nothing becomes something and the mind handles it well and awesomely. And what among finite things is more awesome than the sea, the Deep? Most people, in fact, in the olden days of speculative thought considered the sky itself—Space, Heaven—to be another sea, another deep. The stellar depths. The abyss above.

The Community Book, the *Popul-Vuh,* of the Quiché Maya begins with a time when there was only Heaven (Space) with boundaries toward the four winds. There was no body, nothing that clung to anything else, nothing that balanced itself, or rubbed together, or made a sound. There was nothing below but the calm sea alone in the silent darkness.

The sea alone in the silent darkness became a popular image with humans attempting to say how the world began. Semitic peoples before Babylon created Apsu and Tiamat, sweet water and salt water. As for the ancient Egyptians, Max-Müller wrote:

"Usually the 'ocean' (literally 'the Great Green') is identified with Nuu (or Nûn), the god of the abyss. Originally he represented not only the dark unfathomable waters that flow under the earth and can be reached in the south, i.e. at the source of the Nile, but also their continuation which surrounds the world as the all-encircling ocean; the ends of the ocean disappearing in darkness and endless space, lead back to the subterranean waters. . . ." *If a ray of light travels through space for 500 billion years, it will return to the point from which it came.* "These abysmal floods represent the primeval matter from which all dieties arose, so that their personification, Nuu, is called the oldest and the wisest god who existed when there was no heaven and no earth, the possessor of all secrets, and the father of all gods and of the world."

In the year and in the day of obscurity and darkness, when there were as yet no days nor years, the whole world was a chaos sunk in darkness while the earth was covered with water. So believed the Mixtecs, the Cloud People of Sierra Madre del

Sur. Present-day geologists also believe in the evidence of vast seas that have covered parts of the earth, that have filled up, receded, and returned though neither they, the geologists, nor the Cloud People will undertake to say when or how those seas began. The geologists more or less agree that the newborn earth, whether it was conceived by Mother Sun from the propinquity of a passing star or thrown out as a nebulous homunculus in some monstrous act of immaculate parturition, was, at first, hot and dry; that somehow and sometime as the heat subsided, gaseous elements created themselves, hydrogen became hydrogen, oxygen oxygen, and when those elements compounded, they became water. Steam swathed the baby globe until its surface toughened and cooled enough for rain to form and fall. How long the rain fell no one knows. Long enough to fill the cracks and wrinkles and depressions of the heaving skin, long enough to fill an ocean.

Of the two billion years that have come and gone since that beginning, three-quarters of them have left no trace of life though life must have lived and evolved through those millemillennia—soft life, life without bones. Creatures with bone, even though it be only a bit of calcareous secretion, deposit evidence—fossils—while soft life becomes part and parcel of the ooze. Those first things, whatever they were, spawned by the sea, used seawater for fluid, for blood. So, with changes, did life that came after—hard or soft, crusty, scaly, feathery, furry. So did the Babylonians, the Maoris, the Incas, the Eskimos. So do the geologists, so do you and so do I. Walking sacks of seawater we've been called. No wonder that early examples of our human kind, far-flung and estranged by time, knowing nothing of each other or of hematology, but with saltwater coursing in all their veins, should conceive of the sea as their beginning, as the nothing from which something came.

"I should have been a pair of ragged claws/Scuttling across the floors of silent seas," T. S. Eliot's Prufrock sang. Perhaps he very nearly was a pair of ragged claws scuttling across the floors of silent *shallow* seas. For the abyss, scientists suspect, has always been a void, a nothing. Those sunless depths where prowl weird fishes, all fangs and headlights, is as much a periphery of earthly life as the depths of Space. Life began on the sun-touched shelves of continents that once were; soft plant-animal life that evolved through hundreds of millemillennia into diatoms and foraminifers, seaweed and jellyfish, sponges, mackerel, pythonomorphs, salmon, eighty-foot sharks. As time went by, rhinoceroids as big as houses thundered around Baluchistan; stupid six-foot pigs and horses with long claws roamed Nebraska; and other strange Cenozoic creatures wandered around Los Angeles where, near the corner of Wilshire and Fairfax, they frequently sank from sight in quick pits of tar. And as time passed, the earth, of course, quaked and cracked. Volcanoes reared up, blew up, wore away. A shroud of ice encroached from the north, and beyond its edges, the woolly mammoth and the giant saber-toothed cat abided until, except for bones and teeth and a rare whole corpse deep-frozen in Siberian ice, they vanished. The dire wolf came and slunk away into glacial dusk. Slant-eyed men from Mongolia invaded North America by way of Alaska (or so many anthropologists maintain); squint-eyed men with blond beards invaded North America by way of Greenland; black-haired greedy little men invaded Mexico from Spain; pious outcast men invaded Massachusetts from England; men from the East invaded the West; my grandfather renounced strong drink and Kentucky saloons and migrated westward to Iowa where, in Keokuk, he built the house my mother was born in and lives in still, not having moved a foot in eighty-seven years, and where, bye and bye my brother and sister were born. I, the youngest, child of progress, surfaced to the light and air in the hospital and, twenty years later, set out for the sea, for The Deep, for The Great Green, for the Possessor of All Secrets and the Father of All Gods and of the World. That's where I was heading anyway, but I took a long way around.

Contents

THE
GREAT
GREEN

Between . . . us there was the stewardship of the sea and also the fellowship of the craft, which no amount of enthusiasm for yachting, cruising, and so on, can give since one is only the amusement of life and the other is life itself.

"Youth" by Joseph Conrad

Getting Around To It

I had no intention of being a writer. In fact, I wanted to paint pictures, at least I thought I did. I was godawful restless. I was a prime victim of that gnawing, unspeakable and unnameable restlessness the young are possessed by if they are not possessed by paralyzing inertia instead. The yearning we feel at that age, the downright fear and the dismay with the species to which, we discover, we inescapably belong. It is a compound of emotions that Pascal refers to as Man's *embarrassment*. ("Man would fain be great and sees that he is little; would fain be happy and sees that he is miserable; would fain be perfect and sees that he is full of imperfections; would fain be the object of love and esteem of men, and sees that his faults merit only their aversion and contempt. The embarrassment wherein he finds himself produces in him the most unjust and criminal passions imaginable, for he conceives a mortal hatred against that truth which blames him and convinces him of his faults.") These things make up that cosmic restlessness which is also combined with native greed and a joy in the prospect of new places where no one knows who you are, far places, strange populations who have not yet found you out, continents unexplored, deep seas uncrossed, other worlds unravaged.

That restlessness.

Many years ago Dennis Murphy and I were sitting outside his grandmother's "big house" which he and his wife then occupied in Big Sur. It was early spring and late at night. I was young, but he was younger. His first novel, *The Sergeant,* had been a success. He had spent most of the money in Las Vegas, and he was attempting to write another book and having trouble, serious trouble, with it. He thought that perhaps I could help, could tell him something. His private trout stream, hidden in the little canyon above the house, made that wondrous night music of gentle water over stones. The Pacific Ocean, lit only by a sliver of a moon and some stars, lay black as a pit before us with only the running lights of a tanker offshore to mark the end of the sea and the beginning of the sky. The conversation went from agony and despair to violent words and gestures in the dark to heavy silences; and in the course of it all, Denny asked me his version of the ancient question, not "Who Am I?" or "What Are We?" but "What the fuck do we *want* anyway?" and I said, "Everything!"

A blank shadow, he paced the grass clutching his bottle of bourbon by its neck and laughing. Finally he came out with "Yes!" And he laughed some more and said, "Yes, yes, you're right, that's what I want. *I want ev-ry-thing!"*

Restlessness indeed!

The Second World War. Not since the headlong days of Manifest Destiny has there been in this strange nation such an uprooting and milling around, such a wondering and wandering confusion as took place during those years. Like the Black Death in the fourteenth century, that twentieth-century war wiped out the heads and heirs of families, uprooted the women and the young. Everybody moved except my mother. Some moved by order, some moved to keep a family together, some moved to get away from a family, some moved to make more money, some moved because everybody else was moving or because they were possessed of that same restlessness. Older people, who had never opened a road map because they already knew the way to wherever their lives were likely to take them, bought atlases and globes to follow the movements of their sons and daughters, cousins and nephews and grandchildren as they passed on darkened ships from one unpronounceable place to another across unimaginable seas. Domestically, it was the time of trains; of passing the time through Kansas playing poker in the vestibule; of crying babies and weary families without fathers crossing the continent in two seats of an icy chair car; of sex across the lap in the snoring vacancy of Wyoming. It was the time of damp terminals, duffle bags, belongings roped in cardboard boxes, KILROY on urinal walls; of changing trains in Omaha and sleeping standing up on the bus from Tehachapi. Places like Stuttgart, Arkansas and Dothan, Alabama entered the Midwestern or the New England consciousness for the first time. People in Sioux City spoke of Mare Island as if it were just across the wide Missouri. San Francisco was still Frisco, and mothers and daughters and grandmothers left their homes in Burlington and Bend and Tonapah and Webster City to emigrate to the defense plants and shipyards around Frisco Bay. Girls who had taken the College Preparatory Course at Guthrie Center High—with typing and shorthand on the side in case they should have to work awhile before they got married—became welders and riveters and boilermakers, living on their own, raking in the loot, living their own lives. Some folks said they never had it so good and wished the war would go on forever.

For me the war rolled on in the letters from my older brother, from my sister's husband, and in the newsreels. When I became draft age, the war, though no one knew it, was nearly over. Though I was in excellent, in fact exemplary, health—I was six-two, weighed 175, and, except for the baroque scar of an appendectomy performed when I was fourteen by a new surgeon in town, unmarked—I was slightly cross-eyed and, as a child, I had been asthmatic, so I was not a likely candidate for those specialized programs of the armed forces that required perfect specimens. But presumably, however flawed, I was draftable. I had enrolled at the University of Iowa at Iowa City only a hundred miles from home, and I was getting A's in the subjects I liked and F's in the things I despised. But I knew without even thinking about it that I would never last. Nothing made much sense to me, and the university people couldn't make much sense *out* of me. I was obviously a bright kid, but I was just as obviously strangely erratic, a homegrown eccentric.

Eventually, of course, the Selective Service called me, and since somebody at home, my scoutmaster or somebody, had told me that I would get a better deal from the Army if I had references, I asked the president of the university to recommend me. We had met twice before, once when I had passed through the reception line at the usual "tea" given for all incoming freshmen at the presidential mansion, and once again in the college barber shop while we occupied adjoining chairs having haircuts, so I figured we were not total strangers.

When I asked him, he smiled, but he couldn't very well have refused such an incredible request. Within the hour his secretary had typed up on official stationery and placed in an unsealed envelope a letter which began To Whom It May Concern followed by some lines to the effect that I was a good boy and undoubtedly had potentialities. His name was Virgil Hancher, and he is now deceased, poor soul, having succumbed in India barely six months after his retirement. When, in the course of writing a magazine article on the university, I interviewed him twenty years after the war, he remembered that I had asked him for that letter, the only one of its kind he had in his long career been requested to compose. I had also obtained a letter from Dr. Earl Harper, the unctuous, funereal, ex-Methodist preacher who functioned as head of the School of Fine Arts, a part of the university in which I had elected to enroll. He, too, complied, though in later years we came to thoroughly despise each other.

Naturally, the letters were of no use to me when I went up for induction. Standing stark naked in a long line of other naked men, I had no place to put them, and even if I had clutched them in my fist, I would have had no one to hand them to unless I had pressed them upon the medic who asked me to cough and inspected me for syphilis.

The Army rejected me out of hand when they found out I'd had asthma and was allergic to cats and coconut. My embarrassment was acute. I did not regret, however, being 4-F. Twenty-four hours at the induction center in Des Moines showed me vividly that my natural inclination was not to be a doggy; but three-quarters of the human race was involved in a controversy that, at the time, was considered to be crucial to its survival, and I was spending my time in Dr. Cousins' class worrying the profundities of *Pierre et les Écrevisses* and passing from one class full of girls to another making charcoal drawings of bowls and drapery and looking at slides of the Italian Renaissance. I loved the Renaissance, I still do, particularly the *quattrocento,* but under the circumstances it didn't seem to make much sense. During those war years time and classes were set forward and "History of the Italian Renaissance" was a seven o'clock lecture. I set my alarm for six, five o'clock normal winter time, rising while the stars were out. With the temperature at twenty below and an icy wind blasting down the Iowa River valley, I was compelled to cross the ice like Little Eva—the frozen river was the shortest way to the art building—in the pitch black to sit through a session on Paolo Uccello.

Well, I stuck out the year through spring, but in the back of my mind I knew I was heading elsewhere though my directions were vague. At the back of my mind was the sea, but the river was closer at hand, so I tried the river first.

I had been brought up on the banks of the Mississippi during the Depression when the landings of the river towns were still busy from time to time if a showboat tied up or an excursion boat—the *Capitol* or the old *J.C.*—came to town with its rolling calliope blasting away across the water and all the way up to our house on Billy Goat Hill. And the river freight traffic was heavy, the tow boats often lining up along the shore below the Rock Island depot waiting for a turn at the locks through the Keokuk dam. As I grew up, Swinburnean dreams, a Romantic nature, and some adolescent *Weltschmertz* possessed me on still moonlit nights overlooking the great stream.

> That no life lives forever;
> That dead men rise up never;
> That even the weariest river
> Winds somewhere safe to sea.

The sound of whistles round the bend, the throb of engines across the dark water.

Mark Twain, whose home country I shared, had died over a quarter of a century before, but Tom Sawyer and The Raft were still heady symbols for those of us who formed our early daemons beside the middle river.

(At college, one of my most successful smart remarks in undergraduate beer parlors was that T. S. Eliot, a St. Louis boy, never got over the fact that he was not Huckleberry Finn.)

So that summer, toward the end of the war, I took to the river which was a good enough idea except that I chose the wrong boat, a dredgeboat that quickly came to be known as the drudgeboat *Rock Island*. Because I confessed that I could use a typewriter, I was made a clerk. I will not detail the story of that boat here, I refer you to the appendix, to the short story called "A Place for Lovers in the Summertime" which tells the tale the way it happened, straight experience ever so thinly veiled as fiction. The point was that I was intolerably bored, so bored that it was a relief to go back to school in the fall though I was more restless than ever. After only a couple of weeks I was convinced that I wouldn't be able to stick it out particularly after a friend of mine, Raymond Parker, who eventually has become a highly regarded painter in New York, came back to the university to see old friends. He's older than I am, and he had left Iowa to go to sea as a radio operator. When he came visiting between ships, every pocket in his pants was bulging with money. He bought whole bottles of whiskey at a time, sometimes two at a time, and his duffle was packed with cartons of cigarettes, even Phillip Morris which was our cult smoke at the time chiefly because it was the hardest brand to find. And there was a party almost every night. At one of them he easily and skillfully maneuvered a French refugee, Marjorie, who looked like a Marlene Dietrich of the Midi and whom I had been cautiously dating and circumspectly trying to make out with since September, into the bedroom where they remained for hours. When they finally emerged, Ray looked cool but Marjorie was all wispy and distant and languorously disheveled. The party was a mixture of young teachers and students, Philip Guston was there, and Mary Holmes and her sister Sara Boutelle, and Buck Hanson and Robert Fletcher, and we all remarked upon the transcendant change in her. And though I felt painfully juvenile and an incipient cuckold besides—after all, I had brought her to the party—my admiration and envy of Ray were unbounded and I knew that, art or no art, I had to go.

I dropped out of school and went home briefly to Keokuk to put my thoughts together and explain to my parents my intentions whether I knew what they were or not. Though I was past eighteen, and therefore technically no longer a dependent child, my father, who was a conductor on the C.R.I.&P. railroad (Chicago, Rock Island, and Pacific), the Rock Island Line, managed to juggle some papers and get me a free pass on the train to California. My mother didn't want me to leave school and go so far away, but my father understood and gave me twenty-five dollars. Roosevelt had died that year, the bomb had been dropped, and the war was over. I started out for Los Angeles in the coach of a slow train. Unless he paid a surcharge, a railroad man or a member of his family traveling on a pass could not ride the crack fancy expresses such as the Santa Fe *Chief* or *Superchief,* the Union Pacific *City of San Francisco,* the Rock Island *Golden State Limited,* or the Burlington, California *Zephyr;* he rode the intermediate trains some of which, such as the *Grand Canyon,* were lovely trains; or he rode the locals. I spent a lot of time on sidings in Missouri and New Mexico while slicker trains went by, but I made it to California bye and bye with most of my twenty-five dollars intact.

In Los Angeles I looked up Mary Schlotter, a former school teacher who had abandoned Keokuk and her profession and moved to the sprawling jungle of Southern California to open an arts and crafts shop. She was nearly as tall as I am, and she gave me a place to sleep in back of the store until I found a boarding house. She also helped me find a job at Michael's Art Supply on Sunset Boulevard. Except for a girl named Sonny who was from Chicago and who was visiting her aunt and uncle in Westwood, Miss Schlotter was the only person I knew west of the Rockies and south of the Oregon Trail. Though she's been dead for years now, I still think of her as Miss Schlotter as I did in sixth grade though I called her Mary in Los Angeles. She lived behind the craft store near Wilshire and Western with a very fat young lady named Miriam who wanted to be a singer but whose natural lethargy nearly always overcame her ambition, especially in hot weather. Though Miriam had help from her aunt and sometimes sang for pay in some of the studio choruses, it was Mary who, from the meager proceeds of her shop, supported the bizarre little ménage of which I, for a short time, became a part.

Miriam whined a lot, and Mary was often very gruff with her. They fought a great deal and had very few friends since both of them had descended alone into the golden savagery of Los Angeles from simpler, friendlier locales. If I ever knew I've forgotten how they came together. Miriam did have an uncle or a cousin or something who ran a liquor store in Inglewood and an aunt who had for years been housekeeper for the movie director Raoul Walsh which gave the aunt, in her own eyes at least, a higher social standing than her relatives or Mary or me. Having retired on a handsome pension and having made some shrewd investments while in the domestic service of the Industry, she frequently took Miriam and Mary to dinner at restaurants on Wilshire or Sunset that they would not otherwise have been able to afford. And she made regular visits to the back of the store where she sat, bulbous and antique, by the kitchen stove with her hat on, cigarette drooping from her carmined lips, her nylons rolled, her horny old hands encrusted with emeralds and rubies and her fat liver-spotted arms dripping bracelets of gold—or what she professed were gold, emeralds, and rubies—and talked incessantly of her glittering life backstairs at Raoul Walsh's. She always called him Raoul Walsh, never Raoul or Mr. Walsh, and the people with whom she was, seemingly, in constant intimate company were always referred to by their full screen-credit names. She also criticized both Mary and Miriam mercilessly even suggesting one time that the way they lived together the neighbors and particularly the customers might think they were, well, you know what. Mary could generate murderous anger in a flash. (All of us in her sixth grade used to agree that she didn't get mad very often, but when she *got* mad, she *really* got mad, and many of us went home from school with swollen knuckles and stinging cheeks to prove it.) On this occasion she picked up a crock and slammed it, after a sliver of hesitation, into the kitchen sink rather than, as was obviously her desire, over the old woman's head. Miriam's aunt got up slowly saying, Well if they were going to act like that, if that's the kind of thanks she got, they could just take her home right then and there.

"All right," Mary said. "I'll *take* you home."

But the old woman sat down again and somehow the tensions were eased and sensibilities mended. They put up with the old woman because Mary was beholden to her for help, "financial assistance," in starting the shop; and because she was old and alone and her legs were bad so she couldn't get around very well and she was, well, Miriam's closest kin and—

I don't know what she thought of me, I tried to stay out of her way.

Mary sometimes put my 12″ × 16″ watercolors in her shop window hoping someone would want to buy them and to add a little up-to-date class to the establishment. Most of her customers were leathery old parties who painted sunsets on the ocean or dawn on the desert. Some of them became outraged at my modestly abstract landscapes. Mary loved to argue with them in my defense, but I tried to stay out of their way, too.

I don't know what I meant to those two odd women. Mary

would complain to me about Miriam and Miriam would complain to me about Mary. And sometimes Miriam would sing the Habanera, *L'amour est un oiseau rebelle,* rose in teeth and all, seductive wiggles and dark looks, and she had a lovely voice, but she ate too many gum drops and chocolate creams to perform Carmen effectively.

One night, against my better judgement, I accompanied them on a visit to Miriam's aunt who lived in that older Wilshire section of Los Angeles where the ground is flat and the ambience is rather Southern and slightly decayed with large houses set back from the streets and buckling sidewalks and big flowering trees along the curb. It was a terrible masochistic evening of us sitting there in the old broad's medicine- and cat-smelling apartment being bored by her interminable tales of high life at Raoul Walsh's. You'd think that no one in Hollywood had ever heard of beluga before she introduced it to the community through Raoul Walsh. It was Raoul Walsh this and Raoul Walsh that and fitted sheets and priceless rugs and monogrammed soap and Towle sterling and, Christ! when we emerged from the apartment into the warm starry night I felt like a kid let out of school for the summer. I said, "Let's *run!*" and I began leaping up and down on the sidewalk. "Come on," I cried, *"Let's run!"* So we began to run. My old schoolteacher, six-feet-two, past fifty, lumbering down the sidewalk in Los Angeles, roaring with laughter, and fat Miriam bobbing down the sidewalk in Los Angeles in the Wilshire district on sidewalks no one ever walked on let alone ran on, under the chinaberry trees, then into the wide empty street, all of us in the starlight, roaring with laughter.

And when we wound down and came to a stop, Miss Schlotter, her huge horse face truly convulsed with merriment, catching her breath, finally managed to say, "Cal, do you remember?" She could hardly breathe. "Do you remember when you were in sixth grade—"

"I remember everything from the day I was born," I said.

"—I was teaching you art."

"I remember, I remember."

"And you were supposed to draw a picture—"

"You taught us music too. We sang 'Home On the Range,' 'Oh give me a *ho-ome!*' and 'Flow Gently Sweet Afton' 'My Mary's asleep by the murmuring stream,' and you told us how Napoleon cut a door in 'The Last Supper' and you showed us Rosa Bonheur's 'Horse Fair' and said how Raphael didn't have any canvas so he painted the 'Madonna of the Chair' on the top of a barrel and that's why it's round. I remember, I remember!"

"Do you remember how mad—"

"I remember everything!"

"—How mad I was at you because you were supposed to draw a picture about a song and you drew 'The Man On the Flying Trapeze'—"

"*'He floats through the air, with the greatest of ease!'* "

"Only you made him bulge out in front instead of in back where his posterior should be, and I said, 'Look at yourself, you don't bulge out there, you bulge out *here*—' "

And she slapped her butt, gaining her breath. Miriam was puffing and listening and laughing.

"I remember, I remember," I said. "And you got mad at me because I drew a flower once."

Miriam, with a full lung of air, burst out with *"Ah! tu sol comandi amor."*

" 'What's a boy doing drawing a flower,' you said. I remember the flower, a simple sunflower it was, admired by all except you. 'What's a boy doing drawing a sunflower.' I remember."

"I didn't say that!"

"You did too, I remember. I still love sunflowers. I love them more than cowboys or airplanes."

"I must've been mad at the whole damn world that day. You kids never realized how lucky you were some days to get back home alive."

Miss Schlotter became, with some cosmetic and regional alterations, the character, Maude, in *The Angel and the Sailor,* a short novel I wrote several years after; and she became very bitter in her later years having suffered business failure "at the hands of the Jews" and the physical collapse of her mammoth frame. She died in loneliness, and poverty, and agony.

I met other people in Los Angeles of course. There were young people who worked at Michael's, all artists of one kind or another. And there were the customers who came in or called in. I often drove the delivery truck taking illustration board to the studios or dropping off orders of paint and turpentine and canvas into the hands of Harold Lloyd or Claudette Colbert or Lew Ayres.

And there was Stanley Holtzauer, the store manager and the sweetest boss in California. All of us, all the employees, were outrageous thieves carrying home paints, brushes, inks, everything. Stanley knew we were crooked but he always managed to be looking the other way when a studio tube of cadmium orange dropped into the pocket of our khakis. If I took off on a sketching trip, as I did frequently, hitchhiking up or down the coast or into the mountains, sleeping on the beaches, taking off on Friday and not coming back to work until Tuesday or Wednesday; Stanley would shake his head and scratch his gray hair and mutter something about young people being irresponsible, but when next payday came, he would hand me the envelope and say, likely as not, "Here, I managed to get you a few more beans."

On one of those trips I went to San Francisco and tried to sign up at maritime school to become a merchant marine officer, but one of my eyes still looked here and there in a wayward manner and they didn't want a cross-eyed mate. I took the night train back and fell in with another young fellow about my age who was clutching a portfolio of drawings. My luggage was my Army-surplus musette bag containing my painting gear and my 12″×16″ sketching block, so we admired each other's work, played some poker with some soldiers, and exchanged a few bits of personal information while the ocean went by. His name was Gregory Hesselberg, and when I told him I had just tried and failed to enter maritime school, he revealed that he had quit, only the week before, being a ship's plumber. He didn't know fuck-all about plumbing, he said, but he'd been alone in the hiring hall when the call came in for an instant plumber. The dispatcher had said, Are you a plumber? and Greg had said, Sure. Now he was pursuing painting and drawing again though he was seriously thinking about going to college to become a physicist.

When the train drew into Los Angeles Union Station, it was full daylight and, though I was supposed to be at work that morning at nine, when Greg said why didn't I come on up to his house for breakfast, I said, Sure. At that time the red streetcars of the Pacific Electric Railway still ran in Los Angeles though they have long since given way to smog-shrouded freeways. We took the streetcar to Hollywood, then we found a cab. Being at the end of my trip and having, as usual, lost in the poker game, I was nearly flat broke; but Greg seemed to have plenty of money. We headed up into the hills from Hollywood Boulevard and kept climbing almost as far as Mulholland Drive through what was then near-wilderness. We finally drew up at one of those new sprawling Southern California houses, low of profile with terraces and patios and a swimming pool. Once we were inside, Greg said, "I don't think anybody's up yet, you want a swim before breakfast?" I said sure. In the kitchen, hair wet from the pool, we had ham and eggs and homemade pecan rolls laid on by a round black lady of dour demeanor. Then Greg's grandmother appeared and a few minutes later Greg's father in his bathrobe. Greg's father turned out to be Melvyn Douglas neé, of course, Hesselberg. Greg had not told me his father was a movie star, and I realized he was watching with amusement for the shock to register on my face.

"This is Calvin Kentfield," Greg said. "We met on the train coming down. He's a painter. This is my father."

We shook hands and finished our coffee. Then I said, "I have to go to work," and Greg said, "I'll drive you down in Helen's car."

Greg's stepmother, Helen Gahagan Douglas, prior to her defeat by Richard Nixon in the infamous campaign that he waged against her in 1950, was a congresswoman, and she had at her disposal an enormous black vehicle with congressional plates. Greg had just passed his driving test after he had signed off the ship the week before. We climbed into the limousine, and Greg took the wheel and began to engineer our descent to the Boulevard. Because he had been driving such a short time he did not wish to appear overly cautious or insecure nor did he, given his own Far Left political persuasions, wish to appear to be intimidated by his stepmother's liberal-establishment machine, all of which meant that he negotiated the torturous curves of the Hollywood hills at screeching breakneck speed. Fortunately at that hour and in such a remote and exclusive neighborhood, there was not much traffic so we reached the Boulevard safely. Greg smiled at me, very proud of himself. As we approached the intersection of Highland and Sunset, however, the car ahead stopped abruptly as the light changed to red, and Greg rammed its rear bumper. Greg, who was nothing if not intense, leapt from the limousine wildly waving his virgin license, crying, "I've got one, I've got one!" at the bewildered driver of the car ahead, a lady who was herself intimidated by the Hollywood traffic, the horns that had begun immediately to blow, Gregory's wild behavior, and the imposing gunboat with the congressional plates. She apologized for pulling up so short on the stoplight, we surveyed the damage which was scarcely noticeable on either car—a few flakes of bumper chrome—and Greg calmed down and put his license back in its holster. The lady thanked him for forgiving her and drove off down Highland. Greg, still shaking a little, turned left onto Sunset and dropped me off across from my art store.

I was two hours late for work. Stanley scratched and muttered and said why didn't I just come back after lunch because business was slow, and I could take my bag home and shave and change. He was a real sweetheart, Stanley was, and we all took advantage of him. He knew it, but I think he was pleased we did. He had a wife in housecoat and curlers in a tract house in Van Nuys and a couple of lumpy kids he seldom saw and to whom he did not relate. The three of us who worked in the store were all young and perhaps talented, and if we weren't talented, we at least gave off an insouciant energy which he enjoyed and which he did not and probably never had possessed. He indulged us. Of course, he didn't pay us very much, but we weren't worth very much either. He had a sharp wit though, and he knew how to sock it to the studios for the canvases we stretched and the bushels of paints and varnishes and air brushes we delivered. He could make a scandalous profit and still have the studios blessing him for their professional discounts. And he had an uncanny ability to produce, during that immediate postwar period of dire scarcity, genuine Rembrandt oil colors from Holland, Fabriano papers, fine linen canvas, prewar stretcher bars, Winsor and Newton Series 7 sables and Designers' Colours. At that point in Hollywood history he was indispensable to the society portrait painters of Beverly Hills, the Industry, and the eccentric scarf-bound and bangled ladies who, holed away in art-deco grottoes in the Sunset hills, pulled in fortunes from their depictions of kittens and puppies and roseate nudes that turned up each new year on the calendars from Talarico's Grocery, the Tip-Top Market, and Dugan's Garage. Harold Lloyd loved him.

Gregory came by the store frequently and we spent a lot of time together. We discovered we had a mutual girl friend, Zaida, who worked in a bookstore on the Boulevard and whom we both took out separately with pleasure but without much sexual advancement. The three of us often went places together, Greg and I finding it amusing that we were both after the same thing from the same girl and neither of us getting it. We went to concerts and the ballet with the elder Douglases in the congressional machine, and we spent a lot of time at the vast remote house on Senalda Road, in and out of the pool, the ice box, and the liquor cabinet. We often got drunk or the hour got late and Greg didn't feel up to driving us home so Zaida and I flaked out on couches in the guest room. That was more than twenty-five years ago and I still remember the luxury of falling asleep on a davenport that was longer than I was.

Aside from Grandma Hesselberg's occasional reminiscences of life at home in Georgia, the conversation in that house was almost exclusively political (with a little show business for leavening). The three of us youngsters listened without comment while Mr. and Mrs. Douglas discussed the Truman administration and the mess in Sacramento. Indeed, when Mrs. Douglas spoke of political matters there was little else to do but listen. Very intense, she was, and very articulate. Years later, in an afternoon four-bit movie house on Forty-second Street way over near Eighth, I saw her famous film of Rider Haggard's *She* which had been fairly successfully suppressed after her transformation into a public servant. A hilarious and inoffensive bit of footage it was; and, though she, Helen Gahagan, movie actress, was very beautiful indeed, I realized she had been much more valuable to us all in politics which is something I can't say about other film stars who have more recently followed her direction.

Greg and Zaida, who were very very far left, could not trust themselves to enter into political conversation with seasoned professionals, but when the three of us were alone, they tried hard to militantize me; but I did not then nor do I now militantize easily, and at the time I was much less interested in politics than I was in art and sex and movies and books and hiking and swimming. I enjoyed talking to Mr. Douglas and listening on the edges when visiting celebrities of the theater and films came around. I liked hearing his criticism of Gielgud's *Hamlet,* for instance ("essentially female"), that he had caught on his last trip to London, or his description of a trip to Mexico when they had "pushed their way into Yucatán." Years later, I made use of him as a minor character—and of Gregory as a major one—in my novel *All Men Are Mariners,* a brief section of which I include in the appendix.

Greg and I took bicycle trips to Laguna Beach, made sketching forays into the Malibu hills, and once, while scavenging the local beaches, we insinuated ourselves into the Bel-Air Bay Club and spent the afternoon on the terrace drinking gin-and-tonics, swimming off the private beach, pretending to be members. It pleased his reddish mind to thus confound the establishment. I learned from him that he had not particularly enjoyed being at sea, except that, as a visual artist, the sea itself excited him, the architecture of the waves for instance, but Greg forever thought of painting and sculpture as tools of politics, a notion to which I could not subscribe. Though he never said exactly why, I put together from his remarks and from what else I came to understand about him, some of his reasons. Unlike me—who at the time was large and physical and who, in spite of the paranoia and morning terror that may have set in in later years, was taciturn and easygoing (though burning with the indescribable impatience at the core), and largely innocent of Man's wickedness, a kind of corn-fed Billy Budd—he was physically slight, excitable and vocal, enormously aware of, though confused and frustrated by the social and political forces around him. This was the time of the Truman-Commie hysteria that was so directing our national lives, a hysteria that, a few years later, burst out in the House Un-American Activities Committee's investigation of Hollywood that produced the Hollywood Ten and the defeat by Nixon of Mrs. Douglas who, so as not to be attainted, hid all her copies of Tolstoy and Dostoievsky and Chekhov and her recordings of *Boris Godunov, Swan Lake* and *The Sleeping Beauty,* and even the *Symphonie des Psaumes* though Stravinsky was an expatriate Russian. Once a Russian always a Commie. What Truman, Nixon, J. Parnell Thomas, and the crazy congressmen didn't know was that, while they were screaming about the Red Menace, a ship which I later spent a year on and which was originally christened the *S. S. Kettleman Hills* was, while being leased from the United States government by our friend Chiang Kai-shek, carrying crude oil and high-octane from the Russian refineries at Batum to Chinese communist ports while flying the American flag.

Greg loathed taking orders since he felt, justifiably, that his superiors giving the orders were in all ways, spiritually and intellectually, beneath him. Greg is crushingly bright and, in fact, he was always opening his mouth and getting into trouble. He'd pop off on some controversial subject (he held sharp and generally unpopular opinions on most of them) and some big primitive bozo would threaten to deck him. Like nuns. He had strong views about the iniquity of the Catholic Church in relation to The People, and one time he told me he had in the crew's messroom opened up on nuns and was almost clobbered by a six-foot bosun whose sister happened to be one. But whatever philosophical problems he had, he did not discourage me and the more he spoke of his sojourns upon the body of the Great Green, particularly the quality of the sea itself—the waves, the storms, the lights, the colors, all the wild elements that engage a painter's eye—the more I wanted to go. He never spoke of going ashore in perfumed ports and screwing beautiful island girls; almost all he could talk about were living conditions and the American imperialist oil octopus. O.K. I'd heard about the perfumed ports and the beautiful island girls from Ray, so I wanted to go; and one day I did.

I quit my job at the store and said good-bye to Stan and Greg and Zaida and Mary and packed the few things I had in an Army-surplus overseas bag and shipped it to New Orleans. My painting gear with a sweater, a change of clothes, razor, comb, and toothbrush, I stuffed into the musette bag and started off hitchhiking. The simplest thing would have been to go to San Pedro, which is the port town for Los Angeles, and try to get a job out of the seamen's hiring halls there, but I had no idea how long I might have to hang around before I got a job, *if* I got a job, and Southern California was beginning to get to me just as, in later days, New York would get to me after a while. The Manhattan syndrome I came to call the "dreadful island disease," but at the time I had no name for the Los Angeles malaise; all I knew was that I wanted out.

I had never seen the Southwest or the desert except from the night window of a train; I had a couple of friends in New Orleans, and it seemed only right if I really *was* going to sea, I should cast myself upon its bosom from the mouth of my own river. It was a romantic notion, but in those days romantic notions attained far greater reality for me than more practical, less poetical ideas. They pretty generally guided my movements whether I was conscious of them or not. This sometimes made some of my actions appear precipitous, illogical, and inexplicable to others as well as to myself. At any rate, with what little money I had, but with a great deal of anticipation of what might lie ahead, I hit the road heading east from Los Angeles, over the mountains, east to Palm Springs. Palm Springs was an expensive town even then, but it was still small and drowsy enough for me to sack out on a couch in the lobby of a little hotel without anyone taking the barest notice. A couple of years ago during spring vacation, thousands of young folk, descending upon Palm Springs with sleeping bags and knapsacks and, undoubtedly, a number of rolled joints, were hassled by troopers and police, and riots ensued. Times have indeed changed. The next morning I was the only hitchhiker on the road to Indio. The date palms are still there because they grow and bear to a prodigious age, and there are still some camels, and the people still dress up like Arabs during the harvest. (Arabs on horseback once upon a time delivered mail in Los Angeles.) The desert was a revelation to me, as much a revelation as the sea later on, particularly toward Yuma where the highway passed through great waves of scorching sand. Had it not been for the dozens of stalled Fords and Chevies, radiators steaming, alongside the road, I should have expected to see Victor McLaglen or Reginald Denny scouting for the *Lost Patrol.*

The heat was prodigious, stupefying, desiccating. Fortunately, the young man who had picked me up in his '42 Plymouth Six had been that way before and had, in Holtville, thoughtfully provided himself and, consequently, me with several quarts of Budweiser which, though it grew warmer minute by minute, got us through comfortably, though stinking with sweat, to Yuma where enough more of the same was effected to last us, stewed and glistening, all the way to Phoenix.

"I know a right dandy whorehouse in this town," my benefactor said. "Five bucks short time."

"That's a lot," I said as if I knew.

"Yeah, but they're American cunts, no chili beans, and clean sheets. You want to have a go?"

"I can't afford it," I said, truthfully.

"Shee-ut, I can't either, I blew my allowance on that guzzlin' beer. But I like to think about it."

"Yeah," I said, thinking about it.

He said he went to school in Tempe and, who knows, maybe he did. He was heading out toward Arizona State, but he took me to the north edge of town because he knew I wanted to go to Flagstaff.

Through the sagebrush and the cactus desert. And up, up into the cool mountains where Hoot Gibson and Tim McCoy chased the blackhats. Prescott to Flagstaff and over 66 to Indian Gallup and Mexican Albuquerque to Tucumcari where the *Golden State Limited* switched off Rock Island tracks and onto the rails of the S.P. Then Texas. A gray hotel in Amarillo with a bare bulb dangling from a twisted cord, dust-clogged window screens; but a shower in the bathroom down the hall, a shave, a change of tee shirt, underpants, and sticky socks. A ride from Amarillo in the morning to someplace like Childress or Quanah. A long wait, then a ride in a new Buick from a couple with a Mexican Hairless wearing a pink sweater and a rhinestone collar. The man, about fifty, wore a straw Stetson and a loose sport shirt that revealed a line of white shoulder beneath the creased tan of the back of his neck. His thirtyish wife, clutching the Mexican Hairless, turned full around in the front seat so she could face me. Her red hair, heightened with henna, clung to her skull in tight ringlets. Pancake makeup covered her face as far as her temples and the tragi of her ears. Beyond the pancake the pale skin of her jaw and neck was peppered with freckles, and tiny drops of sweat freckled her upper lip. She had the chicken eyes, the beetle brows, and forward-gaping nostrils indigenous to the region.

"Tyler and me never pick up hitchhikers because they might be murderers, but you looked so hot and lonesome standing there by the City Limits sign, I said, 'Tyler, he looks like a nice clean boy, let's give him a ride, he don't look like a murderer to me,' so Tyler stopped."

Her Okieland speech was softened and modified by what I presumed was a recent rise in affluence and social standing (the Buick, the Mexican Hairless), and by some modest exposure to education away from home. Abject snob that I was, I fell maliciously into the cadence of her speech.

"No ma'am," I said, "I'm not a murderer and I sure do appreciate you and your mister giving me a lift. I *was* gittin' pretty blamed hot and lonesome out there, yes *ma'am.*"

I really overdid it.

"My name's Eloise? spelled L apostrophe little l-o-u-i-s-e. L'louise. My daddy was French from Baton Rouge. This is my husband, Tyler Bartholomew Quitman."

(I'm not using their real names.)

"Pleased to meet you, son," Mr. Quitman said cordially, without turning his head.

"Likewise," I said.

"In case you're wondering I'm so young, I'm Tyler's second wife. His first wife, Mary Henrietta, passed away last Christmas of natural causes in her brother's house in Waco."

"I'm sorry to hear that," I said. "I've known a number of personal tragedies where I come from, too."

"We all got to go sometime," Mr. Quitman said.

"Tyler's in grain," L'louise Quitman said. "He made a bushel during the war."

Laughter.

(I was right. A recent rise in affluence and social standing.)

"L'louise, that boy don't care to hear about—"

"My Daddy always said it did his heart good just to see somebody get ahead," I said.

In the rearview mirror I could see Mr. Quitman smiling. Pleased, he said, "Quitman Elevator Company, Hockley County."

"Let me introduce myself," I said, giving my name and my address as California.

"Say hello to Calvin, Pepe," L'louise said, thrusting the little dog in my direction. "His name's Pepe and don't you call him Peppy because he's a *Mexican Hairless.*"

Tonsured and bug-eyed, the little beast stared at me malevolently. I made no move to pat it.

"I though it might be a Chihuahua," I said.

"A Chihuahua's a different breed of animal altogether," L'louise said, almost indignantly, "but a lot of people make that very same error."

"Isn't it pretty hot for it to wear a sweater?"

"Wrong again," L'louise replied delightedly. "It's not a sweater, it's a serape."

"A *serape?*"

"Pure Texas cotton. I crochetted it myself. It protects Pepe from the vicious rays of the sun, otherwise he'd get sunburned. They don't tan like you and me, you know."

"Oh," I said. "No, I didn't know."

Somehow, in the course of the next twenty-minutes' conversation, I mentioned that I was an artist and really let myself in for it. All the way to Wichita Falls, then, I got the interminable tale of the Hockley County Painting and Poetry Society of which L'louise was past president. There were eight ladies, she said, and a sixteen-year-old boy named Arthur. They were trying to get more young people interested, but it wasn't easy these days, she said. The girls were mostly interested in shorthand or matrimony and the boys, well, they were interested in what boys were mostly interested in. She giggled.

"Girls, you know," she said. "Isn't that what you boys are mostly interested in?"

"I believe," I said.

"Well, not *you,* I know you're an *artist.*"

"Traditionally," I daringly replied, "artists have been known to take a keen interest in girls . . . particularly naked ones."

Mr. Quitman bellowed though his face went red, and L'louise, past president, tried to remain coolly professional.

"Well," she said, "we tried using models at our Thursday meetings, but it's not easy to get anybody to take their clothes off in front of other people in Hockley County. Arthur posed for us once in trunks, but that didn't work out, he didn't have much of a build and his girl teased him so we went back to cow skulls and watermelons. The boys all think art is sissy."

Some of the ladies, she said, wrote poetry instead of painting; and some of them, like herself, did both. She then recited one of her poems which, blessedly, I do not remember except that it had something to do with "passion" and "wild horses 'gainst the sun." Then she said, "Why don't you come and be our guest tonight in Wichita Falls."

I could see in the mirror Tyler Quitman's ruddy face darken for the first time in disapproval.

"We're going to visit my mother and I know she'll have dinner ready," L'louise said. "And there's plenty of room. Mama's all alone in that big house, and we could put you up, and you could see some of the oils I hung on Mama's walls."

Quitman began to fidget in his seat and lean a little heavily on the wheel.

"Well," I said. "I—"

"Tyler, don't you think that's a good idea? I'll just bet he's got no place to sleep tonight, and such a big house and all."

I was desperate. I only asked them to give me a ride, not adopt me. Quitman's distress was as deep as mine. His wife was, after all, boring him as well as me, and I realized that regardless of what she had said earlier, I was not the first young man they had picked up on the road and invited home. Had not Quitman's dismay, flashed to me from front to back through the mirror, been so patent, I would have considered the invitation to be an act of creditable charity and kindness, but as it was—

"Aa, ma'am," I said, "I—"

"L'louise, I don't think this young fella wants to—"

"I really have to keep going," I said. "I thank you all kindly for the invitation, but I have to keep on going. I have to catch a ship out of New Orleens—"

"A *ship!*"

"Yes ma'am, a ship. I said I'd—"

"Well you sure don't want to miss your boat," Quitman said, relieved.

"No sir, I sure don't," I said.

Dusk was gathering as we approached Wichita Falls, but it wasn't dark yet, and the Quitmans insisted upon taking me to the far edge of town on the road to Fort Worth and Dallas.

"Do you need any money?" Mr. Quitman asked, and I replied that I was all right for the moment, but thank you very much for the offer. They turned around and went back into town, L'louise waving at me out of the window and waving the insectivorous paw of the Mexican Hairless at me as well. Though I could not hear her words, I knew what she was saying. She was saying, "Say good-bye to Calvin, Pepe." I know she was.

I should have stayed with the Quitmans.

I hung around the edges of Wichita Falls watching the sun go down, feeling a cool breeze come up. I was wearing khakis and a tee shirt, my hair was cropped short in accordance with the fashion of the day, and I was wearing white sweat socks and loafers. I could have put on my sweater, but I figured a ride would come along before long, and before long, one did. It was dark by then, and I stood visibly, but shadowed in the blinking neon light of a roadside café, a light that switched from red to blue to red again. Juke box music. If my memory serves me accurately it was "Cigareets and whusky and wild, wild women, they'll drive you crazy, they'll drive you insane;" but if my memory deceives me, it could have been " 'Way down yonder in the Indian nation, ridin' my pony on the reservation, in the Oklahoma hills where I was born," or, perhaps, it was neither; it doesn't matter.

Juke box music, flashing neon: CAFE, GRAIN BELT, PABST. I decide that I am not hungry. A car drives up. Two men debouch and enter the café. Which is also a liquor store. Two, perhaps three, cars go by, pass me while I wait. Eventually, the two men who had entered the café emerge, both carrying weighty brown-paper bags. I can't see them in close detail, but in general shape in the off-and-on neon, one of them is medium height and the other is large and husky. The car is a four-door Pontiac sedan, '39 or '40, dark-colored, dull, well-used. The slighter of the two men slides behind the wheel, handing his paper bag to his companion. I show up brightly in the headlights, and as the car rolls forward toward me, I can see the two men mean to pick me up. As they pull up beside me, the large man leans out of his window and says, "You lookin' for a ride no doubt. You lookin' for a ride? Git in."

I open the door, toss my bag in ahead of me, and scoot into the back seat. "I can sure use a ride," I say, and before I get the words out, almost before I get the door closed, the man in the driver's seat steps on the gas and we take off of the shoulder and onto the blacktop.

"We're going to Mexico," the big man said. "Right straight down to Mexy-co. Ain't that right, Dad? Ain't we going right straight down to Old Mexico?" He laughed very loud as if he had made a very clever joke.

The other man, Dad, the driver, did not laugh, but he said, "That's right, Son, that's where we're heading, Fort Worth and San Antone, and all's the way down to Laredo."

"Fort Worth'll do for me," I said. "I'm heading east from there though I'd sure like to go to Mexico."

The big man, who I could see was considerably younger than Dad, loudly paraphrased a line from the jukebox, "Chili-beans and tequila and wild wild women—"

"Shut your mouth, Son, and break out that bottle."

Son, then, reached down between his feet and, after some rustling of brown paper, held up a bottle which, when uncorked, gave off the familiar and aggressive smell of blended whiskey. Each of the men took a deep swig from the bottle then handed it back to me.

"No thanks," I said.

"Drink some whiskey," Son said, and I could tell by the tone of his voice that he would be deeply, perhaps permanently, offended if I didn't, so I took a swallow. It was pretty hot going down to an empty stomach, but it was not unpleasant and certainly not unfamiliar. Twice more this ritual took place, the passing of the bottle, but after that I was ignored in the exchange and I was just as glad I was. The flat fields sped by in the dark and some little towns as well. There was almost no traffic, coming or going. Not only did the bottle become private in the front seat, so did the conversation. I settled back into the shadows and watched the night go by, and I listened to what snatches of talk came back to me. One bottle went out the open window and another rose from the rustling paper bags and passed from side to side. Dad, the driver, threw up out the window without slowing down, and the car swerved into the opposite lane.

"Shit, Dad, where you goin'?" Son said.

"I'm goin' to Mexico, Son, lickety split," Dad said, wiping his mouth on his shirtsleeve.

"Well take the road, will ya? And keep the fuck outta the pasture."

"You buy any beer? I need a beer to warsh that whiskey down."

"Whiskey."

"No beer?"

"Whiskey."

"Shit!"

The older man straightened out and slowed down, and I could see by the way he leaned forward on the wheel that he was concentrating mightily upon the road. Their conversation became more and more *sotto voce,* punctuated with sudden bursts of loud laughter and covert glances back at me as if every now and then they remembered I was there and wondered if I were listening.

Appearing in the darkness ahead, a red glow gradually formed into a flickering sign saying EAT. Dad pulled up and he and Son got out. Son opened the back door and said to me, "Come on, soldier, let's eat. You hungry?"

By that time I was starving. I followed them inside and sat down opposite them in a booth. In the bright light of the café I could see their faces well for the first time. Dad was about fifty and son about thirty. From the look of their eyes and faces, and the stubble on their cheeks they had been drinking heavily and steadily and they had been traveling for quite a while without stopping to freshen up. We ate fried chicken and mashed potatoes with pan gravy, and we drank beer. When it came time to reach for the check, the two of them were giggling like girls over who was going to pick it up. By the time they had reached the cash register at the front of the café, Son had left a twenty-dollar bill as a tip on the table, and Dad was clutching the check in his teeth while one hand held his pant leg and the other withdrew from his tight Lee Rider pocket a wad of bills the size of a wrestler's fist. He peeled off one—a hundred—and dropped it on the counter in front of the florid gat-toothed woman who had come out of the kitchen to take the money.

"You ain't got nothing smaller?" she asked. "I cain't break up to nothing like that," a remark that sent Son and Dad into a dizzy, hacking, sputtering fit of laughter. Son danced and slapped his thighs while Dad leaned on the counter and went into gasping convulsions of mirth which spread to the cook-cashier who also began to laugh aloud.

"Well, give us a bunch of Grain Belt to take to old Mexico," Dad, recovering, said.

The woman disappeared through the kitchen door and reappeared shortly with both arms burdened with paper bags that must have contained a couple of dozen bottles of beer. By this time Son had stopped prancing around and digging into *his* jeans for *his* roll of loot. Flipping the greenbacks he finally came across another modest twenty. "You keep that, Mother," Son said. "I can't handle no change." Only then did I notice the printing on the mirror behind the Milky Ways, the Hershey almonds, the cigarettes and the LifeSavers. EAT MOTHER'S KITCHEN, the mirror, in big red block letters, said. We had done just that. We departed then, and, from the oil-stained gravel outside, I watched Mother for a brief moment through the lighted window. She was chuckling to herself, clearing up the dishes from the booth and tucking the other twenty into her apron. The light from within also fell upon the Pontiac, and I could see that it bore Oklahoma plates. I could also see into the front seat when Son opened his door. Lord knows where he put his big feet. Besides the brown bags of whiskey there was also a sawed-off shotgun and a submachine gun. There was a Luger on the front seat just like half a dozen I had seen brought back from the war. Dad, still the driver, slammed shut the door and turned on his key while Son plopped the heavy bags of beer on the seat and shoved himself in after them. I reasoned that, although I hadn't the foggiest notion where I was, I would most likely maintain myself in better health here with Mother than on the road with Son and Dad and all that hardware. I stepped into the back seat to pull out my bag, and Dad took off.

"Close the door, soldier," Son said. "You fall out and break your ass."

I pulled the door shut against the motion of the car and sank back, trapped, into the dark seat. I heard Dad say to Son that there was an opener in the glove compartment. I heard more paper rattle and more bottles pop open, then I saw Son turn around to me and shove a beer in my direction.

"What outfit you with, soldier?" he asked amiably.

I accepted the beer and replied, "I'm not a soldier."

"You're not no soldier?"

"Nope," I said.

"Hey, Dad, he's not no soldier."

"Shit," Dad said.

"You not in the service?"

"Nope," I said.

"Shee-ut, we wouldn't never of picked you up but what we thought you was in the service. Shee-ut!"

"Shit!" Dad said.

It occurred to me to suggest that if they were so disappointed in me they could let me out, but Son turned forward again in the front seat and said no more. He didn't pass me any more beer either.

A gothic hour ensued.

Shadows in the front seat, heads and sometimes profiles

lighted by the dash. A bottle passed from side to side. Giggles. Animated whispers that grew now and then to indiscreet proportions. Nudges from Son to Dad and Dad to Son and glances back at me indicating one of them might have gone too far in their reminiscences or spoken too loudly. And they had. Several times the word "bank" and the expressions "old bank bastard" and "fuckin' banker" came out loud and clear. And several times the shape held high before the windshield was not a bottle but the Luger. Among the sounds of caps popping and Dad gasping as he swallowed whiskey, I heard a cartridge clip being snapped home.

Silences.

Belches.

Some solemn, deep, and carefully guarded conversational exchanges. Nods of agreement.

Someplace in the black starless ends of Texas nowhere, the car stopped. Dad did not even pull off the road. I could not remember when, if ever, a car had passed in either direction. Son got out his side and Dad got out the other. Dad immediately began to throw up more of his chicken on the highway while Son opened the back door opposite me.

"Come on out, soldier."

"I'm O.K.," I said, maintaining a level cool in my voice. Son was standing on the shoulder weaving from side to side. One arm was cocked to his fly, and the other hung by his side terminating in the Luger. While one vomited the other pissed, and when they were finished, Dad leaned against the rolled-up back window on my side of the car and Son stood outside the open door on the other side buttoning the fly of his Riders and swaying to keep his balance, his legs set apart for stability.

"Come on out, soldier," he said, "and take a leak. You have to take a leak, don't you?"

"No thanks," I said. "I'm O.K. here. I'm O.K."

Son leaned against the top of the car, hulking before the open door, tucking the Luger behind his back as if he thought I hadn't seen it. He coaxed me.

"Aw, come on," he said. "Come on out and take a leak, you

know you got to, drinking all that beer. You pee in your pants if you don't."

There was, under the circumstances, some possibility of that, but I held tight to my bladder and my desperate resolve.

"That's O.K.," I said. I'm O.K. here."

They both stood there nonplussed. I sat hard in the back seat. I figured if they were going to shoot me they were going to have to splatter my blood in their own car, not in the absorbent countryside. After a short period of dead, dead silence with only the faint wailing of the prairie wind in the night, they got back in the car and we drove off again.

The bottle passed some more. Dad wandered all over the highway until Son told him to slow down before the ranger came along and picked them up for speeding.

"Oh, oh, oh!" Son exclaimed. Then laughing, he said, "Whew, would the shit really hit the fan."

Dad laughed too, but he slowed down to an absurd creep and assiduously kept his nose on his own side of the road. A minute later, Son turned back to me and said, "I bet you think we robbed a bank, don't you soldier?"

"You said it," I replied. "I didn't."

Some bright lights appeared far up the road ahead. "We better git some gas," Son said.

"Sinclair," Dad said. "I don't feed this baby nothing but Sinclair."

"Shit," Son said. "Look at your gauge. We got to git to the border if we have to feed it horse piss. Hold up now, Dad, pull over, pull over to the shoulder."

Dad, who was only driving about ten miles an hour, eased the Pontiac onto the dirt and stopped. Son got out, went to the rear, and opened the trunk. In a very businesslike manner with only an occasional stagger, he moved his arsenal piece by piece from the front seat into the trunk, except for the Luger which he shoved into the glove compartment. There were even more guns than I had seen. Finished with that, he threw out all the empty beer bottles, an empty whiskey bottle, and a couple of empty paper bags. Then he put the remaining liquor supply into one sack and put that in the trunk, too. Clean and innocent, he got back in the car, and we drove on to the filling station which sold Mobilgas.

Clutching my musette bag, I leapt out and bathed in the gorgeous bright light of the station like a parched desert wanderer bathing in shade. Gas pumps, Coke cooler, cigarette machine, oil drums, radio, road maps, gonfalons saying GRAND OPENING. Beautiful they all were, just beautiful. The bright new Dr. Pepper clock said half-past eleven.

"This is a beautiful station," I said to the attendant. My voice was quick and animated, a little hysterical. "You just opened, I guess, I'm sure glad you opened, I mean, it surely is a beautiful station."

The lessee, a short knobby youngish fellow in Texas boots, jeans, and a company shirt, looked at me and smiled then proceeded directly to Son who had stepped out of the car.

"Dad wants ethyl," Son said. "Fill 'er up."

While the attendant was squeezing the pump handle, Son took me aside and said, "Soldier, I'm telling you, if we git picked up—" He narrowed his eyes and bent toward me. "—I'm coming after you."

The line was so ludicrous, so straight out of the Hollywood I had just come from, that I laughed. "You've got to be kidding," I said, giggling helplessly.

"Don't laugh, soldier, I mean it."

He did mean it, of course, though he didn't see fit to explain how he could come after me after he was picked up; and I, feeling suddenly very secure with the lessee at my side and backed up by a posse of gas pumps and knowing the guns were all tucked away, replied, "Son, if you get picked up, it'll be for drunken driving not because of me. Thanks for the ride and the chicken. And the beer."

"That's O.K., soldier, just remember what I tol' you."

Dad got out then, leaned against the car, and said to me across the hood, "We're still a good piece out of town, don't you want to ride in?"

"No thanks, Dad, I think I'll just stay here."

"He's staying here, Dad," Son said, prudently turning his back on the attendant, as he withdrew his parcel of bills from his jeans. He skinned off a hundred then searched out another twenty and shoved the rest back in his pocket. He gave the twenty to the attendant who went inside to make change and he handed the C-note to me.

"You can use this, I bet," he said easily but without smiling, "anybody can."

I shook my head. As much as I could indeed have used a hundred dollars, I couldn't see myself accepting what I had good reason to believe was stolen money. Drunk as he was, Son took my meaning. "I get it," he said, switching to a threatening tone. "O.K., you jist remember not to forget what I said, you hear?"

I nodded.

The attendant returned the change, and Dad came around the front of the car. Dad was clearly fading. He put his hand on the younger man's shoulder and said, "If we going to git to old Mexico, Son, I b'lieve you better drive."

He dumped himself into the passenger seat. Son cleared his throat, spat, hitched up his belt, clawed loose the crotch of his Riders, slid into the front seat, shut the door, and gunned up for the border. I raised a finger as a gesture of good-bye.

"You should've stuck with them," said the filling-station man. "There's not much traffic hereabouts this time of night and I shut up at midnight."

"Naw," I said, "they're not going my direction. Maybe I could ride into town with you."

"You mean Fort Worth? I don't go to Fort Worth. I live jus' t'over the rise. I walk to home ever night."

"How far is Fort Worth?"

"Downtown? Twelve miles."

"Is there a bus?"

"This time anight? No bus. No bus atall, day or night. Trailways takes the other road. You shoulda tooken the other road."

"I didn't have a choice," I said. "Do you have a telephone? Maybe I can call a taxi."

"You can do that. Yes, you can do that if you get the lead out. They just naturally don't care to come all the way out here this time of night. You like my new station?"

"It's the most beautiful filling station I ever saw."

"Business is slow, but the town's bound to grow. Growing already."

"Where's the phone?"

"Inside. It cost me plenty to lease this station. I'm glad you like it. Here, have a Coke while you're calling. The number's by the phone. It's a new outfit. Veteran's Cab. They'll come out because they know me. Fred, he runs the outfit, we was in the 36th together. You want a Coke?"

"Sure," I said. "Thanks."

I'll skip Fort Worth. I looked over my shoulder frequently for a dark Pontiac with Oklahoma plates. I scanned the papers in Fort Worth and Dallas, but I saw no mention of a bank having been robbed or of robbers being apprehended. I suppose they made it to Monterrey or Juarez. By the time I reached Shreveport, I felt safe enough and no longer gave Son and Dad much thought. Greg had provided me with the name and address of his mother and stepfather who lived in a little town in Louisiana called Natchitoches (pronounced Nakatosh or Nakitish) on the Cane River, a dulcet bayou-like branch of the Red. Laid down by the French as a trading post in 1714, the town was an historical curiosity said to be the oldest living settlement in Louisiana. Greg's mother, Melvyn Douglas's first wife, who was a painter, resided outside of town in a small tidy house set in a broad green lawn. A pretty place, given that lush iconography of the South. Her husband, James Aswell, now deceased, wrote books one of which, *There's One in Every Town,* enjoyed substantial popularity in the early fifties. He was also, I found out later, an upstate politico with some clout. I hitched into Natchitoches from Shreveport. Though it was less then eighty miles, it took me most of the day, and a hot, sultry day it was, too; but the reception, coming as I did out of nowhere, unknown and unannounced, made up for all the cars that had passed me by as I stood sweltering and suffocating alongside that dreary, flat, dirty, cotton-country road. They accepted me as their son, showed me to the shower, gave me a drink of gin and some supper and a deal of pleasant conversation. Greg's mother even washed my clothes in her new Maytag. After supper they called in friends to meet the wandering artist. Most of the people were middle-aged professors and their wives from the local college (Northwestern State), but there was one contemporary girl from Shreveport who provided me with some amusement. She had thick legs and freckles and she wore hornrims, blue jeans, and a pork-pie hat, but she was jolly enough and she drank bourbon as if, as they say, it was going out of style. The more she drank (and they all drank—heavily, heavily) the louder her raucous laugh became, bursting into the long serenity of the Cane River twilight like a jackhammer. She had just graduated from Northwestern State and planned to enter graduate school at Baton Rouge in the fall. She invited me to come to Shreveport at once, or any time, because there was *nobody* alive in Shreveport, and she went *mad* there with her Mama and Daddy who had struck oil before the war.

"We're filthy rich, and we've got this big old house full of family retainers and a Coke machine. And a swimming pool full of sour mash from Daddy's distillery he picked up in *Tenn*essee, Ol' Gran'paps Galoshes, so you come on up, you hear?"

I said I would with pleasure, but I had to ship out on the Great Green first and see the world. I didn't say just exactly that, but I said that I was thinking about going to sea from New Orleans, but sometime, I said, before the pool dried up, I'd come around. I never did though. I've lost her name.

The Aswells' little house did not accommodate overnight guests so Jim took me into town and put me up at the one hotel, a fine rickety old country place on the main street by the river. I stayed two days and when I left, deeply marinated in gin and bourbon, Jim drove me to Highway 71 across the Red where he left me with notes to be presented to a friend of his named Bernie or Barney who was a reporter on the *Item,* and to the mayor of New Orleans.

"They'll do anything they can to help you," he said. "Just tell them I sent you."

I had friends of my own to look up in New Orleans, fellows I had known from a previous summer at Camp Mondamin in North Carolina where I had once been, at a more tender age, leather- and wood-craft counselor. Blake West was my particular friend, and Marvin whom we called Ding-Dong. I never turned Blake into a fictional character, but years later I met Ding-Dong by chance in Copenhagen and fell in love with his girl. That was 1952, the summer of the Olympic games and the summer that King Farouk absconded from Egypt for Capri. Gregory was in Copenhagen that summer with a new wife, and I put us all into a novel. Perhaps it was the only thing to do.

Blake's a corporation lawyer now, but he was going to Tulane when I knew him in New Orleans. His was an old family from, as they say in New Orleans, "across the lake" which means on the far side of Lake Pontchartrain, in this case, St. Tammany parish. Blake and Marjorie—Blake's very pleasant and very bright sister—lived with their parents in an old jigsaw house on Octavia Street on the river side of St. Charles Avenue. I bunked with Blake in that house while I looked into the prospects of the Great Green. Blake's father was a lawyer and a member of the oldest and most conservative clubs; and his mother was a joy. She ran a taut, elegant ship with the help of Alice, an ancient black lady with snowy hair and the muted disposition of Nora Barnacle (who was, you remember, James Joyce's wife and famous for her belligerent disregard for the sensibilities of practicing, unmonied writers).

Though Mrs. West was a very proper lady, a bit naive and pretentious regarding art, and readily shocked, she was so *kind* that I never spent one moment in her company without feeling I was welcomed and loved, stray wanderer or not. Such a considerate order prevailed in that house, an elegant regard for the true and solid amenities of life. No show, no fuss. Fresh garden flowers were brought in each day. The table settings were simple and polished as a ship's binnacle. The linen napkins were soft and old, perfectly white and perfectly pressed. The crystal shone. The Wests were not rich, not rich the way some of Blake's friends were who lived in flamboyant mansions with swimming pools and darkies padding the forest-green carpets of the halls; but everything Mrs. West had accumulated had been selected or accepted in regard for taste and intrinsic worth. This was before the days of planned obsolescence so neither that nor any philosophy as vulgar as conspicuous consumption had ever entered her mind. When she bought her Waterman fountain pen that resided on her escritoire, she bought it with the idea that it was a good pen, well-shaped, and would last her lifetime. I learned a great deal from her house about quality as opposed to money. Dinnertime, I have to admit, could become a little stuffy. Drinks could be mixed at five thirty, but they were limited to two; and though all my life I had been told to go wash my face and hands for supper, I seldom was required to change my clothes. But after drinks on Octavia Street, everyone changed. My duffle had not yet arrived by slow train from the Coast, so my wardrobe was limited. One time, in my natural uncouth manner, I came down to the evening meal in a sleeveless tee shirt; but, though Mrs. West was visibly shaken, her eyebrows darting up, she said nothing to me and I was served with consummate grace, naked arms and all, though Alice took a dim view of exposure. Blake told me quietly later that, though it certainly made no difference to him, I should wear long sleeves at meals.

With some of the other ladies of the district, Mrs. West was into a number of afternoon things, charitable things, and, briefly, at one time, spiritualism. From Blake's mother through Blake I first heard the story about the little girl who wrote with the hand of a dead sailor, a spooky gothic New Orleans tale that, after many trials and failures, I turned into a multilevel fable of demonic possession set in a deep snowy winter in the Middle West, a far cry from its original location in the fetid swamplands of the lower river.

And it was through a friend of Blake's that I circuitously maneuvered my way to sea.

I'll call him César because he was a kind of little Caesar and because he was a notorious young rakehell known to all of Uptown New Orleans. He was very young, in fact, younger than I was and equally restless. He drank indefatigably and was forever getting into what used, in polite society, to be called scrapes, little scrapes to be sure such as leaping off French-Quarter balconies while drunk, "disorderly conduct," climbing in and out of St. Charles' Avenue street-car windows and stopping traffic, pissing in broad daylight in somebody's front-lawn azaleas, involving himself in morganatic affairs in very wrong parts of town and getting the girls "into trouble." The usual things. His family was extremely well-connected so he never received more than a reprimand from authorities; but he had, in a few short years, driven his grandmother, with whom he lived, to despair. Since he had been left unlimited funds of his own, he subsequently moved out of his grandmother's mansion into a sinful-sex pad on Dauphine Street in the Quarter. His padmate, a native of Algiers (a hard-hat suburb on the west bank) whom I shall call, well, I'll go all out, I'll call her Gloria, was slightly older. She was not particularly bright, but she wasn't dumb in any usage of the word. She was wonderfully educated about human bodies, her own, of course, being exquisitely formed. Uptown and the Garden District were fascinated and appalled, and César was spoken of in subdued tones in magnolia-scented parlors between Coliseum and St. Charles. His grandmother received much sympathy, but what could she do? César, after all, had his own fortune and he was over eighteen. He was a very pretty little fellow with heavy dark lashes and wet lips, the kind of girlish stud that round full women like Gloria couldn't keep their hands off. Certainly her hands were on him every time I saw them together, and even when I saw him without her he was almost never fully dressed as if she had just left or was just about to come; and he was nearly always supine with a drink in his hand. Such concupiscence was, however, debilitating and ultimately boring. And, too, apart from sybaritic appearances, he suffered from a serious turn of mind. He worried about Mankind and Who He Was and Injustice and Adventure, so he left Gloria, shut up the love-nest, and shipped out as a wiper on a freighter to South America.

He did this by way of a whore named Marie who lived across the hall in the Dauphine Street apartments. She kept a couple of clever girls there, and she knew the dispatchers at the hiring halls, the Union patrolmen, a great many old-time seamen, some of the shipping officials themselves, and she liked to exercise her influence over old friends even if she had to apply a little friendly blackmail in a good cause. She, of course, adored César as every motherly female did.

In order to go to sea, every man (or woman) must have "papers" issued by the Coast Guard which has jurisdiction over merchant seamen. (Because of one of the odd circumstances of American history the Coast Guard, until a very few years ago, was part of the Treasury Department, having been instituted as a Revenue Marine by the First Congress. Its authority over merchant seamen was assumed during the Second World War. It is now part of the Department of Transportation.)

But the Coast Guard will not issue a man "papers" unless he has a "letter." A "letter" is a written statement from either a shipping company or a maritime union as hiring agent stating that they are willing and able to employ him.

Since nearly all shipping companies obtain their employees through union contracts, there are very few jobs a company can offer aboard a ship (purser is one). A "letter" from the union then is the only feasible way to the Great Green. So if César needed a "letter" to get "papers" all he had to do was tell Marie who said, "Go down to the hall and tell Moon that Marie sent you." That was the way it worked. (Marie, of course, could have been Charley or Joe or Blacky or Dolores, but in this case it was Marie.) Because I was a friend of Blake's who was a friend of César's who was a friend of Marie's who was a friend of Moon's, *I* got a "letter," too.

But before I did I went to see the mayor of New Orleans. We were both deeply embarrassed. There I was, jackboots and blue jeans, standing before his grand desk not really knowing why I had come. And there he was taking time out from a meeting of some board or other to discover what gesture he was expected to make to satisfy his old political buddy from upstate in Natchitoches parish. I don't even remember which mayor he was. I know he was an Irishman and not politically favored by Blake's family. After some fumbling pleasantries and lame silences, he finally said:

"Well, Mr. Kentfield, what *can* I do for you," and it was clear he meant, Tell me what you want and let's get on with it. Since I really didn't want anything except to go to sea and I didn't see how he could help me do that, I said that I supposed I didn't want anything, that I guess I had just dropped by to say hello.

He grinned an enormous politician's grin and replied, "I can't believe it. You're the first person to come into this office who didn't have his hand out for *some*thing."

He came around the desk, laid his arm across my shoulder and walked me to the door, clearly disarmed, saying how good it was to make my acquaintance, wondering, I'm sure, what kind of crazy kid I was, but adding, "If you ever *think* of something you want, let me know."

I liked him. He may have been outrageously corrupt, but I had never met a mayor of a big city before and he seemed like a nifty fellow.

I also called up Bernie or Barney, but he had just been fired from the *Item* and wasn't feeling like being helpful to some punk from out-of-town.

So I got my "letter" through Marie. A highly fictionalized version of that maneuver occurs in my first novel, *The Alchemist's Voyage,* in which Marie becomes Doris, "Queen Mother of the Deep," because, in such a heavily symbolical book, all names had other meanings and Doris in Greek mythology was the wife of Nereus, a sea god, and mother of the Nereids. A little of César, too, went into Bobby Blacky, one of the main characters of that book. And Moon was there. The real Moon had another name, I'm sure, but whatever it was it could not have been more apt, for his face was perfectly round and deeply craterous; and if we have now discovered that life as we know it cannot exist on that dead speck of matter revolving around us, we might easily have come to that conclusion years ago by observing Moon himself. It's possible that his implacable obesity could have warmed a tender soul, a finer sensibility, a mordant wit, a spark of some kind of human vitality; but the chances are very much against it. He sat at the door of the hiring hall like some perverted Cerberus, the three-headed dog who guarded the gate of Hell allowing anyone to enter, but preventing exit. Moon did the opposite. Anyone could leave but no one could enter unless Moon knew him personally or verified his credentials. Even then he would often trip the entrants or whack their butts or their calves with a cane he kept perpetually in his hand or by his side. He particularly enjoyed laying the hickory to the backsides of those he considered punks, meaning young neophytes like César and me. He, well, I would say accrued to his post as doorman to Hades except that verb is intransitive so I'll say he came by his position because of an old injury on shipboard. His official friends in the union, feeling sorry for him, set him up at the entrance to the cave. It was the old S.I.U. (Seaman's International Union) hall on Chartres (pronounced Charters) Street, and it was deep and dark and windowless. It was only three blocks from the Customs House where one obtained, if one had one's "letter," one's "papers."

Marie's influence was only as strong as the times. At that particular historical moment in the Port of New Orleans, shipping was "good." Ships were moving in and out of harbor with considerable frequency and several ships were being drawn from the war fleet to handle the increasing volume of new postwar civilian trade. Entire crews had to be found for these ships as well as replacements for ships in transit. Skilled men were in short supply, and the union was hard put to fulfill the demands.

César got his papers a couple of weeks before I did and went off to South America. I encountered Moon at the door, told him that Marie had sent me, and he bade me pass with a whack on the ass from his Public Health Service Hospital cane.

(Merchant seamen were entitled to free medical care at marine hospitals which function as part of the United States Public Health Service. And from olden sailing days seamen have been wards of the federal government. In a short story called "Sailor's Grave" I have a character nicknamed Mr. Solly [short for Solomon] say to his two companions, Davy and Blades:

"Well, you know— I mean, *officially* we are. Crazy, I mean. We are officially designated by the gov'm'nt of the United States to be officially *in*sane."

Davy asked, "What do you mean?"

"Well," Mr. Solly said, "back in the olden days, when seafaring was really rough—you know, before the unions and all—they figured that a man that went to sea was nuts. I mean, if he wasn't plain *in*sane, he wouldn't never of gone. So they made ever seaman a ward of the United States gov'm'nt."

"Can you beat that? Now, I never knew that," Blades said.

"Look it up and you'll see," said Mr. Solly. "It holds sway to this very hour. Jist like we was a maniac, or orphan, or minor, or something.")

As Marie had instructed, I went directly to the rear of the hall where the shipping board and the dispatcher's cage were. The dispatcher's name was Joe. He was a small, balding man out of Dickens, harried because of the shipping squeeze, probably dyspeptic, certainly dyspeptic by disposition whether he had an upset stomach or not. Obviously he did his best. He shaved every morning and changed his shirt, and he answered the phone with as civil a voice as possible when the bosses from Waterman or Delta or Alcoa called in and demanded an electrician, a plumber, two firemen, or five able-bodied seamen. When I told him Marie had sent me, he swore and said, testily, "Who does that bitch think she is?"

But he typed out the usual "letter" for me because he knew, wet and green as I obviously was, he could probably use me in some fashion sooner or later. I walked down the street to the Customs House where the Coast Guard examiners inquired of my race, color, creed, and national origin. They determined my height, weight, hair color, eye color and complexion. They asked if there had ever been insanity in my family. They counted my toes, thumped my chest, fingered my balls, looked up my ass, peered into my eyes and ears, told me to bend down and touch my toes. They also took a photograph of the front of my head and a print of my thumb. I was then told to come back in twenty-four hours to pick up my "document" which had become that week the brand new official term for "papers." It turned out to be a wallet-sized card laminated in clear plastic that said: U.S. MERCHANT MARINER'S DOCUMENT issued by UNITED STATES COAST GUARD.

An old-timey anchor decorated the lower lefthand corner, a four-bladed ship's propellor decorated the lower right-hand corner, and across the bottom in tiny letters appeared, just as it appears on Egyptian piasters, Spanish pesetas, Brazilian cruzieros, Tunisian dinars, Guatemalan quetzals etc., the name: American Bank Note Company, Litho. On one side or the other it identified my place of birth, citizenship, home address; and it said when I was born, that I was 6-2, 180, with ruddy complexion, brown hair, blue eyes. It gave my social security number, and a new number, the merchant mariner's number. And it authorized me, Z-864231, to ship out on any waters as an ordinary seaman, a wiper, or a messman.

(A couple of years later at the beginning of national Red paranoia when liberals like the Douglas's were hiding their Modern Library editions of *War and Peace* and Joe McCarthy was warming up to his life's work, all of us merchant seamen were required to deliver up our "documents" to the Coast Guard so they could check us through the FBI. If we were "clean" we got our "documents" back stamped VALIDATED FOR EMERGENCY SERVICE in big *red* letters. Though I had attended a couple of boring Communist get-togethers and proselytizing sessions disguised as folk dances in Hollywood, Mr. Hoover's men apparently failed to find me out and I won my red letters. Others did not. Noah Greenberg didn't. Noah sailed as chief cook or night cook and baker through the National Maritime Union (NMU) in New York. During that organization's internecine power struggles which pitted half-a-dozen political factions within the union against each other—some parties were anti-Red, some were Stalinists, some Trotskyists—Noah belonged to a *very* special little group called Shackmanites of whom I knew and still know nothing, in fact, I'm not sure I've spelled the name correctly; but obscure as it was, the FBI found it subversive enough for its taste and refused to validate Noah's papers. Deprived, thus, of his usual livelihood, he turned full time to his special love, the unearthing and performance of ancient Western music. He organized a group of singers and musicians that evolved eventually into the enormously popular and highly esteemed New York Pro Musica, a very going group even today though Noah, himself, a big expansive man who loved the beautiful and delicious things of life and who once told me, "There's no other way. One simply must live beyond one's means," dropped dead of heart failure a few years ago. So all lovers of Okeghem, Josquin des Près, and the miraculous Christmas performances of the Plays of Daniel and Herod can light candles of gratitude to the memory of J. Edgar Hoover.)

When the Coast Guard handed me my original document, none of this had come to pass. I took my card back to Joe at the hiring hall and received my next essential document, my "permit," a folded blue booklet detailing some of the same information as the other one and providing spaces for a rubber-stamp date that would verify my attendance at future union meetings. The "permit" afforded me probationary status as a union participant, but not as a union member though my dues would be the same. It takes years through legitimate channels to obtain the final, nearly irrevocable union document, "the book." A "permit" was revocable indeed, by almost anyone with the slightest authority. "Permitmen" were the peripheral work force. When shipping was "good"—a condition that altered dramatically often from week to week or even day to day —new permits would be issued. When shipping was "slow," the "bookmen" picked up the jobs while "permitmen" sat around and waited, sometimes for months (attending meetings and paying dues the while, of course), or sought out other means of employment or made their way by land to busier ports (New Orleans could be mackerel dead while Mobile or Galveston boomed).

Having progressed from the "letter" to the "document" to the "permit," I then signed the "register" and received a "date," which assigned me a place on the "roll." From then on it was a matter of making the "calls" and waiting.

Each morning for a week I rose early at Blake's house, went down to the kitchen where Alice would already have made thick, black, chicory-laced coffee and heated the milk for *café au lait*. Likely she would have made the grits, too. As I was usually the first white person up (though once or twice Mr. West preceded me), I took my breakfast in the kitchen. If Alice and I were alone, she'd look at me sourly and say, "How long you gonna be here, boy?" And I'd explain and re-explain my situation and intention. Or, as the week wore on, she'd say, "Lord, boy, ain't you found that shift yet? You gonna eat us out of house and home." If either of the elder Wests were present, she'd naturally call me Mr. Calvin, but she'd scowl at me all the same. She'd been with the family since before the children were born. Mr. West, according to the Southern form of *noblesse oblige* and benevolent white mastery then pertaining, had provided her with, among other things, a house of her own and put her son through one of the local Negro colleges. We fascinated each other, old Alice and I. She couldn't make me out, and I, coming from the North, couldn't believe I was in the living presence of such a Southern fictional cliché. She washed my clothes and ironed my shirts and cooked my breakfast and served my dinner and padded around grumbling and muttering ol' black mammy homilies; and though I adored her, I just couldn't believe she was real. And maybe she wasn't. She became predictably senile, poor old soul, in her old age, and she had to be replaced, but retirement was the same as death, and she died at home soon after.

In the aestival tranquility of those mornings I walked the

few blocks to St. Charles Avenue and boarded the streetcar that used to run along the grassy and flowering median strip of the avenue. At that hour the air was still cool, but the promise was there of heat arising as midday approached with perhaps a thunderstorm in the afternoon. A façade of mansions passed by the open windows and the scent of oleander came in with the breeze. Black gardeners and yard men with hoses washed down sidewalks and front walks and watered grass and beds of flowers against the impending heat of the day. Nearing the business district, the car became crowded with men in seersucker suits and shopgirls and office girls in crisp white short-sleeved blouses all heading for work downtown. For all I knew, I was heading that very day for the West Indies or Spain or Africa. At Canal Street I debarked and crossed the wide wet street (it, too, had been washed down during the early hours) to the mouth of Chartres. I always gave myself plenty of time to walk the few blocks into the Quarter to the hall, undergo the little ritual of identification and humiliation at the hands of Moon at the door, and enter in time to study the "board" before the first call at eight o'clock.

The "board" was a long blackboard above and behind the dispatcher's counter. It listed in chalked letters the ships in port, their companies or operators, the kinds and number of men required, the types of ships (Liberty, Victory, tanker, C-2, etc.), and, sometimes but not always, their cargos and destinations. A ship such as the *Steel Maker*, for instance, an Isthmian Lines freighter that made round-the-world trips, would always be listed as "in transit with general cargo," or Alcoa's *Del Norte,* a passenger-freighter, air-conditioned, calling at colorful, exotic Caribbean ports, would be listed in full as well. Such choice berths, of course, were virtually out of reach of permit-men.

On the other hand an old Liberty headed for the "bauxite run" into the snaky jungles of Surinam would bear no indication on the board of its cargo or its destination.

At five minutes past eight, Joe began calling off the listed jobs and anyone present who qualified could go up to the counter and throw in his card. Bookmen, of course, had first choice, and the oldest registration date got the job. (When a man paid off a ship he went immediately to the hall to register and have his registration date stamped on his card, then he went off to spend his pay, playing around or mowing his lawn or hunting jaguars in Central America while his card got "old." He was supposed to attend every meeting and have his card stamped to prove it, but there were many ways around that rule.) At the call, if no bookman wanted the job then the permitman with the oldest date could have it.

As much as I wanted to ship out, I decided at the beginning that I would not take a job in the steward's department or in the engine room. With my passionate love of the fresh air, the serene and violent elements of Nature, I would be a deck sailor or nothing at all.

Sometimes, if the board was full, the call would last half an hour, other times no more than a few minutes. Once the call was over, there was nothing to do but wait for the next one. They came every hour on the hour, except noon, ending at five, the last call. Most men left between calls, but I realized that in my lowly position, my chances were better if I stayed there all the time in case something came up in a hurry. Besides that, I had no place to go. I was stony broke. Blake slipped me a couple of bucks now and then out of his allowance which kept me in carfare and lunch, but I couldn't hang around local bars where most everyone else spent their time. Over the noon hour I'd go out for a few minutes for a hot dog and a coke, or I'd walk as far as the French Market for coffee and doughnuts, but I didn't stay long in case something came up. I read newspapers and magazines that were lying around, but the few chairs there were in the hall were straight and uncomfortable, and the light was poor. Since César had shipped out, I knew no one well. I often talked over what seemed to be the situation with others, mostly new fellows like myself, but customarily I kept my mouth shut so my ignorance wouldn't leak out and made myself as invisible as possible. That wasn't easy considering my size and the fact that I was often the only one in the room. Joe the dispatcher, grumpy as he was, must have recognized my position and my dedication, for he seemed to develop a kind of primeval pity for me.

Late on Friday afternoon my time finally came. An able-bodied seaman's job, which had gone on the board at the ten o'clock call, was still there after five. It was for the *John Ringling,* a Liberty, Alcoa. No other information. I had not thrown in for it because I was not qualified as an a.b. But when the job was still there after everyone else had gone for the weekend, Joe called me over and said:

"You shipped a.b.?"

"No," I said. "I've never shipped at all."

He knew that of course. It was a form to follow. According to Coast Guard regulations, no ship is supposed to sail without a minimum quantity of qualified able seamen.

"You can steer," he said.

I shrugged.

He looked vexed and impatient. "Well, you can drive a car."

"Sure," I said.

"O.K., gimme your card."

When he handed me my instructions and job form, he said, "This ship's sailing in an hour, can you make it?"

"Sure," I said.

"O.K., get the lead out."

I hurried down to the Alcoa office which was at the foot of Canal Street only a few blocks away and found that the ship had already left its berth for the downstream fueling station at Chalmette. The company port captain said we still had time. They were waiting for an engineer and a purser.

"Go home and get your gear, son," he said. "Where do you live?"

"Uptown."

"Well, get the lead out. Check back here when you get your gear and I'll take everybody down in my car. If we can find that fuckin' purser," he muttered as he turned away.

It was a busy time on Canal Street, the streetcars were jammed with limp blouses and rumpled seersuckers going home from offices closed for the weekend. I didn't have enough money for a cab, so I had to ride the steps of a streetcar. Those old St. Charles cars were like Toonerville trolleys or Mexican *tropicales.* If you were determined and agile—and I was both—you could leap on most anywhere and cling to your imagination as long as you didn't mind the seat of your pants being whipped by the azaleas. I leapt off at Octavia Street and ran to Blake's house. Blake and Alice were there but the elder Wests had taken the car to a cocktail party which meant I'd have to take the streetcar back, too. As I quickly packed my gear, Blake asked me where the ship was going.

"They don't know," I said.

"What do you mean they don't know, you clown. *Of course* they know."

Blake was planning for law school and his mind, more ordered and less fanciful than my own, usually reached the crux of a matter first.

"Well, then, they wouldn't say . . . *Shit!* I don't *care* where it's going."

I said good-bye to Alice who managed a grunt that said "good riddance," but then she smiled and said, "You come back and see us again, Mr. Calvin, you hear?"

I said I would.

Blake walked me—or ran me—to the avenue, and while we waited for the downtown car, I told him to say good-bye to his Mom and Dad and his sister, and he said he would, and he said, "Send us a message."

"Sure," I said.

"Put a note in a bottle."

I said, "Sure."

As the nearly empty streetcar clattered away with me, he stood at the corner between an elegant iron lamppost and a deep-red azalea. The unsmiling look on his face as he watched me depart was not one of envy—he was much too serious-minded to want to run off to sea. But he looked deserted; and as far as this narrative is concerned, I am deserting him though we remained friends for many years. As far as I know, at this writing, he is prosperous and thriving. One day, perhaps, I'll put him in a story.

Voyages

The *S.S. John Ringling*— S.S., by the way, stands for steamship, a fact that *you* may know but thousands don't. All oceangoing ships are not propelled by steam. The M/V of *M/V Arcadian,* for instance, means motor vessel, or it could be MS, motor ship, indicating a ship run by internal-combustion engines like an automobile, or that costly eccentricity, the *Nuclear Ship Savannah.* We live in the AAA which not only means the American Automobile Association but also the Age of Abbreviations and Acronyms so some things must be explained or we become needlessly confused. From time to time I will explain certain terms, and if you find yourself familiar with them, please bear with those less specially informed readers to whom they may be a foreign language.

The *S.S. John Ringling,* a wartime Liberty ship, was built, if I remember correctly, in 1944 at the shipyards in Pascagoula, Mississippi. Liberties were named for prominent civilian Americans (other than Presidents), but so many had been built by '44 and '45 that the war shipping administration was groping for new names thus accounting for such unlikely maritime identities as John Ringling, Joseph Smith, and Henry Ward Beecher.

(Chevron Shipping Company, the maritime transportation arm of Standard Oil of California, with deadpan deference to corporate success, names many of its tankers after its own presidents or chairmen of the board; so that Mr. Lombardi, spinning out his days in solid-gold retirement in Marin county has the deep satisfaction of knowing that year after year his name is plying the great Pacific and falling commonly from the tongues of Honolulu executives, French colonials, Tahitian natives, Alaskan Eskimos. Who says men work for power alone, or money!

This reminds me of a true story that I will insert here. Some members of the board of a large New York corporation, whom I shall not identify, bought a Liberty ship from the United States government for reasons that were never revealed. If they had any intention of putting it into service, they never did; but they had to *keep* it someplace so they moored it in the Hudson near the George Washington Bridge. As it bore the corporate name and thus represented the corporate image, a permanent crew was hired to maintain it, to chip its rust and paint its stack and bulkheads just as if it were plowing the Great Green. None of its owners ever visited the ship, but, apparently, they liked knowing it was there. The crew spent most of its time drinking coffee, playing cards, and watching television because all they had to do was paint and scrub one side, the side toward the bridge, so the owners, when they crossed over on their way to or from their homes in Teaneck or Tenafly or to Upstate vacations could be proud of how bright and beautiful it was. So for years one side shone while the rest fell into a state of rust and corruption—I suppose there's a lesson there.)

If, during the war, a Liberty ship was able to safely deliver one cargo to the troops and allies abroad, it was considered to have been worth its cost. Many of them, of course, could not do that. Some were sunk in the North Atlantic or on their way to Australia. And many were sunk on the dreaded Murmansk run, the frigid voyage to Russia over the top of Norway through the Arctic Ocean, the Barents Sea, where the water was so cold that no torpedoed man, life jacket or not, could stay alive in it more than a few minutes. And many were sunk in the warm waters of the Gulf of Mexico by German submarines lying below New Orleans off the narrow Southwest Pass of the Mississippi delta. Seamen were shanghaied by the dozens, knocked on the head on the streets of New York and Baltimore and Newport News and fed Mickeys in the bars of Staten Island and the French Quarter and dragged aboard the Liberties making those runs. Their pay, of course, was glamorous if they survived.

Countless Liberties completed their single runs and many many more. Thirty years later some are still running, decrepit and criminally unsafe, under Greek, Panamanian, or Taiwanese flags. The war in Indochina brought dozens of them out of mothballs to carry Budweiser and Marlboros and Franco-American spaghetti to Saigon and Da Nang. They were good ships though many of them had a tendency at first to break in half under stress. Seamen called them "floating cigars" and "floating weenies" because they were almost all cargo space and they looked, when they were fully loaded, like a Roi-Tan or a fat hot dog with an absolute minimum of housing on top; and like any overstuffed sausage, the skin was prone to split. When so many of them did that, after so much cargo was lost and so many men were drowned or left bobbing on the waves clinging to half a ship (the crucial cracking place was just forward of the midship house), the shipbuilders began taping them together with long steel Band-Aids welded to the decks or along the sides.

The *John Ringling* was a taped-up ship, and when I joined it, she had just come out of the yard. (Here's a dilemma. Romantic seafaring tradition dictates that ships are feminine and referred to as "she," but it seems foolish to say she to a ship named John, yet the habit is there so if I alternate between "she" and "it"—no one's ever called a ship "he"—I hope you'll understand.) It was under lease from the United States government to Alcoa Shipping Company, the maritime division of the Aluminum Company of America and its co-corporation, the Aluminium Company of Canada, Ltd. It was not surprising, then, that it was being readied for the bauxite run.

It was rusty and run-down but being fairly new and undamaged by the war, it was basically sound. A shipyard crew had done her up in Alcoa colors—silver (aluminum) and gray with white housing and a red, white, and blue stack (short for smokestack or funnel). The rest of the maintenance would be up to the crew on the voyage outward bound. The bauxite run meant transporting general cargo to Venezuela and bringing bauxite back to the United States or Canada from the jungles of British Guiana or Surinam.

I learned this from the port captain while he was driving us from New Orleans down to Chalmette where there's an Esso fueling dock, a Kaiser aluminum plant, and a national historical park commemorating the Battle of New Orleans.

A port captain is a master mariner employed by the company to handle deck crew problems ashore. (There is also a port engineer for the engine department and a port steward for the steward's department.) In this case the port captain was transporting one last bogus able-bodied seaman (me), a third-assistant engineer, and a last-minute purser to a ship that was already loaded and on its way.

None of us had been on a bauxite run; and the port captain, part of whose function is public relations between company and crew, sought to allay any apprehensions we might have. I had none because I was beautifully ignorant. I didn't know bow from stern let alone entertain concern about something called bauxite. The purser, however, and the engineer were far more knowledgeable than I. They were the ones the port captain was addressing.

"It's not nearly as bad as they say," he said. "It gets a little hot sometimes, but—"

I didn't know what he was talking about, but the purser whom they must have hauled straight out of a Bourbon Street bar and who shook continuously and may actually have been hallucinating, knew perfectly well and so did the engineer, but engineers are sturdy unemotional fellows who just do their jobs, and, after all, it's *always* hot in the engine room.

"Shit!" said the port captain. "Wye, that bauxite's not bad neither."

A little scholarly research establishes bauxite as the chief source of aluminum ore, and in the South American tropics it is heavily mixed with laterite and iron oxides. It is named for the picturesque and salubrious medieval village of Les Baux in the Provençal hills where it was, presumably, either discovered or first identified. It also occurs in Northern Ireland in county Antrim, in Georgia (U.S.A.), in Arkansas (Bauxite, Ark.) and in the old duchy of Carniola which is now part of the Yugoslavian alps. There it was called *wocheinite* after Lake Wochein near the town that was, in the Austro-Hungarian empire, Radsmannsdorf but is now Radovljica. From this extensive material many things are extracted, but chiefly, by way of aluminum hydrate or sulfate come Boeing 747's and recyclable beer cans. It is not a rock, exactly, more of an earth, and in the jungles of Guiana kilns have been built to dry it for shipment. In my novel, *The Alchemist's Voyage,* which is heavily based upon this first trip in the *John Ringling,* is this description of the loading of bauxite:

"The seamen themselves were busy that afternoon, readying the vessel for the cargo of bauxite which, fine and pink as ladies' face powder, would be dumped into the holds with vicious abandon by a monstrous scuttle named by the sailors, Dirty Dick."

(In truth, Dirty Dick was the huge shovel at Port-of-Spain in Trinidad where ships on the bauxite shuttle between that island and the jungle unloaded or "topped off." Because of the depth of the jungle rivers, it was not possible for a Liberty ship to take a full load at one time, so Trinidad and Dirty Dick became the way station.)

"Every oiled mechanism had to be covered, every hatch, porthole, and door dogged tight against it. At the last minute at the kilns the crew would seal their rooms to try to defeat the insidious dust. Still it would sift like snow through the cracks, get into their food

("What's this we have here?"
"That's proached eggs boxite."

"And what's this we have here?"
"That's boxite stew."
"And here?"
"That's fillit of mackral with drawn boxite."),

steal into their lockered clothes and into their lungs. It would cling to their shoes and track the passageways, work into the flaking decks, and if rain should fall, the ore in solution would gush from the scuppers in ruddy streams, staining the vessel's silver-colored sides. Indeed, if Man was made from dust, that must have been the very stuff. When dry it had the hue of flesh, when wet the color of blood. It was not mined, it was merely scooped up. It was the very earth of the fruitful, peacefully sunny forest where the strange birds sang, the blossoms spread themselves for no man's eyes, and the monkey hung by his tail in the breezy top of the paste tree.

"Would it be so hard to stoop and take a handful and make a man of it?"

The port captain mentioned none of this and I wouldn't have cared if he had. I had a place on a ship, and I was scared and happy.

There was no gangway out at the bunker dock at Chalmette, only a Jacob's ladder so we sent our gear up on a heaving line. (Bunker is a ship's term that refers to fuel tanks and in the case of bunker oil, the fuel itself. It was bunker oil that spilled out by the thousands of barrels into San Francisco Bay and washed in on the coast when two Standard Oil tankers collided in the fog in 1971. A heaving line is a small tough rope about the size of a clothesline though made of hemp, not plastic or cotton, and perhaps seventy-five feet long with a monkey fist on one end. And a monkey fist is an iron weight, usually a steel bearing, slightly smaller than a tennis ball covered with a Turk's head, and a Turk's head is a weaving of small rope that put sailors a long time ago in mind of a turban.)

The first purpose of the heaving line is for dock workers to haul the ship's heavy mooring lines ashore. As the ship moves toward the dock, a sailor on deck, usually an a.b., heaves the line to the pier. The weight of the monkey fist spreads the line out so the dock worker can grasp it. The sailor ties his end to the eye of the ship's hawser or mooring line which the dock workers then pull ashore and slip over the docking bitts. Heaving lines demand a good deal of attention. They must be kept in top condition, they should be of the very best manila fiber, and only the chintziest companies such as Standard Oil will try to cut costs on heaving lines. The ordinary seaman of the watch is required, after the docking or undocking procedure, to retrieve the lines (in poor or unscrupulous nations, dock workers frequently steal them), make them up into neat coils without snarls—or, as seamen say, assholes—and stow them safely and neatly away. The ordinary, however, is seldom allowed to *heave* the heaving line since that is customarily the privileged function of the a.b. who is presumed to be a skilled worker.

I was supposed to be that very skilled worker, that able-bodied seaman, and I didn't know a heaving line from a hawser. I had either to confess my abject ignorance to someone in command or to fake it. Since I was, and am, poor at dissembling, I chose to come clean. Fortunately the fellow who tossed us the heaving line for our gear was a young man about my age whom I had spoken to in the hiring hall. His name was Dave and he recognized me. Though he had been sent aboard as an ordinary, he actually possessed an a.b.'s endorsement. I was an ordinary sent aboard as an a.b.. As that situation seemed perverse, we found the chief mate and presented him with the situation. He agreed we should switch jobs, and though, with that simple decision, I took an instantaneous cut in pay, I felt more secure and at ease because, as I very quickly discovered, an ordinary seaman is expected, indeed assumed, to know absolutely nothing.

Dave, himself, had come aboard only that morning. Our change of jobs put us both on the same watch, the eight-to-twelve. Sea watches had already been set, and before I had time, even, to stow my gear, all hands were called to let go the lines. I had missed supper, but once we were on our way downstream, I made a baloney and cheese sandwich from the night lunch and drank some coffee. By the time I had eaten, unpacked my clothes, and made up my bunk, it was time to go on watch. Dave told me what to do, and I had enough sense to keep my mouth shut and my eyes and ears open.

Since the advent of union strength and labor reforms in the thirties, the twenty-four hours of a seagoing day have been divided on American ships into six watches of four hours each in the deck and engine departments. (The steward department, the third division of a ship's crew, does not stand watches and keeps a different schedule as do day workers such as carpenters, deck maintenances, electricians, plumbers, bosuns, etc. Incidentally, *bosun* is the spoken variant of boatswain, an oldtime word, and not of boss man as some have been led to believe.) This means that each watch, during a normal day, works four hours twice a day—four on, eight off. If, however, a ship is coming in or out of port or if there is additional work to be done on overtime, that simple schedule does not strictly pertain. Except in cases that are crucial to the function or the safety of the ship, a crewman may not be compelled to work overtime and may keep to the hours of his watches if he wishes to eschew the extra money.

Each deck watch (or engine watch) consists of three men who, on a Liberty ship such as the *John Ringling,* live together in a small room that is still called a fo'c'sle. That word has persisted since olden days when all the crew, except the officers, bunked together in the forecastle or forward castle among the anchor chains. British seamen still refer to the living quarters on a ship as a castle whereas American seamen, being more plainly spoken, call it a house. Thus, the structure that to an Englishman is a center castle is to an American a midship house. Whereas, as well, unlicensed men of the deck department live in fo'c'sles, their officers live in rooms, and the master, who is captain of the ship, lives in a cabin. Nearly all the newer ships of whatever nation now provide each man with a private room regardless of his station, but that was not the case on the *John Ringling* or any other Liberty.

Of the three sailors on a deck watch, one is an ordinary seaman and the other two are supposed to be able seamen by Coast Guard regulations. Each watch is commanded or overseen by an officer or mate (in the engine department, the "black gang," he is an engineer) though the term *mate,* when used alone, refers to the chief mate or first officer; and the term *chief* used alone refers to the chief engineer. During my first days on the *Ringling* I was more than once blasted for an idiot by a fat little man named Casselberry whom we came to call Mr. Dingleberry, the chief mate, because, when told to wake the chief—waking people is the ordinary's job—I woke him, the mate, instead. So much now for nomenclature and etymology.

When official departure time is determined, the master tells the mate to set sea watches which are, as I said, four hours on duty and eight hours off. (Certain vessels, sea-going tugs for instance, may set watches at six-and-six; and some foreign ships, not operating under American-union-type working rules may do the same. This, of course, produces a heavier work schedule because you can't get your eight hours of sleep if you want them.) To show how seagoing times have changed since the days of sail, since the "romantic" days of backbreaking labor and wicked captains, I offer Dana's description from *Two Years Before the Mast* of how *their* watches were set on the brig *Pilgrim,* 1834:

> The crew are divided into two divisions . . . called the watches. Of these, the chief mate commands the larboard, and the second mate the starboard. They divide the time between them, being on and off duty, or, as it is called, on deck and below, every other four hours . . . If, for instance, the chief mate with the larboard watch have the first night watch from eight to twelve, at that hour the starboard watch and the second mate take the deck, while the larboard watch and the first mate go below until four in the morning, when they come on deck again and remain until eight . . . in some merchantmen, this alternation of watches is kept up throughout the twenty-four hours, which is called having "watch and watch"; but our ship, like most merchantmen, had "all hands" from twelve o'clock till dark, except in very bad weather, when we were allowed "watch and watch." [The] purpose [of dog watches] is to shift the watches each night, so that the same watch need not be on deck at

the same hours throughout a voyage. In order to affect this, the watch from four to eight P.M. is divided into two half-watches, one from four to six and the other from six to eight. By this means they divide the twenty-four hours into seven watches instead of six, and thus shift the hours every night. As the dog watches come during twilight, after the day's work is done, and before the night watch is set, they are the watches in which everybody is on deck. The captain is up, walking on the weather side of the quarter-deck . . . The steward has finished his work in the cabin, and has come up to smoke his pipe with the cook in the galley. The crew are sitting on the windlass or lying on the forecastle, smoking, singing, or telling long yarns. At eight o'clock eight bells are struck, the log is hove, the watch set, the wheel relieved, the galley shut up, and the watch off duty goes below.

On the *John Ringling* the noon or midnight to four o'clock watch was presided over by the second mate, the navigating officer; the four to eight watch by the chief mate; and the eight to twelve by the junior officer, the third mate. There was no need to dog the watches though that quiet sociable hour after supper when day work is done and dark is falling is still often called the dog watch.

There was still a deep glow in the evening sky as we set off down the twisting river. This was my home-town river, but that far end of it wasn't anything like home. At Keokuk, the Mississippi is very wide. (No. 19 dam crosses there making a broad lake above the place the Keokuk rapids used to be, but even below the dam the river's wide.) The Illinois and the Iowa sides are banked with bluffs and hills that are white with snow in winter, green in summer, and wildly ablaze with red, orange, and gold when the oaks, the maples, the elms, cottonwoods, sycamores, hickories, buckeyes all turn color in the fall. But there below New Orleans, the river is narrow and deep and winds through the marshland of one of the broadest deltas on earth.

(I became familiar with that delta in later years while working as a deckhand and sometime mate on an eighty-five foot seagoing tugboat called the *Maxine McDermott*. We towed oil-drilling rigs mounted on barges and crew barges from location to location to wherever the geologists wanted to probe for oil, and we often left the busy Intracoastal Waterway and plowed through the marshes, through what was called "the trembling prairie," through solid acres of tall floating grass and blooming hyacinths that turned back like furrows of fragrant earth as we passed through. Every creature that lived in the swampland hopped, leapt, swam, or wriggled away from the *Maxine*'s bow—fish, shrimp, crawdads, bullfrogs, even alligators, and, of course, snakes. A deckhand's routine chore was to patrol the tugboat's decks with a heavy stick to knock off cottonmouths as they slithered aboard.

Someplace in the vicinity of Bayou Penchant, while cutting through virgin marshes, we came upon an enormous lake, open water clear of vegetation, that had never been charted. We threw out an anchor while we searched every map and chart we had with us. We knew where we were except that where we were wasn't there. And it wasn't a little lake, it was a big lake, it wasn't a lake anybody could miss. It was just one no one had ever come across before.)

While the *John Ringling* followed the outgoing river channel through the marshes, Dave told me what to do. A novice ordinary on his first night watch is not expected to do much of anything except "stand lookout," so that's what I did. I stood on the bow as far forward on the forepeak as I could get, and I watched the river wind out ahead of me toward the sea. A lookout's job, of course, is to look out for other vessels coming or going ahead or for anything else that might prove dangerous to the ship's passage. There's a telephone on the bow. And there is also a bell. The ship's bell. The usual way to signal, David told me, if anything showed up, was with the bell, but if anything really odd appeared, I could ring up the officer on the bridge on the phone. But the bell is the customary and ancient signal. At sea, the ship runs by the bell. There is an obscure and perverse little story by Edgar Allen Poe called "The Devil in the Belfry," in which the inhabitants of a town in Central

Europe called Wundervatimitiss perform their life functions by the stroke of the bell. When the bell rings they all eat, they sleep, they breed, they die. Then the Devil scales the belfry and all Hell breaks loose. As far as I know, it's Poe's only social protest story.

So it is with a ship, except that on a ship the bell's a comfort. A ship, after all, like a prison is a controlled environment, and the bell brings human order to the inhuman revolutions of Nature, to the vaster order of Time and the Deep. It marks out the day into sections, into watches; and it warns of danger and announces the ship's presence in a fog. Though nowadays the daily bell, like the ship's whistle, is recorded on tape, on the *Ringling* it was struck by hand. The lookout on the bow passed on the time that was first struck on the bridge's clock, then by the helmsman on the bridge's bell. Eight bells changed the watch signaling eight o'clock, twelve o'clock, and four o'clock. Any odd number indicated a half hour. Thus, three bells—struck bong-bong, bong—said it was an hour and a half into the watch, making the time 9:30, 1:30, or 5:30 A.M. or P.M. To the lookout watching for obstructions ahead, a ship approaching on the starboard (right) side was announced to the bridge by one stroke of the bell, on the port (left) side by two strokes, and three strokes meant dead ahead.

Customs at sea change slowly if at all, but in the olden days of sail and steam, the terms for right and left were starboard and larboard meaning the steering side where the tiller was and the loading side that lay alongside the dock. The similarity of sounds caused so much confusion and so many accidents and so much questioning of authority.

"Excuse me, cap'n, sir, did you say starb'rd or larb'rd?"

"I said starb'rd, son."

"Didn't you mean larb'rd, cap'n?"

"I said larb'rd and I *mean* larb'rd."

"I know, cap'n, but I heard you say starb'rd, if you have me haul larb'rd, sir, we're going to hit that—" After hundreds of years of misunderstanding and disaster to English-speaking ships (other nations didn't have that trouble, *tribord* and *bâbord* are quite distinct in French as are *Steuerbord* and *Backbord* in German), larboard was changed to port.

I wasn't halfway through my first lookout when the third mate called me on the telephone and told me with sarcastic politeness that the pilot said it was not necessary for me to report *every* light I saw. "Just report the ships," he said. And in the background of the scratchy phone, I heard the voice of the pilot say, "You must have a new kid on the bow."

I was reporting everything. Navigation lights, shore lights, gas flames from oil wells in the marshes, stars, driving the bridge crazy with my bell-ringing.

It's roughly a hundred miles from New Orleans to the mouth of the Mississippi at Southwest Pass, so it was after twelve and my first watch was over by the time we reached the sea. But I remember lying in my bunk—being the newest man, the green man, I was left the upper bunk which was the most private and which, in later years when seniority and able-bodied status gave me first choice, I always chose for myself—I remember feeling for the first time the movement of the open sea. And each time thereafter, moving from a river's mouth or a harbor onto the bosom of the ocean, the sensation returns in calm weather, a fresh new experience that in between times I forget. It's like a water bed. It's sensuous and stilling. And if one is prone to *mal de mer,* it's sickening as well, the rising and the falling, the vast breathing of the Great Green.

I have never been seasick, but I have come close. And the closest I came was not from debouching from the Mississippi onto the Gulf of Mexico nor from hurricanes in the North Atlantic or the Bay of Biscay, but from a norther on the Louisiana coast aboard that same tugboat mentioned earlier, the *Maxine*. A norther or *norte* is a high wind out of the Mississippi Valley not unlike the notorious *mistral,* the cold Alpine-Rhône Valley wind that freezes the bones of the winter tourists on the Côte d'Azur. The *norte* terrorizes the Gulf of Mexico and the coasts of Tabasco and Campeche. The *Maxine* was towing across Atchafalaya Bay a barge loaded with enormous steel pipes three feet in diameter and over two hundred feet long. They were to be used as pilings for an oil-drilling platform that the J. Ray McDermott company was preparing to construct in the Gulf of Mexico. High winds in shallow water produce high choppy seas. We tied the *Maxine* to the barge to ride out the norther. For three days the little craft leapt and dropped and rolled and tossed. It was too rough to cook, too rough to sleep or do any work on deck. There was nothing to do but eat cold food, lie in my bunk with the seasick cockroaches, and fight the churning in my stomach.

My watchmate and therefore my bunkmate was a three-hundred pound bariatric case named Tiny who was so obese he could not squeeze into the shower so he never bathed nor did he change his clothes. We all did a lot of sweating in the swampy country working out of Morgan City. Tugboats are made for small lean men. I was lean enough, but I was much too tall and my skull is a study of scar tissue to prove it. And Tiny was much too fat but he was the captain's cousin and in Cajun country, kin counts. Our fo'c'sle was directly over the engine room and behind the galley, and the stench, even with the door and the single porthole open, was remarkable; but I never got sick. I came awfully close, as I said, and I got sick of the wind and the relentless waves and cold horsecock and the stale perfume of Tiny, but I didn't get seasick.

The sky was clear and we listened on the boat's radio to Cajun shrimpers cussing out the weather and each other in that bizarre and cleverly obscene bastard French dialect they use among themselves; and we watched, helplessly, as the wind and the waves tore loose the steel pilings on the barge deck and sent them rolling off to the bottom of the bay. I wrote a story about that boat, seasickness, a drilling barge, and the kinship of those people from the delta marshes. It's in the appendix and it's called "Mortality." And I liked Tiny however much he stank. We had to wrestle buoys and haul in the tow line. It was very hard and dangerous work and Tiny could plant himself on the tow-line deck and do with one fat arm the size of an elephant's leg what it took my whole spare body to do. We liked each other, Tiny and I, and we got along. The waves washed him every now and then so he could have smelled worse than he did.

That first night on the *John Ringling* I felt the queasiness in my stomach and the slight dizziness in my head for a few minutes, then I was all right. I dropped out of my bunk and went on deck, onto the still afterdeck, the deck behind the house out of the wind that the ship made in its passing. I leapt up on the battened canvas of hatch number four and surveyed the Great Green which lay all around me in a great moonlit circle. We had dropped the pilot at Pilottown and were heading south under stars and a late gibbous moon. The weather was superb. Sultry days followed warm clear nights full of stars with a dark moon and a sickle moon. Sudden squalls churning the emerald-indigo sea into high, scrolled, ecclesiastical waves, passing on with a crack of thunder and a flash of lightning, a dark cloud shadow on the sea like Jehovah's scowl and a cool washing of the tropical air, some hailstones and starlight or sunlight or moonlight again.

(Years later, on a moonlit lookout in the Persian Gulf, I stood on the flying bridge which is that part of the midship house above the main navigating bridge. The captain had ordered lookout there because the ship, a tanker, was so loaded with Arabian crude that even in calm seas the water broke over the bow. It was a better place in many ways to see what there was to see. I was on the twelve-to-four watch then, and my officer, the second mate and navigator, was a man without eyelids whom I used in a story and called Mr. Love, Mr. Clarence Love ("An Uncivilized Man"). He was very smart, intelligent smart, superbly schooled in his profession, a really brilliant navigator deeply interested far beyond his job in the mysteries of the Heavens and the phenomena of the sea. This made him a heretic, of course; but he was a fool, too, and so paranoid that if I said "Good morning," he'd worry all day about what I meant by it. We talked a lot and shared our enthusiasm for the manifestations of Nature, but I couldn't get too familiar with him or he would think I was challenging his authority. After all, he *was* my superior even though I was the only other man aboard who even approached his level of interest and knowledge.

That moonlit night, though, coming out of the Persian Gulf toward the "big turn" where all ships must make a sudden and incredibly radical change of course—almost double back upon themselves—to leave the Strait of Hormuz and enter the Gulf of Oman, I watched the ship plow its way through those dark Oriental waters with the moon behind me. It was still as still could be. Not a cloud in the sky. No wind but our own. The foredeck lying before me was black against the silvery water. Below me, in the wheelhouse, the second mate, of course, was keeping watch, too. He was not talking to the helmsman because he seldom spoke to anyone but me. For some inexplicable reason, then, the ship and the sea changed values. The black vessel swiftly turned bright, and the bright sea turned black like the emergent development of a photographic negative. For a minute or two, I watched with astonishment and, I confess, some apprehension as we, a shimmering silvery ship, cut through a pitch-black sea. Then, as swiftly and deliberately as we had first changed places, we changed back. The ship became dark again, the sea moonlit. Nothing had happened in the sky. No cloud had passed. Every element was in its proper place, but we had reversed ourselves as in a dream one finds oneself, for an instant, standing upside down on the ceiling. Having been deprived of women for sometime, I was enjoying sexual fantasies and I thought that perhaps it was me that had turned things over. All kinds of thoughts can come to a man alone on lookout in the Gulf of Persia, but to check my sanity I called down through the speaking tube to the wheelhouse to the second mate. I said, "Mr. Second, did *you* see that?"

"Yes, yes," he said. "You saw it too. Thank Christ you saw it too."

The helmsman hadn't seen it because it took place in such a short space of time and he had been, righteously, looking at the gyro marking our course. But *we* had seen it, the second and I.

"What was it?" I asked.

He hated not to have an answer for any question I might ask, so he said, "It was a phenomenon."

"*Phenomenon!* Your fuckin' A, Mr. Second, it was a phenomenon. We turned inside out. *What happened?*"

"I don't know," he said. And he slammed the tube shut.

Full fathom five thy father lies;
Of his bones are coral made;
Those are pearls that were his eyes:
Nothing of him that doth fade,
But doth suffer a sea-change
Into something rich and strange.
Sea-nymphs hourly ring his knell:
[Burden, *ding-dong,*]
Hark! now I hear them, —ding-dong bell.
(W. Shakespeare
The Tempest)

A ship's routine is simple. The "black gang" (a vestigial term from the days of stokers and coal-burners—nowadays, with diesel for fuel and computers for firemen, the engineroom is as immaculate as a surgical arena) keeps the engines running; the steward's men, the cooks and the messboys, keep food cooking and serve it appropriately at rigidly prescribed hours; and the sailors, the men of the deck department, maintain the outward body of the ship, keep it on course, and look out for other ships and general obstructions. (Though "sailor" is a general term, on modern ships, which, of course, have nothing to do with sails, it is applied fairly strictly to an unlicensed man on deck. It's improper to call an oiler, for instance, a sailor. Deck officers, having risen above the appellation, often use the term scornfully when referring to their inferiors, as in "O.K., sailor, move your ass." The single term that applies to all men aboard a merchant ship is seaman. When women's liberation eventually invades the fo'c'sle, I suppose the ladies will be called sea-nymphs or seapersons.)

An ordinary seaman, which I was on the *John Ringling,* is primarily a watchman and a janitor. He "calls" people at certain hours as at one o'clock, say, when the day workers—the bosun, the electrician, the deck maintainance—have had their hour for lunch, or the succeeding watch twenty minutes before eight bells. He makes coffee for the crucial coffeetime, a twenty-minute break at ten in the morning and three in the afternoon of every working day. He cleans the showers and the "heads," he distributes clean linen to all department hands on linen day. (Linen day, usually Tuesday, provides each officer and man with clean sheets, pillow case, bedspread, bath towels and hand towels, soap and matches. Since even by assiduous bathing and heavy smoking it's nearly impossible to use up a bar of Palmolive, a bar of Lava, and a full carton of Diamond Dominos each week, these two issues, stacking up in the top of one's locker, became useful bartering commodities in some underprivileged parts of the world.)

And the ordinary sweeps up a lot. Broomwork is very important on a ship. The decks, the fo'c'sles, the passageways all have to be swept continually. He also chips rust. All sailors do that. He lays on rust-discouraging red lead after the rust has been chipped and wire-brushed, and he paints the areas after the red lead has dried. At night or in the daytime if the day is foggy or inclement enough for the captain to feel more secure with an additional pair of eyes on the fo'c'slehead, he stands lookout. And if the captain is so inclined, he'll allow the ordinary to stand a wheel watch. A wheel watch means steering the ship, and a man is supposed to have able seaman's papers to perform this function. But an ordinary seaman must learn to steer in order to become an a.b. so most captains consent to his learning on the open sea. (The captain may, with the pilot's acquiescence, permit an experienced ordinary to steer in a harbor or a ship channel, but that is technically illegal and if anything happens, if you run into something as I did once in the Houston ship channel—I ran into a barge, it wasn't my fault, the barge was out of control, but I hit it just the same—both he and the pilot are likely to be in for it.)

Steering at sea, in the open ocean, is the most boring task a sailor must perform (though it can be exciting in close quarters or busy places) and if the four hours of the watch can be split three ways instead of two, it makes it easier on everyone. The a.b.'s don't have to spend two-hour stretches on the wheel, and the ordinary's lookout can be reduced to an hour and twenty minutes. Most post-World War II ships have automatic pilots or "iron mikes" that keep the ship on course in smooth weather by electronic means, though the newest ships are likely to be operated by computer, but not the Libertys. They were steered strictly by hand either from the main wheelhouse or from the auxiliary wheel on the flying bridge. (Because a Liberty was a wartime ship, there was also a steering wheel atop the gun-crew's quarters on the stern in case the bridge should be damaged in combat.)

In the daytime, while one man of the watch was steering, the other two would be working with the bosun on deck—chipping, scraping, painting, washing down, sweeping up, splicing lines, stowing hawsers, overhauling lifeboats, greasing davits, slushing rigging, or any of a hundred other constant maintenance chores. At night, since union rules forbade unnecessary work after five, one man stood the wheel, another lookout, and the third standby. Standby was usually in the messroom by the telephone or, if the officer so ordered, on the bridge. Standby in the messroom was a convenient time to read or play cards or, in later years, watch television.

All through the Gulf of Mexico and the Caribbean, the *John Ringling*—except during rain squalls—was steered from the flying bridge. There was no wheelhouse there, only a canvas-shaded shelter for the wheel and the helmsman. In fact we steered by magnetic compass up there because there was no gyrocompass repeater on the flying bridge. Captain O'Sullivan, at the urging of his officers who were urged by the seamen on their watches, permitted the ordinaries to steer, so I learned almost immediately to take the helm. It is, after all, very easy. As Joe the dispatcher said, if you can drive a car you can steer a ship, except that in heavy weather or a crowded place like the English Channel, a sharp and experienced helmsman is essential.

I loved steering the *Ringling* from that top flying bridge through that dulcet turquoise sea that spread out around us like a summer meadow or a Peaceable Kingdom, with porpoises leaping and silver flying-fish sailing through the china-blue air, with phosphorescent creatures—millions, billions of noctilucae—turning the water bright and shimmering in the night.

I quickly became an excellent, dependable quartermaster, so reliable in fact that Captain Dantzler, master of the *Seatiger* on which I worked for a year, used to call for me especially when things got really rough and dangerous. "Mr. Parker," he'd say to the mate, though he couldn't abide me ordinarily because he thought of me as a smartass or an anarchist or what he called a commonist, "get me that smart ordinary, that Kentfield, up here."

In a story called "Sailor's Grave," I changed myself into a character from Cape Girardeau, Missouri named George Arthur Ferguson who was known to his shipmates as Mr. Solly, short for Solomon because he was forever laying out words of wisdom and settling disputes. In that particular tale, he describes how the captain (Dantzler) called for him (me) in the Red Sea:

But in the Red there, there's a place everbody calls the Hole in the Wall, because it's—well, it's kinda like a hole in a wall, see? So, going south from the canal, you can take your choice. I mean, you git down at the skinny end of the Red, and there's this bunch of islands that are smack in the middle of the track, and you can go around them or you can go through them, and if you go through them, then you're going through the Hole in the Wall, see? So the Old Man, he had one of these things—these split personalities that you read about so much these days, only this was several years ago, and he'd already had his for quite a time . . . I mean, you could see daylight where it come apart . . . One minute, all he could talk about was how safety was the best policy and he wasn't going to risk nobody's neck for a few hours or a couple more knots, and then he'd turn around and chew out the chief engineer for not putting on the strain. So he couldn't never make up his mind. Half a dozen times we come up on this Hole in the Wall, and ever time he'd take the long way around . . . He'd see other skippers go through there, and he didn't have the nerve. I mean, it was a real skinny place and there wasn't hardly any water, but when you was light you could do it with a T-2, if you was careful.

So one time there was jist him and me on the bridge, high noon. I mean, he was standing the bridge for the Second, who was in the chart room working out his figures. And I was on the wheel, and we was coming up on them rocks, and I'm all ready to change course to go around. I mean, man, I've drove that Red so many times I could do it with a bucket on my head. Only, he don't give me no order, and we keep gitting closer, and I says, 'Cap'n, you want I should haul over seventeen degrees?' I mean, that's what we always did. So he says, 'Haul? Haul? Who do you think you are, son, telling me to haul? You haul and I'll haul your tail *over*side! *I'll* tell you when to haul!' he says. So I says, 'Sorry, Cap'n, only—' 'You jist keep her steady as she goes,' he says. And we're heading for the Hole in the Wall.

So I keep her steady, and he says, 'Nothing to the right and nothing to the left,' and I says, 'Nothing to the right and nothing to the left, Cap'n.' And then he turns to me and he says, 'I'll take her through here ever trip from now on,' and . . . the whole rest of the trip I was Lady Luck to him . . . Whenever we come to a tight place, like one time in them Straits of Messina, between the Eyetalian boot and Sisly . . . he called for me. He said to the mate, 'Git that cracker up here.' He always called me a cracker because he figured I was a hick, judging from the way I talked, and where I come from and all.

A quartermaster, in the merchant marine, is merely a man who steers the ship. Bigger, fancier ships such as passenger liners often hire quartermasters separately to stand the wheel watches rather than relying upon the regular deck sailors. Since such quartermasters have nothing to do but stand by the wheel while the automatic pilot steers the course, or shine the brass doorknobs of the wheelhouse, they suffer from pathological boredom and usually overnutrition. Excessive weight is an occupational disease of quartermasters.

As accomplished as I was at steering, I let my enthusiasm for the colors and patterns of the sea get the better of my responsibility one spectacular Caribbean day. It was about the fifth or sixth day out on the *Ringling*. In those days wherever I went I carried an old Model 20 movie camera tucked into my gear. I took the camera up with me that day to the flying bridge where I became so seduced by the sky, the sea, and the pastures of golden seaweed and the purple rain squalls on the horizon that I abandoned the wheel to make sure I recorded everything on Kodachrome. It wasn't until Mr. Kusic, the third mate, came leaping up the ladder from the chartroom—all stairways on ships are called ladders—three treads at a time, that I came to my senses and glanced at the white wake that curved vagrantly like a sickle behind us.

"For Christ's sake, Kentfield, you trying to turn around and go home," Mr. Kusic said. "Where the hell're you going?"

Fortunately, Captain O'Sullivan was having his pre-luncheon nap and wasn't aware of my severe departure from his course. "We're going to send you back to the farm, boy," Mr. Kusic said as I madly turned the wheel and aimed the ship back in the general direction of South America. "I wonder what's happening to our noble profession," he said, "when you clods from the sticks ship out." Then he laughed. He laughed and shook his head in mock amazement. He was a young man of more than usual sense of humor. I liked him and I used him in *The Alchemist's Voyage* as one of the alter egos of my protagonist. The better I came to know him, the more I came to realize he possessed a mordant wit that he used very effectively against Captain O'Sullivan and Mate Casselberry.

I gave him a proper turn one night, though, as we were fetching up on the coast of Venezuela, the tail end of the Lesser Antilles in fact. Besides the main islands of Aruba, Curaçao, Bonaire, and Margarita, there are many little ones like Los Roques and Los Hermanos, Las Aves and La Orchila. Most of them stand unlighted in the sea off the mainland. I was on lookout on the bow one night. The moon was bright, and I saw the island, certainly, but I didn't ring the bell because it seemed so *obvious* that I couldn't believe Mr. Kusic didn't know it was there. We came closer and closer until it was looming up in front of us like a big black bank building. I could see the white line of moonlit surf along the shore and both ends of the island so I knew it wasn't South America. It was alarming. I cranked up the telephone and called the bridge. Mr. Kusic must have been in the chartroom or else he and Dave who was on the wheel were so deep in conversation neither of them noticed what was ahead. At any rate he didn't answer. I struck the bell three frantic times and wound up the phone again. This time Kusic answered.

"Third," I said. "There's an island or something, dead ahead. Is that where we're going?"

"Criminy, Kentfield, why didn't you report it sooner? You know fuckin' well that's not where we're going. That goddamed second mate's put us off course."

The second mate was Mr. Kusic's best friend. They had sailed together for years. In fact, Mr. Kusic, who had passed his chief mate's examination and received his mate's ticket, had signed on the *Ringling* as a lowly junior officer just so the two of them could continue to be together. Whereas Kusic's wit was sharp and often nasty, the second mate told hilarious stories in an Irish accent—he was, as was Captain O'Sullivan, a Boston Irishman—stories that stayed gently in one's memory for days, mostly about his father and his uncle, professional Irishmen both. He and Kusic were very far left, possibly even Party members though I doubt that because Communist regulars are well known for their lack of humor, and those two were very funny fellows.

"I thought you saw it," I said. "It's really *obvious.* Jesus, it's a *whole island.*"

Even as I defended myself, I could hear Mr. Kusic giving the order to Dave to haul left twenty degrees, and very shortly the ship's heading changed and the stars shifted, and the black loom of the island fled to my right. (I'm using *loom* inaccurately there insofar as maritime usage is concerned. On a ship the first sighting of an object or a light, before it actually breaks the horizon, is called the loom. On superbly clear nights you may get the loom of the moon, or as we did when we finally came upon Venezuela, the loom of a mountain, the tip-top of the Cordillera de Mérida, the northern transverse spur of the Andes, that shows up on the horizon long before you're really there. If a lookout reports the loom of a lighthouse such as the dangerous and important Cabo San Vicente on the Portuguese coast that the master is watching for, he, the captain, might very well say to the mate, "There's a good lad," which is an old-time expression that never fails to please. Most captains, however alcoholic or corporate or feckless, still possess a sense of the history of their profession.)

"Kentfield," Kusic shouted into the telephone, "if you *see* something, *report* it. I don't care if it's a fuckin' *continent!*"

"But Mr. Third," I said, "it was so *obvious.*"

"You fuckin' farmer," he replied, "we'll transport you back to the soil, lad." He laughed into the telephone. "We could've piled Cap'n O'Sullivan onto the rocks, *then* wouldn't he hit the fan."

I said to myself that if he'd been watching instead of shooting the breeze with the helmsman, he would have seen the island too, but I didn't say that into the telephone because I didn't know him well enough yet to talk back to him.

And that wasn't the last time. Much later, on the return voyage, the second mate, our navigator, and the master arrived at diverse conclusions about the same course. We were supposed to be heading for the mouth of the St. Lawrence to deliver our load of bauxite to the Aluminium Company of Canada. Personally, the master was very sour, more Scots than Irish, with an ulcer of the blind gut, the pylorus, or, perhaps, he had chronic appendicitis. I don't know if he was the lousy navigator or if the second mate was. Since I liked the second mate and couldn't abide the captain, my personal prejudice tells me it must have been the master himself who couldn't tell the sun from the moon, but one of them set a course that, had it been dutifully pursued, would have taken us, the *John Ringling,* directly onto the shoals of Sable Island. I got the story later from the third mate. The second mate claimed his calculations were the correct ones, and the master argued for his own. He, the master, ultimately laid down the law, of course.

Sable Island, the famous Atlantic graveyard of ships, is a small low lie of land off Nova Scotia. Wild horses live there, and it must have been named by Arcadians before they became Cajuns for its sandy character and not for the furry and expensive *Martes zibellina* which make up into dark, warm coats. *Sable* in French, after all, means sand, and there are îles de sable in the French South Pacific. Where the wild horses came from, I don't know. Some say from wrecks of Spanish galleons. Elizabeth Bishop probably knows, she's been out there. But there is no doubt that under the sea to the south of the island lies the Sable Island bank, invisible shifting sands that bear covering water often too shallow for large ocean vessels though codders and lobstermen have no trouble. Because of the fickle nature of these sands, no chart can accurately show the depth of the water or the boundaries of the bank, so ships or ships with prudent masters stay wide and clear of the place.

Though Captain O'Sullivan was conservative, he was not always prudent, and like so many ship's captains, he stubbornly refused to admit error, being victim of that pigheadedness that inflicts so many men of command as they advance through middle age, particularly if they dislike or resent their juniors. Captain O'Sullivan, by the time the *Ringling,* over two months through the voyage, was approaching the treacherous banks of Sable, had come thoroughly to resent and detest his officers, especially the sharp-witted navigator whose calculations he invariably challenged. Often the second mate would have to set a course he knew was wrong because the master insisted upon it, and such was the case with the course that was taking us straight toward Sable Island and inevitable disaster.

I was the lookout when we raised the loom of Sable Island light on the east end of the island, but I was not nearly as green as I had been on the approach to the Venezuelan coast. I reported the light, three bells for dead ahead, even before the light cut the horizon. Mr. Kusic, who by that time was a good friend of mine in spite of the broad chasm between our stations, had apprised me of the feud between the captain and the second mate and the peril of our course. I knew the island was there and I rang the bell again the second the light cracked the horizon. The weather had not been perfectly clear, there had been rain, and the air was still misty which meant that visibility was limited and we were nearer than the ultimate reach of the light. Each lighthouse has a designated range for perfect weather. One might be a five-mile light, another an eighteen-mile light. I don't remember the range of Sable Island, but it's a strong light, and it was blurred that night by residual rain. Though to do so showed signs of panic, I rang the bell a third time. All the while the captain and the second mate were arguing about whose course was the right one; and it wasn't until the captain was confronted with the indisputable fact of the light itself, dead ahead, that he acknowledged that his course was wrong. Acknowledged is probably too strong a word. Facing the evidence, he probably said something like, "All right, mister, have it your own way," or "If you think that's the right course, take it," with the tone of a man washing his hands of the whole thing. At any rate, the second gave the order and the helmsman hauled over to the right in an abrupt and dramatic change of direction. By the time I went off watch at midnight, Sable Island light was well abaft the beam on the port side.

I made Captain O'Sullivan the master character in *The Alchemist's Voyage* calling him Faircloth and giving him, for fictional purposes, a dimension I'm afraid he did not, in real life, possess. My first description of him was this:

"The master's name was Faircloth, and at birth he had, indeed, been cut as truly, as squarely from the fair and limitless fabric of Heaven as any other, but after journeying sixty years he had come to that spot, seven nights from shore and outward bound, a wry and bias old man. All his life he had cursed misfortune and had evoked it, it had seemed, with his curses—"

Captain O'Sullivan wasn't all that old, probably no more than fifty; but the pun on "old man" is the same regardless of age. On a ship, the "old man" is the captain even if he's thirty.

After the Sable Island scrape, Captain O'Sullivan had us put in at Sydney, Cape Breton Island, because his innards were hurting and he wanted to see a doctor. He was all right as it turned out, he just worried a lot and when he worried his gut tightened up on him. I know the feeling, I've had ulcers myself, in fact, in recent years I've had most of my stomach removed and my vagus nerves snipped so that I now function upon what medical men, without the tiniest nascence of a smile, refer to as a "gastric remnant." As I had a tendency to bleed a lot, and often at sea, the operation was necessary to save what was yet to come of my life. The operational project was called a Billroth II named after the German practitioner, Dr. Christian Albert Billroth, who not only performed wondrous gastrointestinal feats in Vienna in the middle of the last century, but also performed Mozart superbly on the piano. Equally superb was the surgical performance of Dr. John Myers upon me though he, himself, died of heart failure at only thirty-nine while riding uphill on his bicycle. However, the purpose of setting down this chronicle is not to talk about my or Captain O'Sullivan's operations.

Our first port of call in Venezuela was La Guaira, the seaport for the high capital of Caracas. La Guaira is not a natural harbor, it's not a harbor at all; it's a long manmade mole sticking out into the Caribbean. Because there was no dock space for us, we were compelled to anchor out for a couple of days in the roads. (Roads is a Conradian term, short for roadstead which means the area adjacent to a harbor where ships may drop anchor before going into or after coming off the pier. In San Francisco, for instance, the roadstead or anchorage is off Alcatraz Island and the Bay bridge, in Copenhagen it's the Sound, at Antwerp it's the Schelde, at Port Said it's the east side of the mouth of the Suez Canal, at London it's the Thames below Tower Bridge and at Limehouse Reach.) This delay in discharging cargo probably triggered Captain O'Sullivan's initial indisposition. That and the fact that one of his old friends from Grace Line days (a year or so before, because of some transgression I never uncovered, he had, well, O.K., I'll say it, he had fallen from Grace, and the Alcoa bauxite tub had been his first command since then), that old friend had become master of the new *Santa Rosa,* Grace Line's combination freighter-passenger liner that had preceded the *John Ringling* into dock. Captain O'Sullivan toured her newly upholstered cabins, basked in her air-conditioning, drank good whiskey with his old friend at her first-class bar, dined in elegance in the master's spacious quarters, inspected her glistening engine room and wheelhouse with its radar, sonar, and automatic pilot, and then returned to the gray, minimal security cell that passed for his own cabin and, I surmise, got sick to his stomach. Captain O'Sullivan, being shanty Irish and emerging from a Boston kitchen with threadbare oilcloth on the table and a plaster Virgin in the vestibule, aspired to be lace-curtain. He held cocktail hour at sea, serving Rob Roys to the chief engineer and the radio operator. (Mr. Casselberry, the mate, was on watch at that time, but he could, with the master's indulgence, pop in for a quick one.) But the captain never invited his fellow Bostonians, the second and third mates, or his purser whom he considered, with some justification, to be a common drunk. He required his chief steward to order Lawry's Seasoned Salt which he considered the ultimate in gourmet finesse.

According to maritime law and union rules, American ships must carry a long list of prescribed provisions—none of the hardtack and maggoty fatback of the olden days. There is the well-known case of the freighter whose crew refused to pick up anchor and move out of the Gulf of Siam because there was no strawberry jam aboard. And the *Seatiger* (née *Kettleman Hills*) often bought its stores in England or Egypt, and when the steward laid on Keiller's tart Dundee marmalade, the expensive and delicious stuff that used to come in a ceramic pot but now comes in a common jar, most of the men refused to eat it because it was not sweet American style. In a short story called "Dancer's Cricket" I gave the menu for that tanker's Christmas dinner off the coast of Arabia:

The tables were laid with white cloths even for the unlicensed crew and from half past eleven to half past twelve the feast was spread. Half of the red and half of the white wine were put out together. Besides turkey and cranberry sauce, there were baked ham and raisin sauce, mashed potatoes, sweet potatoes, broccoli, succotash, coleslaw, hot rolls, corn bread, pumpkin pie, hot mince pie with brandy, hot raisin pie with brandy, melon and coffee. Relishes of celery, olives, and pickles, and a tomato juice cocktail preceded the turkey . . . At five o'clock the rest of the wine was served with a supper of lamb chops. . . .

(Wine is not on the list of required stores, but the wine on the *Seatiger* had been provided out of pocket by Captain Dantzler.)

Captain O'Sullivan required each of his officers to wear a tie at meals (uniforms are not customarily worn by merchant-seamen officers on civilian ships without passengers) and to keep their feet off the settee cushions of the saloon. (The saloon mess is the officer's messroom and the saloon is a lounging, reading, game room for the officers.) With or without Captain O'Sullivan, the standing rule on American ships is that all men, regardless of how hot the weather is, must wear shirts to meals. And the minimum shirt is a tee shirt, not a sleeveless undershirt such as that worn by old Italian men sitting on their front stoops in hot New York summers or a tee shirt with sleeves cut off exposing the hair of the armpits such as I had worn to dinner at the Wests'. Captain O'Sullivan, in fact, once sent down a memorandum by way of Mr. Kusic that, whatever the temperature, I was no longer to work on deck in nothing but my underpants. And he also objected to our sunning ourselves naked on the fantail during our off-watch, but he didn't actually forbid it. When we finally tied up at the dock in La Guaira, he headed straight for the toney hotel bars on the beach at Macuto while the rest of us being mostly young and suffering aching stiffness of the middle leg headed for the whorehouses on the hill. I have not been in Venezuela for more than ten years, but from what I hear and read the beach at Macuto now has high-rise Hiltons and jet-set clientele. La Guaira, as I mentioned, is the port for the capital city of Caracas which sprawls in a high valley of the Andes, and Macuto on the outskirts of La Guaira and fronting on the Caribbean is the capital's ocean playground. The dictator, Gómez, had a beach house there. It's a lovely spot.

We were tied up in La Guaira for a week discharging general merchandise. Once the pressures of the flesh were relieved at the houses on the hill (a chapter devoted to nothing but sex will follow shortly), we did some sightseeing. Dave and I took a taxi up to Caracas, a horrendous ride, rising three thousand feet in less than seven miles. This was on the old road because the new million-dollar-a-mile superhighway hadn't been constructed yet. Now, having visited a number of places both hilly and flat and having lived for some years in coastal California where secondary roads are likely to be precipitous, I take casual regard of the hairpin turn and the thousand-foot drop into sea or canyon, but they were new to me in Venezuela.

(After my longest trip at sea, a year on the *Seatiger,* I payed off with a lot of money and got married in London. My wife was very young and English. We went to the Canary Islands for a peaceful sojourn, I suppose it was a honeymoon, while we applied for her permanent visa for the United States. She was ever so slightly pregnant then, and on a bus trip over the shoulder of Teide, the volcano that constitutes the island of Tenerife, from Santa Cruz to Puerto de la Cruz, because of the incredible mountain curves, the pot holes, the bumps, the haste, and the pathological indifference of the driver to the feelings of his passengers—there were two nuns who, afflicted with intense motion sickness, were vomiting out of the windows, and I was shouting at the driver "Cuidado, cuidado!" because it was the only word in my minimal Spanish that I could think of to approximate "take it easy"—she, my wife, had a miscarriage. When we arrived at the bus station in Puerto de la Cruz, a tiny town on the north coast of the island, I gave her our traveling *sac* containing our bread, goat's cheese, and chocolate to hold in front of her to conceal the blood that was soaking through her skirt; and I rushed off in the middle of a Sunday to find a drug store that was open whose clerks—young giggling girls as they turned out to be—could understand my Spanish and my unlikely gestures soliciting Tampax or Kotex or whatever else an inexperienced young man could find in the Canary Islands on his honeymoon. It worked out all right, there was no damage done except to the sensibilities of the spinster Englishman whom we had met on the bus and who was appalled to the point of indignation that such a thing could happen to him on holiday. We had our honeymoon and we had other children, and we had other edgy encounters with the precipice (vividly described in my story called "In the Caldron") but I have never been so outraged at the insensitivity of male arrogance, however male and however arrogant I might be myself. The Spanish call it *machismo*. There were sick people, and frightened children and bleeding women, but the driver took no heed. He was doing his thing with his machine, and the machine was his sexual partner, whether he knew it or not, and he was getting his rocks off. We, in America, use sex to sell machines—the incredible pandering commercials on television that sell automobiles are part of everybody's home—and those who criticize our culture, as I am certainly wont to do, and point out this country as a leader of social corruption, which it probably is, use the American sex machine as a salient target; but anyone who has seen that machine in the hands of a male citizen of an underprivileged country, an Arab or a Venezuelan, to whom a car is a special thing, to whom flash, speed, noise is power and position and for whom ownership and control are limited and preferential, anyone who has seen a machine under the mastery of a poor Canarian or an Upper Voltan knows that the machine itself is a social object and a sexual weapon. I have done many things, things I was paid to do but didn't do just for money like "slushing" down the rigging in a greasy bosun's chair, a routine but perilous job, or scooping out the belly of a tanker that was still heavy with dangerous fumes or pulling capers in heat and cold and hurricane that were uncalled for except by the urgency of *machismo*. I've done these things, and perhaps the reason I went to sea in the first place was not just to travel and see the world but to prove to myself I was a man and not a boy. Perhaps. Now I question everything, especially me. And after all these years, I'm still outraged by that bus driver on Tenerife.)

When a ship such as the *Ringling* ties up in a foreign port for more than twenty-four hours, sea watches are broken and a gangway watch set. In general practice, the ordinary seamen of the three deck watches guard the gangway while the a.b.'s go on day work which is straight eight-to-five labor and usually involves such tasks as chipping and painting overside, tasks that cannot safely be done while the ship is underway in open sea. It's not a *rule* that the ordinary seamen stand the gangway watches, but it's a convention becuase the a.b.'s are likely to consider the watch a trifle beneath their dignity. One ordinary goes on at midnight and stands until eight in the morning, then another comes on at eight and stands until four, and the third relieves him then and stays until midnight. Immediately after we tied up in La Guaira, I drew the midnight to eight. I realized at once that I had found my proper slot in the maritime world. In retrospect I believe that aside from the money and the chance adventure, the one thing that kept me going back to sea again and again was that midnight gangway watch. I even resisted promotion to able-bodied seaman with all the *macho* pride and extra pay that goes with the position just so I could have that particular watch in port. (Finally, after six or eight months on the *Seatiger*, and after yet another sailor went berserk in the heat of the Gulf of Suez, Captain Dantzler made me an able seaman whether I wanted to be one or not.)

Because the job results primarily from a union rule, many shipmasters, including Captain O'Sullivan, consider a gangway watch to be a featherbed fuck-off job, but in a foreign port where the company has no shoreside employees to come aboard and watch the ship, the crewmen must take the responsibility. This means standing or sitting at or near the top of the gangway and seeing to it that no unauthorized persons come aboard. The gangway watchman is also expected to perform the necessary functions of the ship's official day (or night). He puts up the flag at sunrise and takes it down at sunset. He hauls up the house flag (the symbol of the ship's owners: Matson Steamship Company, for instance, flies a big letter M, other companies fly stripes or circles or stars), and whatever other flags need hoisting. He may have to run up the anchor balls which are two black leather or canvas balls on a halyard that indicate to other ships in your vicinity that you are not under way, not moving but riding "on the hook." Or he may have to run up the anchor lights—two electric lanterns that indicate the same thing at night. Or he may have to wake the cook or the officer of the watch or the captain if he wants a special call. At dusk he turns on the deck lights, and at dawn he turns them off. He keeps track of which members of the crew are on board and which ones have not returned from shore leave. He helps drunken shipmates up the gangway, and if any officers or crewmen bring women aboard with them, he manages to be lacing his boots or cleaning his grubby fingernails when they pass by. As long as the ship's afloat it's a living thing that must be watched.

The watchman frequently checks the tension of the mooring lines—though the ultimate responsibility for that tension is upon the deck officer of the watch—slacking off or taking up slack as the ship falls or rises on the tide. And, accordingly, he regulates the gangway angle, keeping the handropes taut and safe. If fights break out between drunken shipmates, he tries to make peace without getting hurt; and if the captain comes back aboard blasted out of his skull, he helps the mate put him to bed and keeps his mouth shut. It's a custodian's job, a concierge's job, though not quite janitorial because according to union agreement the gangway watchman is not allowed to *work,* that is, except for tidying up in the immediate area at the top of the gangway, he may not be employed at cleaning or maintenance or any other regular day work. He's not even supposed to make coffee for the day crew though he often does. He's supposed to *watch the gangway*. Since most of the time there's precious little to watch, a bookworm can chomp his way through quite a few pages between high and low tide in the perfect climate of a tropical port. I read Proust. (I'll explain later how I came by those seven volumes.)

Such masters as Captain O'Sullivan, therefore, looked upon the lolling, reading, useless gangway watchman as just another saboteur such as the foreign workmen on the dock who stole his company's heaving lines or his bosun who sold cans of his company's paint to the gook-merchants or the thieving purser who kept crooked inventories of the ship's stores, or the chief steward who had charge of everything everybody ate and drank and slept on and was the most notorious subversive of them all. All sapping his dignity, his substance, and all cheating his company for whose property and profits he was responsible. I quote from *The Alchemist's Voyage* one further scene descriptive of Captain O'Sullivan and then I'll say very little else about him. His middle-class-manqué sensibility quickly becomes as boring in print as he, himself, did in the flesh. I will have a more colorful, more complicated, more diabolical master to speak of soon. The Devil, after all, though perhaps more dangerous than a Knight of Columbus, holds the attention longer. As you can see from the following passage, Captain O'Sullivan (Faircloth) was mostly concerned with merchandise:

> For two hours the previous afternoon the master had . . . shut himself up in the slop chest, a hot little room with steel walls hung with shelves, to discover the deception he was certain existed there. Several items, he found, were missing. Some of his private Scotch was gone. This was his . . . solace and daily reminder, when mixed with soda each afternoon at five, of that dear departed other life . . . the executive life which, though hopelessly dead, he kept alive in memory . . .
>
> Gone, as well, was some of the cheaper rye which persuaded the officials of foreign ports to smooth out his entrances into their countries. Discovering this first of all, he set diligently to work. Surrounding him were shelves and shelves of chocolate bars and razor blades, cigarettes and hair oil, watch caps, underwear, dungarees, khakis, socks, shaving cream, toothpaste. All of these became objects of his deep concern. Meticulously he compared the inventory in his

hand with the merchandise remaining on the shelves, checking both against the purser's records. Where discrepancies existed he enlarged them, where they were absent, he invented them. When he had noted it all, he returned to his room to type a report in triplicate. One copy he threw in the purser's face, another he held for General Offices, and the third copy he withdrew from his desk, after leaving the purser's room, to read to himself again.

(Even if you haven't read the novel, you can see that Captain Faircloth is deliberately framing the alcoholic purser to cover his own transgressions. A typical ploy from a mind like his.)

It was nearly four in the morning. The brass-rimmed clock ticked off the seconds as the master with a nicotine-disfigured finger checked off the items. He sat in his squeaky swivel chair and swung and rocked and checked and rechecked, smoking one after another of the cheap foreign cigarettes that infused his chamber with the common smell of far primitive places.

Why he preferred that exotic tobacco was a mystery to all who knew him, for he was so hostile to the ways and differences of strangers. Yet, wherever he was or went, that odor of barbarism was a cloak he wore. It was a warning to his enemies, and there, as his eyes passed down the columns on his paper, that smoke that bore it hovered about his troubled brow like a swarm of murky thoughts or a cloud of gnats.

In real life Captain O'Sullivan smoked Pall Malls which at that time in the late forties, like their contemporaries Tareytons and Parliaments, were considered parlor cigarettes that presumably indicated, since they were longer and cost more, that the smoker was a person of some position and taste. (All of us common sailors smoked Camels and Luckies and Old Golds.) But for the purposes of my story I had to age and encrust his character with a patina of mystery though there was not, in truth, a mysterious bone in Captain O'Sullivan's body. He was Lawry's Seasoned Salt, he was baked potato in foil with sour cream gone to sea.

However much a master might deplore the wasted man-hours of the gangway watch, I, myself, found it a satisfying responsibility. I was on my own which flattered my manly pretensions. And if something went wrong, if a venal barefoot longshoreman slipped past me with the bosun's new oxfords thrust down the front of his baggy *pantalones* or if the local agent for the company, glistening with the master's Rob Roys, stumbled over my casually put down volume of *Swann's Way,* I could be brought to task. In a pinch, of course, I had recourse to the officer on watch but he was usually too busy with the loading or discharging of cargo to be bothered with my petty problems; so it was really up to me to keep the outside out and the inside functioning. But my devotion to the twelve-to-eight —the midnight-to-morning—watch went far beyond my simple-minded devotion to duty.

The midnight watch is the odd, irregular watch that most sailors avoid, and I can best begin to describe my special feelings about it by setting down a passage from my novel *All Men Are Mariners* in which the protagonist, Tom or me, at this point in the narrative, has probably lost his girl. But he's not sure; so to take his mind off his anxiety, he is riding his bicycle around the docks of Copenhagen:

He came to a halt there opposite the long mole. Puffing slightly, he propped one leg against the cobblestones and sat there for a few moments perched on the high seat, shoulders hunched, back bent, elbows resting on the grips of the handlebars. Thus he paused in the incredible stillness of Sunday morning, feeling the cool breeze off the Sound work at the corners of the web or the shadow or whatever it was that clouded his heart, whatever it was that made him turn from time to time in miniature panic to see if someone had come up unseen, unheard behind him. Except for a small coaster tied up between two pyramids of coal, the wharf was deserted and undisturbed in Sunday quiet as far as the twin lights of the harbor mouth.

Slowly Tom joggles along over the cobblestones, pushing his wheel with his leg toward the little ship that lay as still as sleep upon the oily basin water. As he drew near, he heard music with the tinny sound of radio and fragmented by the breeze. No houses were near so the sound came, without a doubt, from the coaster.

Tom drew up alongside the ship, almost close enough to step aboard. Its single hatch was closed; its paint was faded and chipped, but there was no rust on the hull or the house; its mooring lines of good old manila hung slack and safe and softly curved. Its name was plain *Marie*.

The music came from the pilot house and the tune was familiar . . . It issued from the chugger's pilot house where a sailor and a girl were dancing. The house was so small that dancing could scarcely be more than holding and jiggling together, but that, of course, was all they wanted.

Tom could see them only to the waist through the square window beside the helm. The girl was not pretty except that she was young, and her hair was uncombed and wild as the sailor's whose cap sat on his head like a bird on a nest. He wore an open vest over his skin and every now and then he bound his partner in his thick bare arms and spun her round and round the tiny cell, pressing a bottle of *snaps* between her shoulderblades, laughing and kissing her as they danced.

Tom, frozen into watching, felt their turning deep in his heart—the anguish of memory. He remembered the exquisite pleasure of brief desire and safe escape when the ship departed. How often had he, in his short life, been that sailor carousing in the broad daylight and peace of Sunday morning—or going on watch at midnight and sleeping in the sunny hours, eating breakfast at suppertime, leaving when others were coming, turning left when the world turned right, sitting backwards on his chair.

Most of my life I have sat backwards on my chair so the midnight-to-morning watch accommodated my aberration. It fell naturally to me in Venezuela because I was the newest and greenest sailor on board. None of the other men wanted it because of the unnaturalness of its hours. If you got all dressed up and went ashore with some of your shipmates after supper, you had to stay close, stay sober, leave them and break off in the middle of whatever you were doing in order to be back before midnight, an hour at which significant action in many places on this earth only manages to commence. It also meant trying to sleep in the daytime which can be a hot and sweaty proposition on a tropic coastline or an insectivorous jungle, and a horrendously brain-rattling one with winches stuttering and screaming and chipping-hammers banging outside the porthole or on the deck overhead.

But take an odd fellow like me. Being the only man awake on a sleeping ship (there was always a watchman in the engine-room, of course, but I never saw him), tied up at the dock or anchored in the roads of a strange sleeping port in Venezuela or France or Egypt or Arabia—or even in Red Bank or Brooklyn—watching the world when it wasn't aware excited me, touched me like watching a baby innocently sleeping. When Kate, my first child was born in Iowa City, my friend, the great Hebrew scholar, Frederick Bargebuhr, came to the hospital to see her. She had just been born and was sound asleep; and he turned away, saying, "No, I can't look at her now, Calvin, not while she sleeping. It's not fair."

And that was right for him because he felt his intrusion upon her innocence, her unawareness; but Fred's a gentle and sweetly sensitive soul, and I'm a coarsely blatant spy. I read other people's mail and look in people's windows, sometimes with binoculars. I want to *know* what *every*body's doing *all* the time; an impossible ambition, of course, and perhaps a fatal one, curiosity, after all, killed the cat; but nevertheless I watch innocence asleep and knowingness wide awake, and I hold to the conviction first expressed in my hearing years and years ago by Phil Guston when he was a young painting instructor at Iowa and I was a pimply, punky, overbearing student, the conviction that somehow one must be in the world and of the world yet out of the world all at the same time; and those solitary hours between midnight and dawn, riding the hook in a foreign roads or moored in a jungle river placed me in that dichotomous and transcendent location, showed me things and told me things that I never could have seen or learned in daylight.

Sunlight deceives more profoundly than darkness, particularly the light that falls between the lines of Cancer and Capricorn. Describing in *The Alchemist's Voyage* a night watch in Venezuela, I said:

> The night continued as close as the walls of any skull. The sky eventually began to lighten, revealing the *Alchemist* as bathed in dew as any rose in the morning. Like a rose or a precious relic the vessel couched on the orient sea, vaulted over and preserved by the flawless sky, a bell glass. For a few minutes, thus half and perfect half, in just light, the riddle's answer was so boldly shown that any fool that wanted to could have read it. Then the crack of sunrise came, the glass was shattered. Mists and limpid clouds began to form around the edges, shadows fell, and in such an inequality of light another day's deception was begun.

I'll go on to something else now after this brief description by Joseph Conrad of a jungle river. It's from a story called "The Lagoon."

> For the last three miles of its course the wandering, hesitating river . . . flows straight into the sea, flows straight to the east—to the east that harbours both light and darkness. Astern of the boat the repeated call of some bird, a cry discordant and feeble, skipped along over the smooth water and lost itself, before it could reach the other shore, in the breathless silence of the world.

There were other advantages to that midnight watch. Reading, as I said, was one. Another was sleeping. Once the green had faded from my cheeks and I had become slightly seasoned, I found I could usually get a few hours sleep during the watch if I wanted to. It depended, of course, upon the presiding officer. The second mate, though he had become my friend, stayed conscientiously, not to say religiously awake for the whole eight hours. He so despised Captain O'Sullivan that he wasn't about to give him any cause for complaint. We talked—*he* talked—during the night and he told me tales of Irish-America, Boston division, while we drank dozens of cups of coffee. He was in his late twenties and he had dark piercing, knowing eyes and black hair that came down almost to his eyebrows. He also had very bad pustular skin that made him, on the outside, unattractive; but his wit and invulnerable self-assurance drew every man (except the captain, of course) to him. These days the cant word is charisma. Well, he had a lot of that, but he refused to give me the chance for a nap.

The third mate and the chief mate, Mr. Casselberry, both catnapped on the saloon settee. Without a cover, of course, and with their shoes on because to lay in under a blanket in the chill of a tropical morning or to take your boots off would constitute "being asleep on watch" which is like "falling asleep at the wheel," both being serious derelictions of duty. Some officers I came to know learned to sleep not just with their shoes on but with their feet firmly planted on the deck however supine the rest of their bodies might be. When the officers dozed off, I could go to sleep as well. In my chair.

Captain O'Sullivan, for all his petty bourgeois paranoia about gangway watchmen goofing off on company time, did, now and then, exhibit evidences of human kindness such as allowing a chair at the head of the gangway instead of demanding that the gangway watchman spend his entire eight hours upright on his feet or half slumped against the salty bulkhead. Some wicked masters forbid the chair.

While I was an ordinary seaman aboard the *Seatiger,* long after the *John Ringling,* the midnight watch worked to perfection for everybody. This was Captain Dantzler's ship, the diabolical captain, the one who never knew what was wrong, who could never see what he was doing to his men and to himself, the one I called Captain Dancer in "Dancer's Cricket." (See appendix.) Innocence, as Elizabeth Bowen may once have said in that superb novel of hers called *A Death of the Heart,* may be our greatest sin. Innocence is the Devil's cleverest wile, to convince us he does not exist. Though Christian tradition has always depicted a clever Devil, a knowing schemer, an Iago, a Mephistopheles who can lead Man, because of his own faults and follies, to inevitable damnation, we think of him humorously, affectionately. (Oh, you devil, you!) We think he's smart. When I was a child and all of us boys played cowboy and chose up sides, I never wanted to be John Wayne or Tom Mix or Tim McCoy, I wanted to be the blackhat, the villain who kept his own counsel and worked his evil deeds unbeknownst to the others. But I was wrong. Innocence is the Devil, so the Devil being innocent is blameless. Evil is spread abroad by blameless folk like Joe McCarthy, Dean Rusk, John Foster Dulles, Kitchener—and Captain Dancer—by the boy I called Rock in my story "Near the Line," who was "like unto a man beholding his natural face in a glass: For he beholdeth himself, and goeth his way and straightway forgetteth what manner of man he was."

When Captain Dantzler looked into the mirror, all he saw was the stubble on his cheeks, and he turned away without seeing who he was, and often without shaving. But when his ship was broken down for weeks in Port Said, he went ashore to the Eastern Exchange Hotel and stayed there while the *Seatiger* anchored across the canal near Port Fuad waiting for parts.

There was nothing to do. The ship was a tanker in ballast so no cargo was being worked. We just lay there; but because those were touchy times in 1951 when the Egyptians were trying to gain control of the canal from the British and we had English crewmen aboard, we were assigned an Egyptian harbor policeman as an additional watchman. When, now and then, the captain did come back to the ship, he was always drunk and the mate and I put him to bed. Once the captain was safely stowed in his cabin, the mate would flake out in the saloon, I would go to bed on a bunk in the infirmary—both of us fully dressed, of course—and the Egyptian watchman, in that remarkable Arab way, would, at the head of the gangway, squat on his haunches, pull his *jellaba* over him, and sleep too. Should a launch approach, the motor would wake him, he would wake me, I would wake the mate, and, if necessary, the mate would wake the captain—or try to. Because of this arrangement, many things were stolen off the ship by thieves in silent bumboats and canoes, things like cases of paint and new mooring lines, but since the captain had a flourishing private business in ship's gear with the harbor merchants ("They'll steal off your socks without untying your shoes; they'll make off with your drawers without your taking your pants down.") no one bothered about anything but his personal gear.

Having had a good night's rest on the infirmary bunk, I could go ashore after breakfast and not return until midnight. I even paid another ordinary to stand my watch (sleep my watch) and went to Cairo, smoked hashish and ate Turkish delight, took off my shoes in the great mosque, roamed the bazaar and the wrecked tombs of the Mamelukes, visited the pyramids and the Great Sphinx at Gizeh, and wondered—wonder of wonders—at the fantastic loot from poor little Tut's tomb in the National Museum.

The arrangement on the *John Ringling,* however, was not that smoothly oiled, and I was more excited, then, being awake than being asleep, particularly when the ship moved from La Guaira into what, in those years, were nearly uninhabited bays and coves along the northern Venezuelan coast.

Being operated by an aluminum company, the *Ringling's* ultimate purpose was, as I said, the delivery of bauxite out of the jungle, but first it was to deposit some general cargo at La Guaira and then to unload heavy construction material—bulldozers, I-beams, H-beams, etc.—at such primitive places as Amuay Bay, Cabimas, and Puerto la Cruz-Guanta. This was 1947 and the huge American oil companies (Creole-Standard Oil, New Jersey; Mene Grande-Gulf) were building docks and refineries to ship and process Maracaibo and interior Venezuelan crude. They were using native labor, of course, but the bosses and the materials were being brought down from the States.

Puerto la Cruz was a new town of a few corrugated shacks near the tiny old Spanish port of Guanta, east of La Guaira. The gringos who were there to build the pipelines, the docks, and the refinery lived in a guarded compound on the beach. When I went back again a few years later on the *Seatiger,* the docks were finished and the pipelines from the oilfields in the interior of Anzoategui and Monagas states were also finished and pumping, and Puerto la Cruz was a brawling, sprawling new port with all the blessings of American products and appliances, but no running water and fickle electricity. Many people, Venezuelans and immigrant Canary Islanders, were affluent enough to buy Pontiacs and Fords which were often used for houses when the tires went flat, and to buy Maytag washing machines which the women filled by hauling up buckets of water from the creek and heating it on a wood fire outside their hut. And when I went back still again in 1957 on the *Esso Gettysburg,* a fast supertanker, even the whorehouses were carpeted, brocaded, and offering restaurant and floor-show entertainment in addition to their more traditional wares.

But when the *John Ringling* dropped anchor off the beach near Guanta, the docks that would in a few years accommodate huge vessels from all over the world—Dutch vessels, Danish, Norwegian, British, Japanese, Greek—were still in discrete parts on the Liberty's decks. No human artifact was visible from where we dropped our anchor though we were close enough to shore to watch the huge emerald-green iguanas sunning on the rocks.

Everyone has his own daimons which is not to say demons; we have those too and they are something else again. But daimons, daemons, numens, presiding spirits, powers that guide and inspire us or lead us to guide and inspire outselves. Some people are aware of them, most people are not. My onetime, longtime mistress, Rivka, was driven relentlessly by her daemons though she never knew what they were or that they existed. Her guiding geniuses were active and aggressive, others may be implacable and aloof. Mine are natural things like the sea, the desert, a river. And anchored off that beautiful, desolate Andean shore, I found another one, the frigate bird. Here is a short descriptive paragraph from a story of mine called "The Great Wondering Goony Bird." The time and location are slightly different but the point's the same:

It was late in winter. Outside the Dragon's Mouths, the trade winds roared. The sun had just dropped behind the wet green peaks of Venezuela, and high in the blue air above the ship a frigate bird soared and hovered. From the bird's eye, the ship—scarcely breathing on the clear water—might have seemed to be suspended in the air, like a conjurer's device, a mirage, or the manifestation of a poetic image. And, too, from eyes on the ship, the bird, floating on invisible currents, might have seemed to be contained and transfixed to the point of art.

Off Cabo San José at the southern tip of Baja California where the sun sets behind the hills instead of dropping into the Pacific Ocean, I saw a frigate bird (they are the most gifted aerialists of all the species) arrest himself in flight, *stop* dead still in the air, and turn himself completely around on the spot and fly back the way he had come and on the same course. With his long scissors tail and black pointed pterodactyloid wings, he's a devil to watch and king of the air: "The Will of a King is very numinous; it hath a kinde of vast universality in it." *

All the cargo for Puerto la Cruz and, later, Amuay Bay on the bare Paraguaná peninsula where refineries were due to be constructed outside the lake of Maracaibo, all the heavy beams and machinery had to be discharged onto lighters which are barges that come alongside an anchored ship or a ship tied to buoys and transfer the cargo to shore. Native shore crews did the work during daylight hours so my quiet midnight watches lying off that wild coast were seductive and reflective times indeed. This was, after all, the Spanish Main, and though there are now docks, tanks, cities, pipelines, clubs, whorehouses, auto agencies, movie houses, roads, trucks, noise, smoke, and sweet, sickening petroleum stinks, then there was nothing but the immense starry sky over the mountains, the polished obsidian of the gulf, the creak of the ship's chains, the perfumed tropical breeze, and the thoughts of Henry Morgan sacking Maracaibo, sunken galleons, gold and pearls (it's still called the "pearl coast" sometimes), and a lot of other Errol Flynn-Captain Blood stuff absorbed from volumes illustrated by N. C. Wyeth and from Saturday afternoons at the Regent Theater in

* Nathaniel Ward, *The Simple Cobler of Aggawam in America.*

Keokuk where we could get in for a dime if we were under twelve.

> Returning to Maracaibo, he [Henry Morgan] found three Spanish ships waiting to intercept him; but these he destroyed or captured, recovered a considerable amount of treasure from one which had sunk, exacted a heavy ransom as the price of evacuating the place, and finally by an ingenious stratagem eluded the enemy's guns altogether and escaped to safety.
>
> —Encyclopaedia Britannica, 11th Ed.

At Guanta, from my post at the gangway, I could watch the moonlight on the salt-whitened spars of a sunken ship. It was only a coastal schooner not a galleon, but from the atmosphere of the place I exacted a description (minus the wreck) that I used in my first story and that accurately evokes the mood of the pearl coast at a time that was only twenty-five or so years ago but could have been three-hundred, and will, of course, never be so again:

> Far down the arid cactus beach were fishermen's fires kindled among the lizards against the chill that before dawn even in the tropics slips from the mountains to the sea; shuttles through the jungle, putting out the clatter and the roar; settles, cold, like a pall in silence until the sun rises.

And during those dreamy watches, I could remember the song I used to sing over and over at the request of delighted girls in my painting class at Iowa (I was one of the very first of the folksingers way back in those college days when a longhair was not a pole-vaulter or a science professor but merely a piano student or a fiddler in the symphony), until Phil Guston told me to shut up and paint. He often had a hangover during morning classes and my singing got on his nerves. But the song was one called "Venezuela" that John Jacob Niles who, even before the recordings of Burl Ives, performed on one of the precious few 10-inch 78 r.p.m. folk records available anywhere (he was listed in the Victor catalog as a "mountaineer tenor") and who palmed it off as an authentic sea chanty pretending to have heard it from a sailor from Barbados or someplace though in later years he owned up to having written it, and several other of his "folk" songs, himself. Well, I suppose John Jacob Niles was as much a folk as anybody else.

I met her in Ven-na-zoo-way-ay-ay-ay-ay-ay-la,
With a basket on her head,
And if she loved others,
She didn't say,
But I knew she'd do,
To pass away,
To pa-ass a-way-ay the ti-ime in Ven-na-zoo-way-la.

There's more to it, but that's enough for here. It's a sweet song with a sad, haunting melody like so many such songs, and I sang it softly to myself on lonesome decks at night.

I never once saw a girl with a basket on her head in Venezuela, but I'll come to girls later. And no one, after the *Ringling* moved to Amuay Bay and Las Piedras, went ashore because there was nothing *on* shore (the Paraguaná peninsula, unlike the lush east coast, is a bare, dry, dusty, windy fist of land), and because Captain O'Sullivan, in order to economize for the company, refused to request a launch except for himself and a couple of other officers whose visits to the social club over the hill could be construed as official business. The club had been built for the white engineers and construction bosses who were building the docks and the refineries, and even though we were an S.I.U. (Seamen's International Union) ship and therefore carried an all-white crew, the master and the members of the club did not cotton to the idea of sharing the companionship of rough and maybe rowdy sailors. Everyone in the civilized world, of course, knew that merchant seamen from 'way 'way back in the olden days were low scum off the docks, and everyone had seen those movies with Marlene Dietrich or Hedy Lamarr slithering through the strands of beaded portières while drunken sailors broke up the place. Even though seamen now made handsome wages, owned a car, two cars, had wives and houses and children in Richmond and Perth Amboy, the legend persisted. (My mother had a seizure when I first mentioned I wanted to go to sea, but then she had always planned on my becoming a Methodist minister.) There were, of course, some of us who were unpredictable, raunchy, and likely to be wild as will be demonstrated later, so maybe the captain and the club members were right. They had to draw the line somewhere and Captain O'Sullivan drew his right across the top. The radio operator told us the club was nothing but a tin shack with a record player, some card tables, and some whiskey, so none of us missed much.

I know I said I would leave Captain O'Sullivan alone, but inchoate though my character and amorphous though my opinions might have been, he symbolized for me so much of what I despised that to reveal myself in this account, I must also expose him because he represented the kind of man that, given the similarity of our social and economic origins—lower middle-class blue-collar sons though of different environments and different generations—I knew I was in some peril of becoming. He had seen me reading books that were clearly not westerns or mysteries but thick hard-back tomes of substance, and he found out that I had at least visited the premises of higher education, so in spite of the absolute polarity of our stations aboard the ship, he marked me for proselytization. For instance, when the ship first anchored off La Guaira waiting for a berth, I, having stood my first midnight gangway watch and having slept till lunch, found myself in the two o'clock shore-leave launch with only him and the chief engineer. He invited me to come with him to Macuto for a drink. He had friends in La Guaira, he said, whom I would find interesting including the captain of the *Santa Rosa*. I accepted, not realizing, ignorant of the ways of the sea that I was, what an extraordinary proposal he had made. Nor did I realize how difficult my consorting with the master ashore could make my position with the rest of the crew. In those days, enough of old traditions prevailed that officers kept *their* place and the crew kept theirs.

They did not even enter each other's messrooms unless on official business or by specific invitation. (On one long trip across the Pacific, some of us pooled some funds and rented a movie projector and some films in Honolulu which we showed on Tuesday nights in the crew's messroom, and the captain who was as anxious to be entertained as anyone else, stood at the pantry door and watched until someone had the grace to ask him in, even then a second invitation had to be extended for him to actually sit down at the crew's mess table.)

Off the ship, of course, the structure softened, but it did not entirely disappear, so the master and an ordinary seaman drinking together was an unusual occurrence indeed. There was a tradition of which I later became aware of the master having a "boy" from the crew much as Hercules had Hylas or Caesar or Alexander kept boys with them when women were impracticable on expeditions. This tradition which, hundreds of years ago, declined from classical love to simple buggery, is still alive but rears its head infrequently. Ships no longer spend long months and years at sea without the catharsis of the shore; in fact, in the merchant navies of some countries, the captains take their wives along.

Captain O'Sullivan was not continuing that tradition when he asked me for a drink, he didn't want me for his boy in that sense, the idea would have appalled him; and I, though I went to Macuto in his taxi and drank for a while with him and his friends, realized that I had not come all the way from middle America to the Spanish Main to have cocktails with a crowd I would have fled from at home. Since my early youth, being of a romantic disposition, I had considered myself to be a member of a kind of Rousseauian Natural Aristocracy, and the master's bourgeois solicitousness embarrassed me. He did, however, while sitting in an outdoor café on the beach at Macuto, introduce me to a young fellow who lived in the beachfront hotel and worked for Braniff airlines and who, in turn, introduced me to the work of Venezuela's greatest writer, Rómulo Gallegos who, that very year, won the presidential election. I've forgotten the fellow's name, but he went upstairs to his room and brought back a copy of Robert Malloy's English translation of Gallegos' most famous novel, *Doña Barbara.* Though I didn't like the book, which I read later, I appreciated the gesture; but the talk of money and business and airline expansion and dirty, thieving natives; and the ostentatious and imperious manner in which O'Sullivan ordered drinks began to stifle me so I said good-bye to the captain and his friends and hiked back into La Guaira on my own. I was aware the action was an insult to the captain, but I couldn't have cared less.

Weeks later, after we had discharged enough cargo at various ports to cross over the shallow bar into Lake Maracaibo, we anchored again off Cabimas where another oil dock was under construction. A few days earlier at Cumaná, while tying up at the dock, I had suffered a severe rope burn on my right ankle because I had failed to stand clear of the hawser as it sizzled off the deck into the water. It was a novice's accident, stupid and inexcusable, so being ashamed of the wound, I ignored it, pretending it was nothing, but by the time we were in the lake off Cabimas, it had become so seriously infected that I could hardly stand on my right foot and I was forced to reveal my folly to the captain.

I had not seen him face to face since the café at Macuto. Each time he had passed my gangway, he had passed without glance or comment. When I explained my accident, he took great pains to repeat, indeed reiterate, how stupid were the flotsam being currently sent to sea, and he showed no sympathy or concern that I might lose my leg. Reluctantly, he sent me ashore to the tiny Cabimas infirmary where a Venezuelan doctor cleaned the nasty wound and shot me full of penicillin which quickly erased the red stripe that had begun to travel up my shin.

A few days later, having discharged onto the lighters the last of our cargo, we were leaving the anchorage when one of our gantlines somehow got twisted into the propeller. Nobody knew or claimed to know how it happened or where the line had come from. (Gantline is a general term used for a very long rope much heavier than a heaving line though not nearly as large as a hawser. An all-purpose line, it has dozens of uses such as hoisting staging and bosun's chairs, winching, hand ropes and life lines—a life line is a rope rigged waist-high along the deck in heavy weather that helps a sailor move along from one end of the ship to the other, when the roll is deep and the seas are high, without getting slammed against a hatch coaming or washed into the scuppers or overside.)

The anchor had to be dropped again and the engines shut down while the line was removed. A "line in the screw" is one of the most bothersome and potentially expensive accidents that can happen because, to a merchant ship, time is money. It's like losing a contact lens in a taxi with the meter running. It's also embarrassing because, like a hawser burn on the ankle, only stupidity can cause it.

Captain O'Sullivan went into a rage. Everyone aboard including his chief engineer became an incompetent idiot in his eyes. A light skiff used for painting the ship's sides near the water line was let down and I, being on watch, was detailed by the bosun to man the oars. The gangway was still down, its bottom step hanging over the greasy water. (Lake Maracaibo, then as now, was a forest of oil derricks and the water a bath of corruption.) I rowed the bosun and the chief engineer from the gangway to the stern where, since the ship was light—without cargo—and since we had not planned to take on ballast until we had crossed Maracaibo bar (a deep-water channel has since been dredged through), half the screw and the propeller shaft were out of the water. The gantline, twisted into the joint between the screw and the shaft was clearly visible. I nosed the skiff up to the shaft, and the bosun and the chief climbed out and began to unwind the rope while I pulled back a couple of strokes to be in a position to relay their messages to the mate on the deck above. The mate, of course, could not see what was going on below him because of the overhang of the fantail. The captain was also on the taffrail, livid and fuming.

The bosun, finding his sheath-knife inadequate, called for a fire ax.

"An ax!" I cried, cupping my hands around my mouth and

shouting up to the taffrail. Dave, who was also standing by above to carry out the mate's orders (the other a.b., the third man of our watch, was standing by the helm with Mr. Kusic) lowered a fire ax into the boat, and I delivered it to the bosun.

"The motherfucker's jammed on the bottom," he said.

I was a good underwater swimmer, so I offered my services saying I could make some surface dives and cut the line away from underneath, but the bosun refused to let me get in the water because of the wound on my ankle. "Tell the mate the motherfucker's jammed underneath," he said. I stroked back to my former position and shouted up to the deck.

"What did you say?" the mate called down.

"The bosun says the motherfucker's jammed underneath!"

"Well, *cut it out!*" the captain cried. He was so agitated he was bobbing at the rail.

"The captain says cut it out," I called to the bosun on the screw.

"What the fuck you think I'm trying to *do?*" the bosun shouted.

I called up to the deck. "What the fuck you think they're trying to *do.*"

The captain screamed, *"Come get me!"* gesturing wildly toward the gangway. I started to pull toward midships.

"Where're you going?" the bosun shouted.

"I'm going to get the old man."

"The old *man!!*"

"He said to come get him."

The bosun made a fist of despair and passed the terrible news on to the chief who was already halfway in the water with his clothes on. I rowed off toward the gangway, and when I reached it, Captain O'Sullivan stood on the bottom step. He had stripped to his jockey shorts and stood there, his half-rimmed glasses on his purple face, his long, white purple-veined legs ending in feet clad in black lisle socks held up by garters. When he lurched down into the tippy boat, I saw he was clutching a long knife in his left hand.

"Row! you stupid sailor," he commanded.

I rowed him back to the stern where, without taking off his glasses or his socks, and with the knife, believe it or not, clenched in his teeth, he leapt into the foul lake. He treaded and floundered his way to the screw, grasped the trailing edge of one of the bronze blades, and clung there panting. I pulled close with the skiff as the chief engineer said from the water, "There's no need for you to trouble yourself, Cap'n."

"We're getting there, Cap'n," the bosun said.

The captain said something unintelligible over the knife in his teeth.

"What was that, Cap'n?" the chief said.

The master let go the prop blade with one hand and snatched the knife away. "I *said,* with this stupid crew I have to do everything myself."

"We're getting it, Cap'n, slow but sure," the chief said.

The bosun helped the master up onto the prop shaft and explained the problem.

"Has anybody gone under to the other side," the captain inquired, still breathing heavily.

The bosun said, "Cal, here, offered to, but I didn't think he should go in the water with his bad foot."

"Kentfield's a stupid ordinary, you don't depend on a stupid ordinary to do your work for you, what's the matter with you stupid people."

With that, he slid into the water and was about to submerge himself when the bosun said, "Sir, your glasses."

If he was embarrassed at having forgotten them, he didn't show it in his face because his fury masked any other emotion that might have contested there.

"Kentfield," he commanded. "Hold my glasses!"

He whipped them off his face and handed them to the bosun who passed them on to me in the boat. I carefully laid them on the stern seat, trying not to laugh. But I did laugh when the captain put the knife back in his teeth and went gurgling under. He couldn't see in the clear air without his glasses let alone in the dirty lake, but he kept bobbing up and going down and bobbing up for breath and going down again, making an absolute fool of himself while the chief, the bosun, and I looked on and looked at each other with wondrous disbelief.

On one rise, he gasped, "Pull from the *top,* stupid."

The chief dutifully pulled on the line from above, and the bosun hacked away with the ax, chopping out small bits of line and tossing them into water. The captain emerged again, obviously dangerously exhausted. He couldn't even say stupid he struggled so hard to get his breath. He clung with one arm to the chief, with the other to the shaft. He had lost his knife in the murky depths. Without a word the bosun reached down and grasped him by the armpits and pulled him out of the water. When he had retrieved his breath, the captain said, "I suppose you people can take it from here."

We all nodded, and I pulled the boat as closely as I could to the prop shaft and helped the master in. I pulled off my tee shirt so he could wipe his face and eyes and put his glasses back on. He didn't say a word as I rowed him back to the gangway. He climbed slowly, heavily up the steps, declining assistance from me, but gaining strong support from the hand ropes. He went straight to his cabin, where Mr. Kusic told me later, he had a gastric attack.

When I returned to the stern, the bosun had taken off his clothes and gone, himself, into the water, and in an hour or so, between him and the chief, the line was hacked out and piled into the skiff.

Once again underway, we passed over the bar and into the gulf and the Caribbean, putting in at Curaçao, at neat Dutch Willemstad, for fuel and stores, then made our way under the Antilles, rounded the northeast point of Trinidad, and, keeping well out from the shifty effluent of the Orinoco delta, headed down the coast for British Guiana (now Guyana). At Georgetown I found a used copy of the second volume of the Random House edition of *Remembrance of Things Past* (the first three Modern Library volumes I had brought with me in my sea bag), bought a ready-made white duck suit such as Willems and Lord Jim wore and Fredric March wore in "Trade Winds."

Then we went up the Demerara River to the bauxite mines at the Mackenzie, took half a load of ore to Port of Spain, dumped it, went back up the river for half a load more, went back to Trinidad and topped off—filled up—left the tropics and the Southern Cross, eventually delivering our cargo under fantastic displays of aurora borealis at Port Alfred on the Saguenay.

Back in New Orleans I shipped out almost immediately on the *Paul Revere,* another Alcoa Liberty on the bauxite run that, a couple of months later, took me back to the jungles of Guiana, but first it took me to Europe.

Instead of transporting construction material to Venezuela, the *Paul Revere,* on the outward voyage, carried coal to France. Coal is filthier stuff than bauxite though once it was safely dumped in the holds and the dust settled, it could have been rice or beans or wheat or cotton. The *Paul Revere* loaded up in Mobile and "secured for sea" in Mobile Bay before moving out into the Gulf of Mexico. It was already November and even the normally phlegmatic Gulf could not be trusted in the *norte* season.

Before a freighter moves out of the protection of a harbor or a safe bay or a river's mouth, it must be made as invulnerable as possible against the indifferent though often destructive action of the open sea. On a Liberty—as on many other freighters that do not have steel hatch covers that slide hydraulically and lock together, or covered mooring cables that reel in automatically at the touch of a lever or the push of a button as many new ships have—as soon as the longshoremen have finished with the cargo, all hands of the deck crew, whether or not sea watches have been set, "turn to" to secure for sea. First they cover the open holds. On a Liberty there were five of them, and if all were open, the crew, under the direction of the bosun, started forward, usually, at Number One and moved aft, hatch by hatch. One man, usually the deck maintenance or an a.b. or an especially experienced or trusted ordinary, operated the winch. Being winchman was a status job. A ship's winch, of course, is a powered drum that rolls in or lets out cables that raise or lower the steel booms and operate the runners or cables that run through the boom's blocks (pulleys). (The winch on the bow that pulls up the anchor is called a windlass for reasons known only to nautical tradition, and it is part of the anchor equipment—chains, claws, etc.—called, by the same tradition, ground tackle.) There are permanent winches at each hatch. These days, winches are nearly all electrically powered and troublefree, but the winches on a Liberty were steam, and on the *Paul Revere,* they were rusted, battered, and unnaturally cantankerous. The deck engineer worked on them frequently and cursed them continually, and even then they stuttered and grabbed and slipped and complained.

By winching the boom's runners, broad steel strongbacks that supported the hatch covers were carefully lowered and fitted across each open hold, then the hatch boards were laid on by hand across the strongbacks. Old hatch covers, which are two-and-a-half inches thick and about thirty inches wide, four feet long, and fiendishly heavy wood, are, these days, when encased in acrylic resin and made into table tops, very popular with certain decorative persuasions.

This solid covering of hatch boards was further covered with a heavy, oiled canvas tarpaulin. (The exposed edges of the tarp's seams must be laid toward the stern of the ship so wind cannot tear in between the stitches, for, as everyone has heard, a hurricane can drive a straw through a telephone pole, so it can open the tightest seam of a tarp.) The canvas was then tucked against the hatch coaming and held there with long steel battens and heavy wooden wedges laid into place with a sledgehammer. Wielding that hammer was the carpenter's special job.

The booms were lowered and clamped snugly to rest in their cradles, the blocks unshackled and drawn together, and the lines made up and lashed to cleats on the masthouses. The mooring lines were stowed away in the forepeak below the deck of the fo'c'slehead. On the anchor windlass, the brake levers were set and pinned, steel pawls hinged to the windlass by the cathead were flopped into place, and to further prevent any slippage of the mammoth hooks in heavy pounding seas, huge steel claws shackled to padeyes in the deck were dropped into the links of the anchor chains. (On sailing ships, the cathead was a beam projecting over the ship's bow and used to pull up the anchor. The word was transferred on steamships to the turning drum of the windlass that raises the anchor chain. A padeye is a steel half-ring or a bit of steel plate with a hole in it welded to the deck and used for shackling guy lines, securing deck cargo and any number of other things. Padeyes are a menace to a new man until he learns where they are. He can smash toes and fall on his face and twist ankles. In daylight he can see them, but treading the maindeck in the dark of the night can be treacherous until he learns which track to follow.)

The little hatch to the forepeak and all the watertight doors of the masthouse lockers were shut and dogged. The ship, then, was secure for sea. If the season is calm and the weather expected to be fair, some of these precautions may be ignored. Locker doors may be left open, for instance, and the claws left off the anchor chains. Few precautions were required, in fact, on the *John Ringling* in the sunny, summery Caribbean; but they were all necessary on the *Paul Revere* headed for the North Atlantic in winter.

That winter, 1947–48, may or may not have set a stormy record between the 40th and 50th parallels of the Atlantic, but, to the fat-bellied, deep-riding, underpowered, war-wearied *Paul Revere,* it, the sea, set up an obstacle almost as crushing and as defeating as Sisyphus' hill.

(According to Homer, whom, I suppose, we might as well accept, whoever he or they was or were, Sisyphus was compelled to spend eternity pushing a rock up a hill, and when he got to the top, but before the rock went over the other side, a force pushed it back down, and he had to start all over again:

"Also I" [Ulysses—who may have been Sisyphus' son rather than Laertes'; there's a Homeric uncertainty there—visiting the land of the dead] "saw Sisyphos. He was suffering strong pains, and with both arms embracing the Monstrous Stone, struggling with hands and feet alike, he would try to push the stone upward to the crest of the hill, but when it was on point of going over the top, the force of gravity turned it backward, and the pitiless stone rolled back."

This is a popular illustration of the human dilemma, and Albert Camus, whose thought went forward and backward and finally crashed at high speed against a tree outside of Paris, said Sisyphus was happy; well, Sisyphus has also been personified as the sea, as the huge waves that go up, that you struggle to surmount, only to have them fall away under you in the same spot while you start over again.)

That winter was a Sisyphean winter. It took the *Paul Revere* nearly thirty days to cross the Atlantic. And every day was an up and a down, every hour, every minute an assault against the implacable sea. There was no perilous hurricane, only the common stormy waves, a sunless sky. When somebody like Francis Chichester crosses the North Atlantic in a small boat, it's a kind of stunt, and, of course, it can be done; but Conrad, at the beginning of "Youth," aptly stated, "We all began life in the merchant service. Between the five of us there was the stewardship of the sea and also the fellowship of the craft, which no amount of enthusiasm for yachting, cruising and so on, can give since one is only the amusement of life and the other is life itself."

Day after day the sea came over the bow, then day after day it tipped us broadside. On a Liberty, a fifteen-degree roll is a severe tilt—ninety degrees is flat on your side and fatal—and we were rolling twenty, even thirty degrees. On a sailboat that's nothing, but on a 10,000-ton baloney stuffed with coal, it's wallowing. Day after day the sky was wet, gray, overcast, and I fancied I knew each single individual wave. There was a dream image, an image of restitution for committed sins, at the end of my first story which that marvelous madwoman, Eileen Garrett, published in her old *Tomorrow* magazine, a wave image that finished the story:

The air was cold and heavy . . . Suddenly, far off toward the horizon, he saw a disturbance; it was a wave that grew and grew. It approached, a giant tidal wave, fast as a passenger train. He looked up at it coming, blotting out the moon. If it broke, it would send him and the ship and all rolling and dying away in the sea. It rose up over him, starting to break. Then it stopped still, hovering, suspended over him. And he knew there was no escape should it choose to fall.

We'll get to the hurricane shortly on this voyage, but first, after all those monotonously leaping, falling, two-steps-forward-one-step-back days, we made it to France. That was the time, before the heavy hand of DeGaulle, of the confused fingers of the Fourth Republic just after the war. A general strike was on, which, of course, included dock workers, so we put in to Brest to wait it out. I remember going ashore there—we were on the hook, not tied up at the dock, just waiting for the political times to change. We were getting "danger money" which is extra pay for being in potentially perilous zones (seamen have been getting rich for years now, going to Indochina). The waters of the Channel and all the approaches to French ports had been mined, and even though the war was over, the mines remained and we were paid for them.

After all that battling the sea—we could do no work on deck, we couldn't even go out there without clinging desperately to the hand ropes, the life lines; we stood lookout topside on the lee wing of the bridge, and to keep busy in the daytime we tried to paint our fo'c'sles and passageways, but it took two men for every stroke, one to lay on the paint, and the other to keep hold of the can so it didn't go scooting down the passage when the ship pitched—we were ready for some relaxation.

I had some shipmate problems at Brest. First of all I went ashore in the same company as the second mate, whom I didn't particularly like, but because he and I walked past the first gin mill outside the docks—I wanted to see the town and he had some ship's business to attend to—I was accused of ignoring my fo'c'sle buddies and consorting with officers by an a.b. named Whitey. Whitey was blond, lean, strong, and accomplished, all the characteristics that would qualify him as Herman Melville's "handsome sailor," his prototype for Billy

Budd, except that Whitey was evil, not good, a prototype for the devil. He possessed a terrible strength not just in his body, but in his influence on the minds of others. Other men followed him, but I didn't, and he resented that. (Years later, I came across him again in the marine hospital in San Francisco where we both were doing therapy for broken legs. We recognized each other, but we didn't speak.) I have disliked people, but I can't remember knowingly, actively hating anyone other than Whitey. (I won't identify him further, he may have learned to read.) All my notions of human kindness, of forbearance, of forgiveness, of honesty and straightforwardness, all the Boy Scout virtues which I had always felt I should attempt to acquire, all these were turned around, turned inside out in Whitey. He told me, by being quite innocently what he was, what I did not want to be but probably was. He made up lies about me, he accused me of things I never thought of and of crimes I never committed. We never fought. His weapons were not his fists, they were deviousness and innuendo. (Fighting, as I shall describe later on, was a way of easing tension. It's technically forbidden on American ships, but when men live together for long periods, animosities and even murders can result. Only a couple of years ago a captain was murdered by his crew on a Greek ship in the Pacific. On the *Seatiger* I used to fight with a kid from Yorkshire whose name was John Hardy Westbrook Twemlow, but we wrestled like kids, hard, but not trying to hurt each other, just to see who was strongest the way my brother and I used to do. There were two others on that ship, two Scotsmen from Glasgow, who, when the heat and the time and the brooding monotony of the heavy voyages overcame them, went out of sight of the master and beat each other mercilessily, but dispassionately. Sometimes one triumphed, sometimes the other. Whenever I have fought, aside from the friendly wrestles with John Hardy Westbrook Twemlow, it's been in deadly earnest for a cause, or it's been in self-defense. Those two Glasgow men stripped down and fought out a bloody ritual, at least once each trip to Kuwait usually in the hot sandstorms of the Red Sea or the moody winds of the Indian Ocean.)

I put Whitey into the body of an Estonian named Harry in the story "Near the Line" and wreaked my revenge upon him. I don't always fight with my fists either.

And I didn't go ashore in Brest with Whitey and his pals. The second mate and I walked past the dockside pubs that drew them in and climbed the long hill from the harbor, and I left the second mate, too, at the turn of the road.

At sea there's lots of empty time, and reading can fill it. Almost all seamen read something. First off, in Brest, I went to a bookstore and instantly fell in love with a girl who sold me a continental edition in English of *Almayer's Folly*. She also told me the name of the best restaurant, the Grape de Raisin, in Brest, Finistère, France. Though I know by the way she smiled that she liked me and my funny French (I described myself as a *peinture* rather than a *peintre*—I had been known at Iowa as "the bad boy of the French department"—) she would not let me take her there. She was a properly brought-up middle-class French girl, and not only did I identify myself as a painting, but also as an American sailor which meant to the proper French bourgeoisie that I wanted one thing and one thing only from a girl. That was not altogether true, she bewitched me and I would have loved her company though, of course, I would sure enough have gotten around to arranging, if possible, for our bodies to join. As it was, I went to the Grape de Raisin alone and had walnuts for dessert. Times were thin in 1947 in Finistère.

After three weeks the ship moved to Cherbourg, and I took a train for Paris. The captain told me I couldn't go because we had, in two days' time, to shift the ship upriver to Rouen, but I said I was going anyway. The ship could shift without me, and the captain could log me if he had to.

("Shifting" a ship is moving it from one place to another within a general area without setting sea watches. A ship may shift, for instance, from San Francisco to Oakland, Brooklyn to

Hoboken, but it can't shift from New York to Jacksonville or San Francisco to Seattle.

"Logging" is putting a malefactor's name down in the ship's log or record and, at the master's discretion, withholding a portion of his pay. It's the modern version of the lash, taking the place, as punishment, of flogging and keel-hauling. I was willing to be logged in order to get to Paris. Sometimes men "jump" ship which is leaving a ship in a foreign country with all one's gear. If he doesn't take his pants and boots and toothbrush, his books and his cigarettes, then he can't be accused, legally, of jumping ship, he can go back later and claim his pay saying he "missed" the ship. Missing and jumping are two different things. The *Seatiger* was famous, infamous, for men missing and jumping, partly because of Captain Dantzler, and partly because of the horrible long hot run through the Red Sea in summer, from Liverpool to the Persian Gulf and back again. When that ship finally returned to the United States, of the original deck crew, only I and Charlie Goodwin remained. More of the *Seatiger* later.)

An old friend of mine, Warren (Jack) Wirtz, a poet and a composer, was in Paris working on a Woolley Foundation grant at the Cité Universitaire. He was older than I (I've just received a notice from my mother that he has died in Phoenix), but I grew up next door to him in Keokuk. His father was once a grocer and later ran a bowling alley of which the mother and the children were ashamed because it was down toward the river and sold beer and attracted unrespectable types including women like my fallen cousin who slung hash at a restaurant across the street and who was said to live in a state of sin with the owner, the town crook. And Jack had a crazy uncle who, in the silent late nights of summer, stood on the street corner by Rose Neyen's store and, accompanied by the distant barking of Chip Canary's dogs and the barn owl's cry, preached sermons to the sleeping neighborhood. His name was Jess and I think they finally took him away. I kissed the girl of that family, Jack's cousin, before I ever kissed Regine Trautvetter, and I kissed her when I was twelve.

Jack and his sister Dorothy were both incredibly talented and bright, and they exposed me, the enfant next door to so many things that were not commonly accessible in Keokuk during the Depression—art, French, music. (Jack, who was an excellent pianist, tried one summer to teach me the instrument, but I could not stay awake in the hot afternoons of July.) I have never written about Jack or Dorothy, though I still may, but I put their mother, Alma, into a short story—along with my own mother and some of my cousins—originally called "The Tenants of Alma's Garden" ("Dark had nearly come. A chance breeze, like a cat's paw at sea, passed softly through the locust trees and over the short grass, displacing a few strands of ghostly hair, intruding upon the tenants of Alma's garden. Alma herself had long since gone into her house, and she had a bright light in her kitchen window."), but which *The New Yorker* published as "The Bell of Charity."

I looked up Jack in Paris, but I also wanted to see the Corbusier dormitory at Jack's university on the Boulevard Jourdan way out in the left environs of the city. Jack was miserable. Paris was a big, poverty-stricken, hungry, strike-torn, existential city. Jack was poor. He'd always had sinus problems, and, like Katherine Anne Porter when in the early fifties she went to sojourn at the University of dirty Liège, he could scarcely breathe and was going crackers; but he put me up in his dormitory (not the Corbusier one) and took me to lunch at his schoolside café. Fresh from an American ship with all of its provisions, I was well-fed and ate only half my food. The waitress screamed at us in the inimitable way of French shrikes. Times were hard; how dare I not eat every morsel that was set before me. Jack argued with her. He had good French. We left. We went into Paris and got fairly drunk. We listened to Juliette Greco—before she had her nose fixed—in a tiny black *cave* off Boulevard Montparnasse. We looked for Jean Paul Sartre in all the wrong cafés, and when I got back to the ship, it had moved to Rouen.

I was dutifully logged three days' pay, but it was worth it just to have stood like Quasimodo under the gargoyles of Notre

Dame. I found on my return that I had drawn the gangway watch from four to twelve. I paid a Spaniard to stand it. He said he was Spanish, and the thirteen- or fourteen-year-old boy with him he said was his son. Dock haunters, filthy, cold, cadging meals. They could have been anything. They had been, as the Bible probably says, cast naked into the wilderness. Homeless, stateless refugees of the terrible war. The master of the *Paul Revere,* who was a West Indian and quite different from O'Sullivan of the *Ringling,* expressed and evinced a compassion for his fellow creatures which is why, when Whitey said to me, "How can you talk to a guy that's logged you," I shrugged, knowing that logging me was the least the captain could have done, and allowing me to pay the Spaniard and his son, who were freezing and starving and literally quaking with the shock of their blasted lives, to stand my coal-black watch in the grim back estuary of the Rouen docks, was letting himself in for trouble; but he did it, and I crossed on the ferry into the city. It was late in the afternoon, too late to see sights, so I found my way instinctively to the Hôtel de la Poste. It was Christmas eve.

(Flaubert was born in Rouen and used the ancient cathedral town as the setting for Emma Bovary's meeting with her lover, Léon, in the famous scene of the cab that wandered around the cobblestoned streets for hours with curtains drawn.) The Hôtel de la Poste, I believe, had not yet been built or had not attained prominence in Flaubert's day, but it was well-established and well-known by the time of the First World War. In "Rouen in February," a chapter of his *Memoirs of an Infantry Officer,* Siegfried Sassoon says:

> The Hôtel de la Poste hadn't altogether modernized its interior, but it contained much solid comfort and supplied the richest meals in Rouen. Consequently it was frequented by every British officer employed in the district, and had become a sort of club for those indispensable residents—so much so that strong suggestions had been advanced by senior officers to the effect that the Poste should be put out of bounds for all Infantry subalterns on their way to the Line. The place, they felt, was becoming too crowded, and the de-

portment of a "temporary gentleman" enjoying his last decent dinner was apt to be more suitable to a dug-out than a military club.

Leaning back in a wicker chair, I enjoyed the after-effects of a hot bath and wondered what I'd have for dinner. The lift came sliding down from nowhere to stop with a dull bump. A bulky grey-haired Colonel, with green tabs and a Coronation Medal, stepped heavily out, leaning on a stick and glaring around him from under a green and gold cap and aggressive eyebrows. His disapproval focused itself on a group of infantry subalterns whose ungainly legs were cumbered with high trench boots . . . I smiled sardonically at the green and gold Colonel's back view. The lift ascended again, leaving a confused murmur of male voices and a clatter of feet on the polished wood floor . . . Young cavalrymen were numerous, their superior social connections demonstrated by well-cut riding boots and predominantly small heads . . . The large dining-room was full of London Clubmen dressed as Colonels, Majors, and Captains with a conscientious objection to physical discomfort. But, after all, somebody had to be at the Base . . . They were as much victims of circumstances as the unfortunate troops in the trenches. Puffing a cigar, I decided that there was a tolerant view to be taken about almost everybody, especially after a good dinner (and a bottle of Burgundy) at the Hôtel de la Poste.

Christmas eve, 1947, and the *Second* World War had passed through Rouen. The hotel bar was not yet crowded, but it was steamy and warm, a cheerful relief from the raw bone-chilling dampness of the Norman winter. The interior *had* been modernized, apparently, just since the end of the war. It may have been rebuilt for all I know—Rouen had been heavily bombed. There were chrome-plated stools at the bar and red-leather banquettes along one side; and cream-colored walls, gold-framed reproductions of the Barbizon school, chandeliers, and a long mirror behind the sparkling glassware of the back bar produced an effect of some elegance on the likes of one who still had slush and coal-dust on his boots.

The dining room which was not open but which I could see from the lobby when I went through to the head (as continentally casual as I must have wanted to appear, I did not at once become accustomed to the lady in black smock attending the open *pissoirs* of the men's room), the dining room looked older than the bar having potted palms in the corners and those wicker chairs though I can't suppose they were the same that a mellow, contented Sassoon leaned back in thirty years before.

My brief sojourn with Jack in Paris had taught me that coffee and cognac were a good combination for a cold twilight, and very French; so I said, when I returned to the bar and slid onto a stool, *"Un café, un cognac, s'il vous plaît,"* sounding, I thought, fairly authentic. The bartender thought so, too, apparently, because he didn't give back to me that contemptuous cold-fish stare of feigned incomprehension that I later came to associate with French serving folk.

Only three other people sat at the bar. One, two stools away from me, was a girl who had just sat down, and at the end, a middle-aged man and a youngish woman of unbeautiful, but striking appearance with a wide mouth full of prominent teeth in which she clamped a cigarette holder. They were patently English, and they clearly found each other amusing because they laughed together a great deal, she making animated gestures with her smoking holder.

The girl ordered a cognac and fell immediately into a conversation in French with the bartender. It was not a large bar, separated from the hotel lobby by swinging doors; it was slowly filling with the cheerful, heady stink of Gauloises and Player's, coffee and spirits. To be dead honest, they picked *me* up. There was not much to do in Rouen—well, Emma Bovary found amusement and so did Jeanne d'Arc—in 1947, Christmas eve, and I was new flesh in the territory, so we fell into conversation. I spoke with the couple for a long time, then I spoke with the girl whose conversation with the bartender had ended when some other customers, refugees from the season, came into the bar. She was not at all French, she was Australian and her name was Beverly MacClaren, and she was stranded in Rouen of all places with visa problems. The middle-aged man with the woman with the teeth was the British consul. I introduced them, and when Beverly went to pee, the laughing woman bent forward and said to me, "Who *is* she?" and I had to admit that I didn't know. "Oh!" the woman exclaimed, then pushed her exclamation into a roar of merriment, "you're just *starting,*" and I said, "Yes, I'm just starting," and the woman said, "Well, then, who are *you?*" and I said, "My name is, believe it or not, Calvin Kentfield, and I'm from Keokuk, Iowa, and though I pretend to be a painter because I paint pictures, I'm a sailor and we're discharging coal across the river." I stretched out my leg so they could see my dirty boot.

"Extraordinary," the consul said.

"I suppose it is," I said. "She's having visa problems, I don't know why. She's Australian."

"O Lord," said the consul, "Then I suppose she *is* my territory."

I said that because she was a pretty girl, large but pretty, and I had been at sea for a long time, I figured I'd make her *my* territory. The woman with the teeth guffawed.

Beverly came back and ordered another cognac, and I explained to her that I had spent my draw and was broke. She laughed and said, "I'll get some money."

(A "draw" is an advance against salary that the captain of a ship gives out in each port. There's no limit to the advance except the total amount each man has, at that point in the voyage, earned; and the captain must, by law, issue the money in each port of *loading* or *discharge.* But when a master "gives out a draw," he's only required to do it once in a forty-eight hour period, and he's not *required* to do it if the ship, as in Brest for instance, is merely in transit. By custom, however, he does. Some of these fine points of custom and law will be illustrated soon.)

Beverly sojourned at la Poste in a room on the third floor. She excused herself and exited for a few minutes. When she came back her arms were draped with commodities—coats, stockings, scarves. She grinned—she had a marvelous, open, vulnerable smile that girl—and motioned that I should follow. As we went out, the consul touched her arm and said, "Come see me at the office on Boxing Day." His lady swirled her holder in the air, threw back her head and laughed like a French actress, like Edwige Feuillère. I was captivated.

Beverly led me to a series of underground *boîtes* and *caves* where we had drinks and listened to jazz and transformed her black-market commodities into cash. When we returned to la Poste, having eaten nothing, it was nearly midnight, but the consul and his lady were still there drinking and laughing—he drank scotch and soda, she Dubonny. "Du bos, du bon, dubonny!" (I'm probably fictionalizing here, I don't think the advertising slogan for Dubonnet was introduced until the fifties, but you get my point.) They were merry Christmas, drinking in that way that literature, cinéma, and true life have shown us that ranking members of the British Foreign Service, holding provincial posts are scheduled to do.

"Don't forget," the consul called, as I took a bottle of cognac and Beverly upstairs to bed, "Come see me on Boxing Day."

Saving the cognac for later, I was well into the matter when the telephone rang. Being on top and adjacent, I answered, but I couldn't understand a word, so I withdrew and stood quivering, upright, in the unheated chamber while Beverly told me I must go downstairs and book a room. I pulled on my pants and descended, half naked and still obviously excited and barefoot to the frigid lobby where I signed in and was led back up the elevator to a room on the same floor as Beverly's. The concierge—the place was closed up by that time, the bar and all—turned down my bed, raised the shade, indicated the bathroom down the hall, and accepted my promise of payment and a tip in the morning for I had nothing in my pants but my desire. As he descended in the lift I hurried down the hall to Beverly. After all that coal-dust and those Sisyphean seas, I came eight times that night, and the next day, she went out to lunch with the consul, and it was Christmas, not Boxing Day.

A light snow had fallen during the night, and the sky was still overcast, lowdown and gray, when I went out, midday, to walk the old city.

I can never forget that Christmas in Rouen. I mark the

spaces of my life from it. Hungover and my body played out, I was left with the medieval winter—and art and history, both as exciting to me as sex. I walked the crooked streets, saw where Joan of Arc was burned, returned to the cathedral which was hoarded up, boarded over, demolished by bombs. The streets were empty, the shops closed. In the *charcutier*'s window, sausages and geese hung by their necks. By two o'clock, people were beginning to shove their soles—some leather, some wooden—through the snow that had, with coal-dust descending from the air turned to grey slush. Opposite the cathedral, in a stone-paved square, a tiny clutch of acrobats appeared, *jongleurs.* They were knobby-kneed, knotty-muscled little men in patched tights, shivering and putting on a brave show, doing leaps and juggling pins to the tune of a flute and a tambour and a tambourine. For *sous,* for *francs,* leaping and sweating in the icy winter in the shadow and beneficence of Our Ruined Lady of Rouen.

Back on the ship, across the Seine, cold rain began to fall. The Spaniards were still there, begrimed but fed, the older man quaking still, shaking, an incandescent quivering. I gave them soap and matches and cigarettes, and I gave the boy my sweater because I could get another and, besides, we were going to the tropics and I wouldn't need it.

Sea watches were set. The captain trusted me so I stood the wheel as we went down the Seine, ox-bow turns past sleeping villages, the morning turning bright, green banks and white churches, Protestant-looking land in a Catholic country. We had shucked our coal, we were light with a ballast of Seine water, past Le Havre into La Manche, the English Channel, and then to the Bay of Biscay on our way to the jungle.

In a story called "Sailor's Grave" I wrote this introductory description:

It was just past twelve o'clock of a bitter night, off the coast of Europe, in those grim, chaotic seas that fringe the Bay of Biscay and Spanish Finisterre, where the winds come in turn from every quarter, and powerful opposite currents sometimes run side by side.

The waves were mountainous, and each time the freighter *Lever's Wife* tipped over a crest, the vessel's whirling screw came out of the water and shook her dangerously. The cups and plates in the pantry made a terrible racket, and those unfortunate seamen below, lying in bunks that were hung athwartships, rolled irresistibly from side to side, like the swivel chairs in the crew's mess, which banged the edges of the dining tables.

The captain of the *Paul Revere* was not the cold pedestrian counter-jumper that O'Sullivan was, nor was he the neurotic diabolist that Dantzler was; he was a competent, kindly man who, under pressure, became hysterical. The *Paul Revere* was an untaped—and, therefore, unsafe—vessel; that is, it was a Liberty without Band-Aids to hold it together; and in the Bay of Biscay it started to come apart. A crack appeared, just like an earthquake fault, forward of the midship house. It was patent, visible. And as the ship ascended, descended those mountainous waves, shaken like a dead cat shaken by a dog when its tail end came out of the water, the crack widened. The captain cried, "It's a hurricane, it's a hurricane," and though it was not hurricane season, he was right. Though we were in imminent peril of breaking in two and all of us facing the possible ends of our lives, I found those seas exciting. I probably wouldn't now, I may have sense enough to be scared; but when you're young, it seldom occurs to you that you're going to die, if it ever does. Death, after all, happens to other people; but when we began pitching into the incredible trough and watching the crest of the next wave rise and tower over the masthead—from the bridge you had to look *up,* like Holman Hunt's Jesus looking up to the face of His Father, to the top of the wave—the captain called all hands to stand by and called the chief mate and the chief engineer to the bridge though, however many men there may have been on hand, there was absolutely nothing anybody could do. We were helpless, at the total mercy of the sea, and it was the sea, itself, that saved us. It stopped. We came to along the Portuguese coast, and passed out of the storm. The poor *Paul Revere* closed its crack flexing itself back together—the crack didn't heal, of course, a ship's not a human body and cannot produce scar tissue—and sailed into the tranquil spring seas of the Canaries. But the experience, not just the seas of Biscay, but also the long slow crossing (not all the crew had enjoyed the incredible satisfaction of Beverly—and the *Paul Revere* was a slow, exasperating ship) had built tensions and energy to the bursting point; and when we got to the jungle, to Paramaribo in Surinam, all Hell broke loose.

There's a famous eighteenth- or nineteenth-century engraving entitled "American Sea-captains Enjoying Themselves in Paramaribo." I may have quoted the caption wrongly, but the key word is Paramaribo, and in our case it was not the captain who amused himself, it was us, the crew. What I'm about to describe is not extracted from a Hollywood shooting script of the thirties, it's true life from the late forties, 1948 in fact, Paramaribo, Dutch Guiana, Surinam, north coast of South America. The cast: the crew of the *Paul Revere,* featuring, but not starring, Calvin Kentfield.

By the time we docked at Paramaribo, the crew had become an aggregation of rival cliques, some natural, some contrived. (The word "crew" includes in its strictest sense, every man on board a ship from the captain to the wiper and the ordinary, but in common usage—as in the dice game played in West Coast bars, Ship, Captain, and Crew—it describes only the unlicensed men—the non-officers—deck sailors, black gang, messmen.) It was natural for the men who lived and worked together at the same jobs to group together—wipers and oilers, firemen, firemen-watertenders, ordinaries and a.b.'s, messmen and bedroom stewards—and it was particularly natural for those of the same watch. The natural leader of the sailors, of course, was the bosun who was the boss on deck, who was usually an "older" man. (He might be thirty or thirty-five while most of the watchstanders were eighteen or nineteen or in their twenties though I wrote in many of my stories of a character whom I called Blades and whose real name, in fact, *was* Blades, who was an ordinary seaman though he was well into his late fifties.)

The bosun, depending upon his character and his inclination, could make life on deck tolerable or miserable (depending also upon his relationship with the mate who was *his* boss). Most bosuns I have known have fallen over backward to be fair all around, to give every man an even break; but I have known some, too, who have indecently persecuted certain sailors, men that offended him or men he resented. There is nothing really terrible a bosun can do, merchant ships are not military ships, they're just a way of making a living, but there are certain tasks that are less desirable than others. Mixing fish oil in the stifling forepeak on a heaving sea is a disagreeable task, for instance. (A combination of fish oil and petroleum penetrants is often used as a treatment for rusted decks instead of paint. One of the really big jobs on a ship is painting, or fish-oiling, the decks. They get rusted and become scaly, particularly the foredeck, from seas washing over the bulwarks and the bow, and every now and then they must be given a coat of protection. If the job's done properly, it's done all at once with all watches working during the day and with the company, of course, paying overtime. Anytime at sea that a sailor works on deck when he is not on watch, except for emergencies, he is paid overtime. Some captains resent paying that extra money to sailors for treating the decks and wait for the ship to come into port when sea watches can be broken and the job can be done on day work or by a shore gang. Captain Dantzler made a deal in Port Said with an Egyptian entrepreneur—a polite term—to have the decks of the *Seatiger* painted. In one day twenty-five or thirty *fellaheen* swarmed aboard and madly painted the decks of the *Seatiger* black. They looked fine until we turned the corner of the Red Sea, out of the strait of Bab-el-Mandeb into the crashing monsoon seas of the Indian Ocean where, because the corrosion and scale had not been removed but merely painted over, the black flaked off and the decks became bright rust; but the captain and the Arab entrepreneur both made a packet on the deal.)

However equitable a bosun might try to be, he unavoidably has his preferences based, usually, on the simple natural attraction of one man for another—some men he feels friendlier toward than others; often based on the man or men he feels he can trust to do a job right; occasionally, though rarely, based upon sexual attraction. Sometimes an older bosun likes a younger sailor for a bunk-partner or a shower-mate. It's not at all flattering to be known as the bosun's "boy."

The bosun on the *Paul Revere* was a man of exemplary knowledge and accomplishment in the ways of the sea and a strong character who was infinitely fair, and who liked to have men do their jobs promptly and well. He also told good stories and funny dirty jokes, and no one doubted his experience in the ways of anything whether it was women, booze, brawls, or the ways of the world between continents. He was a likeable man who seldom lost his cool, and his following was large. Whitey led a smaller rival faction of neophytes, while many of the rest of us remained simply uncommitted.

Knots of men—showered, shaven, shaggy, in clean shirts and polished shoes—after all those slow, tedious, tension-building weeks from France to South America, went ashore at Paramaribo. I went with a fellow named Bob who was the deck maintenance and who should have been part of the bosun's party because he and the bosun being day men shared a room on the ship (on more commodious vessels than a Liberty, the bosun would have a room of his own); but he was as uncommitted to cliques as I was, and, since we had worked well together on deck and become quite close in thought, we buddied up; but in the end, after the haircuts and the sightseeing and a couple of bars—there's not much to see in Paramaribo though it had a certain forgotten-corner-of-the-world charm—all of us, the whole crew, converged at what I will call the Hotel Surinam, no, I'll just call it The Hotel because there might be, these days, a legitimate Surinam Hotel since Dutch Guiana has been "developing" and soliciting tourism of late.

The Hotel, according to seamen's gossip, was the place where the action was, action, of course, meaning girls. It was hardly a hotel in the usual sense. There were, indeed, rooms, but they were not for a good night's rest—as if any of us wanted *that*—

and there was no dining room; but the whole second floor was a dancing bar. It had a balustrade, a broad posted balcony of white woodwork open to the singing tropical night. (It was the insects and the night birds that sang, not the natives.) Tables and wicker chairs surrounded the dance floor, just like the very proper Queen's Palace Hotel near the Botanical Gardens in Port-of-Spain, though the music was provided—I swear this is the truth—by an unshaven piano player in a dirty white suit with a cigarette dangling from his lower lip and a drink in front of him on the upright piano. I had not brought with me the white duck suit I had bought the trip before in British Guiana, but there were others there—Dutch planters, Dutch foremen from the bauxite mines upriver—in immaculate white suits and white shoes. One of them sat alone at the only table with extra chairs when Bob and I, later than the others, came in; so he motioned for us to sit down. He spoke English and he told us that no one had expected an American ship in harbor that week; that there was a French ship there, a local coaster from Cayenne; and where had we come from; and beware of the girl in pink with the big tits because she was a bruiser and hated men; but the girl with the golden earrings dancing with the blond American sailor was the sweetest bit of jungle pie north of Belém; and would we like a drink. He had a bottle of rum on the table, and he called for some glasses and some Coke.

I began to laugh. I couldn't believe it. In Mobile, just before the *Paul Revere* had left for France, Bob and I had gone to see *Golden Earrings,* and I could still hear that deep hoarse, bosun's voice of Marlene Dietrich singing, "And when my love wears golden earrings—"

"What are you laughing at?" Bob said.

"If you don't know, I can't tell you," I replied.

"Fuck you, Kentfield," Bob said.

He was a dark-haired fellow, about my age, maybe a year or two older, quite handsome but insecure. In sexual discussions, of which, among men on a ship, there used to be many ("Hell, Cal," said a friend of mine who was still going to sea in 1972, "we don't talk about booze or broads anymore, all we do is sit around rapping about taxes and crab grass."), Bob, who knew we'd all seen him in the shower, repeatedly said when Whitey would say, "I've never met the cunt yet that can take everything I've got," or the bosun would say, "In France there, I said I didn't want to catch nothing so she tried, but she couldn't even get her mouth over the end of it," "Well, never mind, you guys, it's not how big it is, it's how you use it, I'd rather tickle a girl to death than stab her."

Except for that diffidence about his physical size, or perhaps because of it, he was a very cocky fellow and quite bright. I lent him *Almayer's Folly* and Edmund Wilson's *Memoirs of Hecate County* which had just been published the year before and which I had bought in Mobile; and we had had a serious discussion, after he had finished it, whether or not, in the story about the golden-haired girl, when Wilson said he had taken her from behind, whether or not he meant he had shoved it up her ass. Bob said no, Wilson hadn't meant that, and he described to me how it could be done in the right place from the rear, "And you don't need a broomstick like Whitey's to do it with either."

I also lent him *To the Finland Station,* but he didn't have much to say about that.

It was Whitey, of course, who was dancing with Golden Earrings, and, I believe, if anyone on the *Paul Revere* detested Whitey more than I, it was Bob (or maybe the bosun). I think he moved in on them not so much because he wanted the girl —though she was a gorgeous East Indian with startling blue eyes like some of the dark-skinned, blue-eyed Maya of Yucatán— but because he wanted to challenge Whitey, which he did though once the general fight had erupted, Whitey squeezed into the background urging his confederates forward. If the battle hadn't begun that way, it would have begun some other. The bosun's group was there, taking Bob's side. Some French sailors got into it. The girls screamed, the piano player played louder, the Dutchmen absconded, one of Whitey's boys crashed through the balustrade and fell off the balcony, the bosun and

I—level heads—tried to herd the clutch of writhing bodies and flailing fists down the stairs and down the street because the whoremonger manager had called the cops. I only saved myself from getting hurt and getting involved because I saw how funny it was. A lot of rum had been drunk. Bob and I had drunk a full bottle between us before we even reached The Hotel, and I was in that state of exhilaration that booze can afford, that can, under one set of circumstances, generate violent acts while, under another, produce laughter. Once in the soft dirt street, the fighting knot broke up, and I found myself on one side of Bob and the bosun on the other. Bob's lip was bleeding. Whitey's group was half a block ahead. We were all heading for the harbor.

"Calm down now, Bobby," the bosun said. "Just calm down."

"You leave me alone," Bob said. "I'll kill that fuckin' Whitey, who's he think he is?"

"Take it easy, Bob," I said. "Take it easy."

"Fuck off, Kentfield."

"Whitey's not worth it."

"Goddamit, Kentfield, come on, you want to fight?"

I laughed. "Shit, *no!*" I said.

"Come on, Kentfield, come on, you son of a bitch."

"You're not going to fight me, Bob, you know you're not going to fight me."

"Calm down now Bobby, calm down you two."

"I'm calm," I said. "Bob's not going to fight me."

"You son of a bitch, Kentfield, you laughing bastard."

"And when your love wears golden earrings," I sang.

Bob dropped to the dirt, lay his bloody white shirt flat back in the dust and bellowed to the stars with laughter.

We, the bosun and I, raised him to his feet. He draped one arm over each of our necks, and when he stopped laughing, he said, "Kentfield, you son of a bitch, let's go have a drink."

Release.

Next time it was the bosun's turn.

There were two dockside restaurant-cafés, of the Metro-

Goldwyn-Mayer jungle type, dark interiors, portiered doorways, chairs and tables on the cobblestone docks where there were also shops and small market stalls, closed at that hour. The *Paul Revere* was tied up in front of them. When the three of us reached the waterfront, one of the cafés was occupied by Whitey's forces and most of the other by the bosun's men; but we found places to sit, either in chairs or on the cool stones. It was late, but the cafés, which had not had so much business in a long time, stayed open the night for us. We sat there laughing and swearing and telling stories, and drinking, drinking, drinking. We had gone separate individual ways in France, but here in the jungle we were all together.

The tide was coming in, and the sailing board hung at the top of the gangway.

(A sailing board is a small blackboard on which is chalked the hour of departure and the destination. The board must be put up at least three hours before sailing time—preferably twenty-four hours—so the men ashore may have time to get back aboard.)

The *Paul Revere* was due to start up the river on the morning tide, and the board was posted for six thirty. About six o'clock a truckload of stores was unloaded at the bottom of the gangway. Customarily the sailors would carry them aboard to the steward's lockers, but almost all the sailors were sitting on the dock, drinking. The mate came down the gangway and walked over to the bosun's table.

"Get your hands together and get those stores aboard," he said. The mate and the bosun had been at odds ever since Rouen. I don't know exactly what their problem was, but the bosun said, "Fuck you, mate." (It's not usual to say that because, not only, according to maritime regulations, may an officer not swear at or directly call a sailor a name, a sailor may not curse an officer.)

"Mind, bosun," the mate said, "mind your tongue."

"Excuse me. Fuck you. *Mr.* Mate."

"I said get these men together and bring those stores aboard."

(I should explain that though the mate could, by law, give us sailors a direct order to obey, by *custom* which, as in medieval France, is stronger than law, in fact, supersedes it, he may not order us except through the bosun.)

The bosun turned his back on him. The mate, helpless, turned on his heel and climbed back up the gangway.

By that time it was good daylight. Traffic along the quay was increasing. Fishermen, passing merchants opening shops, Hindus, Malays, Chinese, Blacks passing by on foot or on bicycles. Dutch housewives with shopping bags. Whitey leapt out of his chair and ran, lickety-split, to the edge of the wharf and screamed *"He-yeouw!"* and dived into the water. He could have killed himself, but Whitey liked to show off by doing wild things. His confederates loved him for it. They followed him over and pulled him out because the bulkhead was too steep for him to climb. He came up soaked and laughing. He sat down again at the next café to us, swallowed his drink, and proceeded to strip off his wet clothes, wringing each garment out as he removed it and spreading it out on the stones to dry. He emptied the water out of his shoes and sat down naked at the table, combing his hair, downing his drink. His confederates roared with laughter as he stood up and shook his long white cock at every woman that passed by.

By this time most of the other seamen who had been aboard ship had come down the gangway and were squatting on the stones drinking rum or Dutch beer. It was past sailing time. The captain, poor soul, was on the bridge watching it all. He sent the mate down again. "The captain says this is mutiny," the mate told the bosun.

The bosun laughed. "I haven't finished my bottle yet," he said.

The mate returned to the ship.

A policeman, a Malay in white shorts, high white stockings and helmet tried to arrest the indecent Whitey, but he was so outnumbered, all he could do was tell him to get dressed.

The bosun ordered another bottle and said, "Cal, you and

Bobby and Heavy and Steve go put on those stores, then come back here."

The four of us staggered to the gangway and lifted the crates of melons and lettuce and milk, eggs, oranges, bananas, and even some papayas onto the deck, letting the steward's men take them from there. Then we went back to the café.

"Put down two hours overtime apiece," the bosun said. "I'll authorize it."

He passed us all rum from his new bottle.

The master was frantic. He shouted down from the bridge, "This is *mutiny!* This is *mutiny!*"

"Fuck you, cap'n," the bosun said.

The captain began to blow the whistle, signaling that the ship was leaving. The tide was full, the dock workers, who had never seen anything like this before, were standing by to let go the mooring lines. Those of the crew, mostly messmen and officers, who were aboard were standing along the rails watching to see what was going to happen.

The captain blew the whistle frantically, he even blew the danger signal which is four sharp blasts in a row. The company agent, a neat Dutchman, who had been apprised of the problem, confronted the bosun. "As company representative," he said, "I must insist you shift the ship upriver. The tide is high and another ship is on its way down. *You must move the ship now!*"

"Fuck you," the bosun said.

"Why don't we go, bose," Bob said.

"We'll go when we finsh thish bottle."

I said to the neat Dutch agent, "The bosun says we'll go when we finish this bottle."

"See that you do," said the Dutchman who spoke English like an Englishman, and he stalked back in high dudgeon toward his office. What else could he do?

Some of the men, enlivened by the ship's whistle, had gone back aboard. Half an hour later, the bosun rose to his feet. Bob and I held him up. "All right," he said, "all right, all hands turn to to shift shit." He shoved Bob and me aside, "Take your cottonpickin' hands off me, you think I can't walk? *Shit!* All right, you guys, *all hands! Whitey!* Put your pants on, you cunt."

The rest of us followed, including Whitey's pack with Whitey last, zipping his trousers and skipping along on one foot and then the other, pulling on his shoes, the rest of his clothes balled under his arm. Bob and I followed the bosun to his room where he flopped dead out on his bunk, drunk, insensible, but clearly boss man.

Letting go was simple, there was nothing to do but pull in the lines and fake (flake) them out. The Paramaribo stop had been merely an immigration stop, a grocery stop, and, well, a rest stop. A lot of poison was antidoted in Paramaribo, and the good captain knew it. After he had calmed down, he never said another word about it, and I'm sure that until right now, Alcoa Steamship Company never knew that it happened.

Fortunately, one of the a.b.'s on the eight-to-twelve, being a Mormon, drank neither booze nor coffee, so he was sober at the wheel. Just as the *John Ringling* had done, we took half a load of bauxite to Trinidad, to Dirty Dick, and returned for another half load then went to Georgetown and Mackenzie for another half load. At Georgetown, we took on a local crew to do the loading upriver. (If seamen do longshore work, they get double pay, so it was cheaper in those days before there were permanent dock-workers at the mines, to transport natives each time from the coast.) There is a short account of the procedure in *The Alchemist's Voyage:*

> Between Freetown [Georgetown] and the ore kilns were a hundred miles of uncivilized forest pierced by the narrowing river and some native paths. Thus isolated, though circled by a settlement of Malays and a compound of whites, the mine kept no stevedores to work the ships that came. The *Alchemist,* therefore, must carry a shore gang with it.
>
> One by one the native workmen, straining under loads of tenting and mats, shovels and pans, boarded the steep gangway . . . There were twenty-five or more altogether. During the afternoon they

went about preparing for the journey—erecting shelters on the after deck, spreading the hatch boards with palm mats and tattered blankets, stringing lines and hanging canvas baffles, fixing an odd latrine to the stern rail. Between the heads of the capstans aft of number five, a cook made a galley from an oil drum and began at three in the afternoon to prepare a stew that would thereafter bubble night and day over the chambered flame.

Once again we took half a load of bauxite to Trinidad and once again returned to the jungle for more. We were on the "bauxite shuttle." Some ships stayed on it for months, Georgetown to Mackenzie to Trinidad to Georgetown to Mackenzie to Dirty Dick or Paramaribo to Paranam to Dirty Dick and back and forth. The *Paul Revere* made three complete shuttles and returned with a full load to the Mississippi River in the spring of 1948.

I hung around New Orleans awhile, seeing friends, then I went to Keokuk to visit my folks, then back on the Burlington and the Illinois Central to New Orleans. Then Blake, Ding-Dong, and I drove to California and worked the summer in a lumber camp in Humboldt county, then I went back to Iowa City in the fall, talked Paul Engle into letting me in the Writers' Workshop (undergraduate division with Paul Griffith), wrote my first story, "The Round Giant," which won second prize in *Tomorrow* magazine's college story contest, listened to Harry Truman's election on the radio, swept out The Bookshop every night for spending money and entered a window-display contest to promote Billy Rose's autobiography the name of which I have forgotten, and split the thousand-dollar first prize with a department store in Cleveland. I split that half prize with the ladies of The Bookshop, took my half, $250 and my story second prize, $200, and went to New York where I became employed nights at the Doubleday bookstore on 52nd and Fifth, was fired for any number of good reasons, but specifically for getting drunk on martinis one afternoon when Blake came to town from New Orleans and having him, who could scarcely enunciate Doubleday, call in an hour after

I was supposed to be at work and say I was sick. I subsequently became broke and hungry, and one morning when I awoke starving, and realized I didn't even have the fifteen cents for coffee and pecan roll at the Fourteenth-street Automat, I remembered my golden guilders.

When I had left Surinam on the *Paul Revere,* I had brought, left over, a wad of guilders that I kept in my duffle as curiosity souvenirs. There was a whole bunch of them from Paramaribo. At that time I lived in a rooming house on 17th Street between Irving Place and Third Avenue across the street from the old French flats. Noah Greenberg lived just around the corner. I was barely subsisting on unemployment and writing my first novel, *The Alchemist's Voyage,* then entitled *Chambers of the South* from Job, chapter nine:

> Which commandeth the sun, and it riseth not;
> and sealeth up the stars.
> Which alone spreadeth out the heavens,
> and treadeth upon the waves of the sea.
> Which maketh Arcturus, Orion, and Pleiades, and the chambers of the south.
> Which doeth great things past finding
> out; yea, and wonders without number.
> Lo, he goeth by me, and I see him not:
> he passeth on also, but I perceive him not.

I hadn't a penny in my pockets, but my jeans were stuffed with guilders. First I walked up to a bank on 23rd and Lexington, but the teller said he could not convert the currency of Surinam into dollars unless I had an account, so I walked down to Julius Goldstein's place at 523 Hudson, rousted him out of his miserable tenement and compelled him to accompany me to his bank in the Village; but his bank was not a commercial bank and could not exchange foreign currency. I must go to Wall Street, the teller said. I could not walk there so Julius reluctantly lent me subway fare and I sped downtown on the IND getting hungrier and hungrier after all that walking, cold-sweat hallucinating in fact since I had not eaten since the

Kraft dinner I had prepared with water instead of milk the previous morning. You cannot write novels on an empty brain no matter what old Alfred Knopf used to maintain; keep a writer hungry, that was his belief and, I learned later, his firm practice.

I found a foreign exchange place down near the Battery, and I laid my provincial guilders on the man in the cage. Surinam paper money of any kind was not common even in New York and the croupier had to look them up. But they were good guilders, and though I've forgotten the rate of exchange, I got something as magnificent as ten or twelve dollars for them. I had an enormous breakfast at Child's on Lower Broadway—ham, eggs, hotcakes, all—and blessed my Puritan restraint for not blowing my wad on Golden Earrings that last night in The Hotel in Paramaribo.

I'll describe just one more voyage, the *Seatiger*'s, of which I've already said a great deal. There were many others because I was never a "homesteader." A character, a mate, in a story of mine, "The Big Surprise," goes ashore and encounters the real world, its complexities, confusions, immoralities, and retires with relief to the safe, simplistic, microcosmic world of the ship. *A ship at sea is the small, safe hiding place in the attic of the mind; it is a prison; and in the round giant of the sea it is the desolate single eye.*

He [the mate] rolled into his blankets, pulling them up snugly around his chin, for the sea breeze through the porthole was cool and damp and salty . . . "From now on I'm *homesteading,*" he said to himself. "I'm going to get me a T.V. and put it in this room right up against the bulkhead. One of those new seventeen-inch portables will do me fine, and I'll string me up an aerial on the radio mast, and I'll have me my programs right here on both sides of the ocean. I won't never have to go ashore again, I mean, except for haircuts and to let laid once in awhile, things like that." His eyes fell closed, the muscles slackened in his rugged face. The vessel rose and fell on the vast, comfortable bosom of the sea, and very soon [he] was asleep.

That's homesteading. I never made more than one voyage on the same ship. I was on the *Seatiger* for nearly a year, but it was really one voyage (Technically, a voyage is a trip from a loading port to one of discharge, and by that definition the *Seatiger* made a number of voyages during that year), for in all those months from sign-on to payoff, we did not once return to the home country.

Before joining the *Seatiger,* I was living in New York with a girl who had a pleasant apartment and a lucrative job on a magazine. Our sexual and social life was splendid, but I was broke and restless and falling victim of the "dreadful island disease" which I diagnose merely as not being able to tolerate Manhattan more than a few months at a time, so to ease my discomfort and fill my pockets, I decided to make another trip to sea. A short one because I was rather in love with the girl and didn't want to leave her for a long time. The dispatcher at the Manhattan hall of the S.I.U. assured me the *Seatiger* was going to Texas to England and back, on a four-week trip at the most. I joined her in Sewaren on the day the previous crew was paying off, in fact, I went straight on watch the minute I reported to the mate and changed my clothes. I was sent to help an a.b. who was about to go overside in a skiff to paint the hull under the fantail with black paint and long-handled rollers. The skiff leaked and one of us painted while the other bailed, then someone appeared on the deck above and called out, "Pay off!" and my fellow workman dropped his roller and said, "I'm leaving, I'm paying off," and scrambled from the bow of the leaky skiff onto the piling we were tied to, giving the skiff a backward shove with one foot as he muscled himself onto the dock. "Send a relief," I said, as the skiff plowed into the water a good deal of which poured over the stern seat. So intent upon his payoff he never looked back at me standing in a foot of water in the boat. I shouted at him but he didn't hear me so I reached out for the piling and tried to climb on to it, but my movements in the boat brought in more water and put the piling out of reach. There were no oars so I tried to pole with the roller handle, but the water was too deep and I finally had to resign myself to sinking. It was like that hilarious scene in "Beat the Devil" when they lower the lifeboat but forget to put in the plug, only in this case I was *in* the boat, standing up, feeling ridiculous as I swiftly sank into the harbor. The five-gallon cans half full of paint tipped over and spread a thick black film over the water that was already full of grease and oil and garbage. I was wearing heavy boots and I went straight down into the paint and guck up to my shoulders. I treaded my way to a dock piling and tried to shinny up, but the piling was slick with oil and creosote and the overhang of the dock was far overhead. I clung to the piling to keep my head above water, and, more furious than scared, began to shout. I refused to cry Help, that would have been undignified, so I just shouted, just made noise. No one on board heard me because they were all midships in the captain's office lined up for pay-off. I must have shouted for ten or fifteen minutes before some dockworkers heard me and searched. They had to lean over the edge of the dock and look under to find me. "Didn't I tell you I heard somebody yelling," one of them said. "For God's sake," said the other. "The boat sank," I said, apologetically. They went aboard and found some more men and a gantline and pulled me up, soaked and stinking and covered with black paint. A portentous initiation that was into the strange ways of that strangest of ships.

The *Seatiger* had been put together at Marinship in Sausalito, California, in 1944 and christened the *S.S. Kettleman Hills* after the bare rolling oil-rich coastal country of central California. After the war she was laid up until the National Tanker Corporation bought her in 1948. I set down part of a letter from a former shipmate, once radio operator of the *Seatiger,* who had access to the deck logs of the ship when it was still the *Kettleman Hills.* My own comments are in brackets.

Dear Calvin,

Well I've spent a lot of time trying to assemble my thoughts and such on this past voyage, without much success it seems. There seems to be some kind of block with sailors, we can recall yarns or "sea stories" for the delectation of coffee-time audiences, but the lengthy and introspective analysis or long-range views of our lives past and future is seldom sought, and so is just not available when desired. Somebody said that men in jobs like seafaring men's are always trying to run away from something, maybe so, maybe that's why serious looking backward is so rare. Anyway, will try to outline first of all the history of the Tiger and save the self-analysis for the next voyage. Incidentally we are loading here [Philadelphia] for as usual but not inevitable for Amsterdam [he's a homesteader], also our customary discharge port. 25,000 tons of fine Pennsylvania anthracite to keep our G.I.s in Deutschland warm when fräuleins fail.

I believe she was first run, when built, as the Kettleman Hills by either Western Tankers [actually it was Pacific Tankers] or "Wet Ink"—War Emergency Tankers Inc.; both of them were corporate devices of a temporary wartime nature for relieving the U.S. treasury of some of its custodial burden. I have heard that then-senator Bill Knowland, later termed the senator from Formosa and even then a big China lobbyist, had a considerable interest in some such companies. Seems likely. Incidentally, you'll remember that the Tiger was what was called an "Elliott Job," that is her motor and turbines were mostly built by the Elliott Company of Jeanette, Pa. Nearly all the other T-2's were by Westinghouse and by G.E. One of those many Elliott guys who used to fly to the ship in all corners of the world once told George Webber [George was the chief engineer on the *Seatiger,* he is now dead] that their company never wanted to build the damn things in the first place, as they had always been strictly builders of shoreside power plants, but the government told them they had no need for shoreside power plants but they did need ship propulsion plants, so get cracking. He held that out as an excuse for the universally recognized great inferiority of Elliott ships. They were all called Hills something, Fruitvale Hills, Kettleman Hills.

At the end of the war, she was apparently bought by the Soong family, Chiang Kai-Shek in-laws. She was operated by Seiling and Jarvis of New York, rhymes with stealing and starve us, which was the colloquial sailors' name for them. Actually S&J was a pretty decent bunch though. I think most of their personnel are now in National Tankers, Inc. The "National" refers to Nationalist China, not the U.S.A.

What happened on the Kettleman Hills I learned from the deck logs, all of which were neatly bundled up aboard, extensive files of radio messages and talking with the guys who were on there.

Apparently the Soongs bought the K.H. and one other tanker partly for investment purposes and partly as insurance of petroleum supplies. The postwar tanker market was very confused and very profitable for some anyway, si no me equìvico . . . As you remember they eventually ended with Hong Kong Chinese for a crew, something like 60 of them, and German officers, except Victor Johnson who was the captain and Larry Parker the chief mate, you remember Larry, and the chief engineer, then a Greek-American name of Katsos. Anyway she made a trip or two to Formosa after the fall of the mainland, and then! Began to run what may best be called Communist Intercoastal. She lifted cargoes including jet fuel, Avgas, and such in Constanza, Rumania, and Odessa, discharging at Tsingtao and Vladivostok. One can only conclude that there was some fraternization at high levels between the Chicoms and the Chinats. No doubt you are fully cognizant of the Chinese attitude that they are always and forever first and last Chinese, etc. etc., against the foreign devils. And further vide la condition humaine in which Malrocks treats among other subjects such as how to fire a steam locomotive with the 1927 hijinks. Also v. April 1968 proceedings of the U.S. Naval Institute, p. 47, the Whampoa Academy which describes Chiang, Ho Chi Minh, and Chou-en-lai as old school buddies under the smiling aegis of Dr. Sun and Uncle Joe Stallion . . . This was some time prior to Eisenhower's "unleash ing" of Chiang. Anyway, the voyages and the cargoes are absolute fact.

Kettleman Hills supposedly detonated a mine while leaving Odessa one trip. Supposedly the mine was buried in the mud, lifted the ship and did quite some damage. Later some Elliott and other engineers felt that this set the stage for her subsequent main-motor problems. Parker told me that they made a survey of the ship and blamed every damned thing they could find on the mine, such as toilet bowls that had been cracked for years, etc. etc. The Russians were not prepared to work on her, so with or without a seaworthy certificate she proceeded on voyage, then went to Hong Kong for several months for extensive repairs, and then, of course, after Orion Steamship Co., that was the Goulandris outfit only I think their operating company was Colonial SS Co. bought her and renamed her the *Seatiger* and Larry Parker accidentally came back aboard as chief mate. The only reason he knew he was on the same ship was that he came aboard gassed and fell down the ladder and recognized the dents in the bulkhead he'd made when he fell down the ladder before. And Cal, I don't have to tell you what happened in Port Said.

Got to close now, wife is due at the ship any minute and we're paying off & must run home to catch up on some housepainting I left about a month ago. Stay tuned for the next installment. Will get this off in haste, Best regards.

Eventually the *Seatiger* was cut in half and "jumboized." A new mid-section was constructed (before the ship was placed under a Liberian flag of "convenience"), the stern section with the dreadful engine and the ghosts of all our talk and lives, our fights and controversies, our dreams and fantasies was towed to Spain to shipbreakers, and the bow section with our midnight thoughts was stuck onto another ship, the *Appomattox* that had been built in Chester, Pennsylvania, in 1943. My friend also wrote me from Amsterdam:

I know about the *Seatiger's* metamorphosis—I was in the Gulf in '62 and first heard her on the air again, a most curious sensation, spooky to sit in a half-darkened radio shack and hear a transmitter you knew like your own voice calling Galveston, "KLO DE KSVO, QTC"—she had been assigned Liberian call letters ELIU when they ran up the monkey flag in '57. But I was pretty sure about the transmitter, not easy to forget after 7 years with it. So I called him later and the guy told me she was now a bulk carrier, Globe Explorer. After she returned to the Yankee flag, she had an explosion and fire in the engine room about Christmas of '66, killed a man, I think. I think she's now running grain to India.

I, too, came upon the *Seatiger* once again when, after having quit the sea for a few years, I went back on the *Esso Gettysburg* which I joined in midstream off Staten Island. In the dim light of dawn with the harbor lights still burning, looming next to me over the launch dock and without a sign of life—no lights, no sounds, dead at the pier—was the black form of the *Sea-*

tiger. Of all the ships that could have been tied up there on that morning of my return to sea—— As the radio operator said, it was a spooky feeling.

That ship still haunts me. Years later, without knowing I had come there, I found myself living and working in the very town, the very spot almost, where she had been built and having friends who had worked on building her. When we left Sewaren, after my original baptism-by-immersion in Arthur Kill and black paint, we shifted the *Seatiger* upriver to Rensselaer opposite Albany on the Hudson where we discharged the remainder of her cargo. Then we headed back down the river and the coast and around the Florida Keys to Texas. At Port Arthur, we filled the tanks with high-octane gasoline bound for England. But we were also presented with twelve-months' foreign Articles to sign.

(A ship's Articles is the agreement or contract, officially authorized and sworn to, between the operator or owner of a ship and the men who sail her. It's part of the ship's "papers," like its passport to get it in and out of foreign ports. Any vessel leaving the United States signs foreign Articles, and each man signs the document agreeing, unless he becomes seriously ill or has some other reason subject to the approval of the master, to stick with the ship—nor can he be fired—until it comes home. Thus, the "List of Persons," which is now contained in the Articles, in 1840, recorded as a sworn member of the crew of the *Acushnet:*

Names	***Places of Birth***	***Places of Residence***
Herman Melville	New York	Fairhaven

Of What Country Citizen or Subject	***Age***	***Descriptions of their Persons***			
		Height		***Complexion***	***Hair***
		Ft.	***Inches***		
U. S.	21	5	9 1/4	Dark	Brown

Articles now put a time limit on the length of foreign voyages, i.e. three-months' Articles, six-months', twelve-months', even, I believe, eighteen-months', so the seaman has some idea before he signs on how long his maximum stay aboard will be; no such thing in Dana's or Melville's time. If a ship touches any American port before the Articles' time is fulfilled, the Articles are "broken," and the men are paid off. If the payoff occurs in a port other than the one the Articles were signed, the company must pay each man's transportation back to the original port whether he cares to return there or not. If a ship stays abroad past the expiration of the Articles, each man who does not wish to sign further Articles, who does not, in a sense, wish to re-enlist, must be paid off and sent home at the company's expense.)

Twelve months are long Articles and usually mean the ship will be tramping around abroad for some time. The reasonable rumors that were circulating around the *Seatiger* in Port Arthur were that the ship had no intention of returning after a short trip to England. The master and the mate and the radio operator were close-mouthed about it. (The master is not required to reveal his orders to the crew though a courteous and humane one will do so. The master of the *Seatiger* was David Miles Dantzler who was never courteous and seldom humane.) The dispatcher at the hiring-hall claimed not to know the ship's destination or ultimate purpose beyond the delivery of that single cargo to Jarrow-on-Tyne though he undoubtedly did. Many men, balking at a year's Articles and fearing the real possibility of the Persian Gulf with summer coming on and also of crossing the foggy busy North Atlantic loaded with highly dangerous cargo and without the assistance of radar, quit. As much as I regretted leaving my girl for a possibly long stretch, I had not made much money on the short trip to Texas (the ship had not gone foreign so I would have had to pay my own way back to New York), so I decided to take my chances. I signed. I described that nervous crossing in a story, "Near the Line."

Near Hatteras the ship veered off to cross the ocean. Four pale-blue evenings of ingenuous summer passed and, during the fourth night, a fog appeared ahead of the ship, rising from the sea like the moonlit ramparts of some alcazar . . . Day after day the sun rolled dully as a pewter plate across the sky. The ship dead-reckoned, feeling its way through ship-infested seas, its whistle blowing a persistent and monotonous warning, its sailors harried by the cries of unseen birds whose voices swarmed about their ears like the tweets and squeals of spirits. Those were very fishy seas, and the birds dove to feed then rose and soared into a world of light and air that opened wondrously not fifty yards above the captain's head as he stood his gloomy bridge. His vessel had no radar. Human vigilance was his only protection against collision.

At Jarrow-on-Tyne, which had been sacked and burnt by the Vikings in 794, just down the hill in fact from the ruins of the abbey of Baeda (who since the 7th century has been called "The Venerable") where Celtic Christianity flourished, we discharged the remains of our touchy modern cargo most of which had already been dropped at Killingholme at the mouth of the Humber. Though the towns on both sides of that river have such industrial-gothic names as Grimsby and Hull and, of course, Goole, Killingholme was apart and rural lying on the maritime edge of the Lincoln marshes in what is called the Parts of Lindsey. The land is green there, and in that late spring of 1950 in the sunshine it was greener than blue eyes accustomed to the two blues or the blues and greys of the open sea and sky could adjust to—almost. As the sun descended and the cooler tones of evening prevailed and the great white swans flew in to land in the fens and glide silently in the spaces of open water among the tall grasses, my eyes did accommodate the changes; and the sight moved me, tenderly—the quietude of that original country that slid softly into the German Ocean. It was Saturday night. The oil-dock at Killingholme was a long mole that reached out into deep water. (Our Pilgrim Fathers, as they are called, left their homes in Gainsborough and Scrooby, separated themselves from the Church of England,

and sailed from Killingholme to Holland in 1609 before crossing the Great Green to set foot on Plymouth Rock and invade in the name of righteousness the world that had been old to its natural inhabitants for thousands of years but was new to them.) It was a long walk from the end of the oil-dock to shore (and a taxi ride to town), but in that lowland a couple of miles away from the dock was a country pub, and, as I said, it was Saturday night. Charlie Goodwin and I (Charlie was then a.b. on my watch though he later became, as necessity and Captain Dantzler dictated, the deck maintenance) made a hike to the pub which, as I recall, was a Barclay's and named, appropriately, *The Swan*. We drank many pints of Barclay's lager (we had not yet become accustomed to English bitter) and pissed against the stone wall behind the pub listening to the sullen beat of the white birds' wings as they rose and settled in the long twilight, and drank more pints in the crowded—glistening, country crowded—"singing room" where a plain, earnest young girl from the village sang "My 'art cries for you," and, yes, I wept and so did Charlie. And George Webber, the chief engineer, was there with tears in his eyes. So plain, she was, so young, so godawful, and so godawful real——

Charlie, who was not a very large fellow but who had a very large heart and who was an intense combination of sentiment and perpetual concupiscence, fell in love on the spot though someone else soon took turn at singing and the country girl vanished in the crowd. The next day was Sunday and we let go for the Tyne. (Poor Charlie. More than once he fell in love that year. His pursuit of girls and sex was truly assiduous, clever, and sometimes perilous. I think he was the only man aboard who managed to assuage his lust in Egypt since King Farouk had, only a short time before, closed up all of what Captain Dantzler called "the houses of assassination," but if, anyplace in the world, there was a warm young passage to slip into, Charlie could find it though the girls he fell in with who were not out just for business invariably deceived him. Charlie was a very kind young man, I think from Texas, and he was frequently taken advantage of. He'll turn up again in this part of the story.)

At Jarrow which is grimy—and not even dirty Pittsburgh or filthy Liège can surpass Grimsby for grime, or Jarrow. Jarrow is just near Newcastle to which one carries the coals only we were carrying another more sophisticated fossil fuel.

Though Jarrow was the last port of discharge for that cargo, the captain still did not reveal that the ship was, in fact, bound for the Persian Gulf. He was afraid he'd lose half his crew, but the dockmen knew and the word escaped. As it was he lost only one man who jumped at the last minute. He almost lost me, or rather, he almost left me. My mother had fallen ill partly from despondency over my whereabouts—it was a cumulative and repetitive condition, and I was a very negligent correspondent—and my father, caring for her, had somehow managed to track me down. The telephone on the dock rang just as we were preparing to let go lines. Sea watches had been set. There was another tanker in the river awaiting our place at the dock. I was on the fantail standing by with the rest of our watch under the guidance of the second mate.

(When a ship ties up to a dock or lets go its mooring lines, which may be ropes or cables or both, the bosun calls "fore-and-aft" and the deck crew splits, half going to the forward lines, the other half to the after or stern lines. The chief mate takes charge of the bow, the second mate takes charge of the stern, and the third mate goes to the bridge to stand by and relay the captain's and/or the pilot's orders to either mate or to the engine room. That traditional polished brass object that stands in the wheelhouse like a clock in a town square, in towns that used to be—places like Mount Pleasant and Fairfield, Morning Sun, Chester-le-Street, Wundervatimitiss—is the "engine telegraph" though its face has words instead of numbers. Full astern, full ahead, half ahead, dead slow, stop, etc. And each time the third mate sets the hand, bells ring above and below. The engine telegraph is, I believe, still mandatory equipment though most ships communicate these days from the bridge to the engine room by telephone or, on some really new ones, by computer.)

When the telephone rang on the dock at Jarrow, I was called off deck much to the master's chagrin. My mother, bless her dear old soul, who was calling from her bed of pain and despair in Iowa, will outlive us all though for centuries she has been, as old family doctor Clark used to say, "nervous"; but like most of the rest of us who insist upon pursuing this life, she fails to realize that whatever age we are—and she's well away into her eighties now—we've never been there before, not in *this* life, there's no banking on experience, habit, perhaps, but not experience. Nervousness was her habit and she wanted me home. And Captain Dantzler wanted me on board.

"Son, where are you?" my mother asked in a voice as tenuous and remote as a voice from an infant dream, transatlantic cable notwithstanding, "Where am I calling?"

"Mother, I'm on the *Seatiger,* we're—"

"The what?"

"The *Seatiger.*"

"What kind of an animal is that? When you was home, you said you was with John Ringling, now you say you're on a tiger. Son, you're not with a circus, are you?" There was admonishment in her tone.

"The *Seatiger* is a ship, a tanker, and I'm on the oil dock at Jarrow, England, down the hill from the abbey of the Venerable Bede."

"I don't understand."

"And I'm going to the Persian Gulf."

"Son, come home, there's nothing you want in— Where? Where did you say you was going?"

"The Persian Gulf, mother."

"I don't know where that is, son. There's nothing you want there."

"Kentfield!" the captain shouted from the bridge. "Get your ass up here."

"Mother, I'm fine. I've got to go. I'm fine, I really am."

"Kentfield!"

"Give my love to everybody . . . No, I'm *fine.* I've got to go . . . I'm fine. Take care of yourself and give my love to everybody. I'm sorry I forgot your birthday, but I'm not very good at things like that, and you know perfectly well I don't believe in Mother's Day, we've been through that . . . Yes, I'm fine. I've got to go. Give my love to everybody."

Captain Dantzler was steaming. All hands turned to and standing around fore-and-aft, his ship shorthanded, the Tyne pilot on the bridge, the tugs standing by waiting for me to hang up on my mother. The gangway had been secured though there was a Jacob's ladder out.

"Kentfield, get your ass up here," the captain cried.

"Good-bye, mother," I said.

Of all the people I've turned into fictional characters, I've used no one as frequently or as exhaustively as my mother (including Captain Dantzler, the Dancer, of course, of "Dancer's Cricket"). She appears in many stories. I seldom wrote about my father though I came to love him more. Boys, I think, need their mothers when they're little, but it's their fathers that count later on.

A word about the Persian Gulf and why Captain Dantzler tried to keep it such a dark secret from the crew. Nowadays, tankers are swift, air-conditioned, electronically equipped with all manner of safety devices, and offer a private room for every man, but the tankers in the years just after the Second World War were not though the T-2 was considered, at 16,000 tons, to be a supertanker. (Supertankers now run 300,000 and building to half a million tons.) And the Persian Gulf, even in the high season, in the winter and spring, was a rotten run. A tanker to the Persian Gulf almost invariably went on a shuttle from the Gulf to someplace, back and forth, thus the year's Articles. No wonder so many men homesteaded a good run like an American President Line's freighter-passenger that circumnavigated the globe, putting in for days at a time at Hong Kong and Bangkok and Beirut and Marseilles with Frisco as home port; or no wonder Captain O'Sullivan envied his friend the mastery of the *Santa Rosa* that cruised the Caribbean from New York.

But the dirt runs, the tramp runs, the shuttle runs, no one but eccentrics like me or Charlie Goodwin, men who sat backwards on their chairs, would want. I looked forward to the Persian Gulf just to see what Hell was like. Sailors call the Strait of Bab-el-Mandeb, that narrow place (no one goes through there now because the Suez Canal was closed by the 1967 Arab-Israeli war) between the Gulf of Aden and the Red Sea, the Gate of Hell, at least that's what George Webber, the chief of the engine room, called it.

In 1950, such tankers as the *Seatiger* were crewed not so much by men who had a choice or even by oddballs like me, but by men who needed jobs and would ship on anything going anywhere, even to the Persian Gulf in summer.

Each day at sea, the chief engineer reports the air and sea temperatures to the captain, that's his job.

(The captain is, of course, master of the ship and everyone on it including the chief engineer; but the chief is master of his own crucial department and his power is so great that if he and the master do not operate in harmony evil vibrations may result because, in reality, there are two masters, two ships. I don't know what the present salaries are, but the chief of the *Seatiger* made almost as much as the captain, and the enmity between them was intense though the chief usually held his tongue and kept his animosity under control.

But the ultimate responsibility for the safety and destiny of the ship and its men is the master's which is why, not infrequently, he comes over all funny and queer. If a hurricane slows him down, it's *his* fault in the company's eyes. He's merely an appendix in the corporate body. The ship may be owned, as the *Seatiger* once was, by Chiang Kai-shek or, as the *John Ringling* was, by the Aluminum Company of America or by U.S. Steel or by the octopus with the bland blank name of the National General Corporation or by any group in any far distant structural steel-and-glass International-style-out-of-Bauhaus vertical catacomb in New York or San Francisco or Athens or London or Tokyo; and the accountants and computers there and the board chairmen hold the master on the bridge responsible for the life habits of *Lepas fascicularis,* the barnacle that clings to his hull, for fog, for Calvin Kentfield's nervous mother in Iowa.)

I, being ordinary and errand boy, often carried the chief's daily report to the captain, and since I cannot remember ever carrying a message that I didn't read, even a temperature record, I observed, one day, that the air was 111° and the temperature of the Red Sea, the *sea,* was ninety-eight. And sometimes the blistering sand blasting from the deserts of Sudan to the desert of Arabia (or vice versa depending upon the season) made a desert out of the sea covering the ship with sand and pelting its decks and houses with the bodies of birds and giant locusts that had to be swept overside when the wind died.

And there was nothing there when you got there, there was no place to go, nothing to see. The sheik of Kuwait was a xenophobe who allowed no tankermen into his country which meant that after twenty-two days at sea—from England to Mina' al Ahmadi—the seaman had a twelve-hour turnaround during which his sole recreation was a walk down the loading dock to a one-room rec-room where he could buy a haircut and receive a free glass of lemon squash and peruse a six-month-old copy of *Country Life.* Even Charlie Goodwin couldn't find a girl in Mina' al Ahmadi though one trip Captain Dantzler and the radio operator received special permission to visit Kuwait city—I think the chief engineer went along too—and came back with a carpet each. Some tankers had even longer Persian Gulf shuttles, from Bahrain or Ras Tannurah to Japan for instance.

(There is the famous story, well, famous among seamen at the time, of the ship in the late forties that was placed on the shuttle from Ras Tannurah to the Clyde and after six-months' running of the Red Sea, the Gulfs of Aden and Oman and Persia, the master went berserk, put in with a full cargo to Beirut, picked up half a dozen Lebanese whores, a couple of hundred cases of Lebanese wine, and took his crew aimlessly, madly around the Mediterranean like a drunken Ulysses until he had to put in to a port in Greece for fuel and stores and the company caught up with him.

He was fired.

A captain may be fired. Dantzler eventually was, I believe, but he wouldn't be able to fire me or Charlie Goodwin or Bob or Scotty without a severe and embarrassing feedback from the union though the union could drop us without a word. But only in the States. The captain belongs to a union, the Masters, Mates, and Pilots, but it's a shadow structure. The master is, as I said, a company creature, and however much I and the rest of the crew of the *Seatiger* deplored the personal habits and inimical singularities of character of Captain Dantzler, I *did* understand his problems, even then.)

When we left Jarrow it was May, as I recall, or early June. The seas across the mouth of the Bay of Biscay from Finistère to Finisterre and along the Iberian peninsula were amenable, not like the ocean that aggressed against the *Paul Revere*. It was five days from Tyneside to Gibraltar, and once inside the Pillars of Hercules, it was five more halcyon Mediterranean days to the Suez Canal. In those friendly seas we cleaned the tanks. If you have ever trod a lovely beach in Sicily or Sardinia, Corsica or Ibiza, the Côte d'Azur or the Costa del Sol, Carthaginian Tunis, Alexandria or Crete, the Greek Isles, the Dalmatian coast, Elba or Forte dei Marmi and stepped on or sat on or lain back in solar slumber on a glob or sand-covered pool of brown, adhesive, glutinous, foul-smelling glop, it was because we, the *Seatiger* and hundreds of other tankers had been cleaning our tanks for years.

I will explain the procedure, but to keep the narrative current, I should also explain that on that first passage of the *Seatiger* through the Meddy (as British seamen call it, just as Gibraltar is Gib) we were a "clean" tanker clearing out gasoline and tank scale in preparation for becoming a "dirty" tanker, i.e., in preparation for carrying crude oil which is the awful fossil fuel, the dirty, dirty stuff, the stinking fossilized bodies of billions, trillions, quintillions of decayed organisms that have collected in the earth's crust above the Mohorovičić discontinuity through the uncountable millennia before we were born. That's the stuff you try to get off your feet at Isola Bella and track into the lobby of the Gran Hotel. (Soap and water won't take it off unless you really scrub, paint thinner—mineral spirits—will, but it burns the skin. It'll wear off eventually in the sand or into the equally fossil polyethylene insole of your go-aheads.)

Unlike a freighter on which, except under special circumstances, the sailors have nothing much to do with the cargo, a tanker requires the active musclepower of an a.b. or an ordinary to load and discharge. Valves must be opened and closed, and cargo valves on deck are eighteen-inch iron wheels that may, on as ill-used and ill-tended a ship as the *Seatiger* had been, take all the strength of one man and often of two to move.

After cargo is pumped out, the ship's tanks are butterworthed. Butterworthing is a cleaning process invented and patented by a man named, of course, Butterworth. Butterworthing equipment—nozzles, plates, and hoses—was leased from the Butterworth Company like telephones or copiers. The butterworth equipment was the ship's delicate gear though it was enormously heavy and cumbersome. Made of brass, which is a relatively soft and vulnerable metal, the butterworth nozzles were kept in their own private bins filled with light lubricating oil. They were huge double nozzles on swivels that were threaded onto special tough black hoses and lowered into the dirty empty tanks through butterworth holes in the deck and secured at whatever depth the mate desired by clamps on the special butterworth plates that covered the holes and were held in place by deck bolts. It was against one of those bolts that I shattered my first kneecap when I fell while working on the *Esso Gettysburg*. The resultant experience in a ward of the old marine hospital in Norfolk, Virginia, after I had been shunted ashore by coastguardsmen from Hatteras, provided me with a short story called "A Good Example," for, as Bob Henderson, my editor at the *New Yorker,* said, "It's an ill wind that blows no good."

When very hot water under extreme pressure is pumped through the hoses, the butterworth nozzles spin furiously spraying the insides of the tank rather like enormous dishwashers. The oil that is knocked and rinsed from the insides of the tanks mixes with the water and is pumped overside. It, of course, does not *combine* with the water, it's only carried away by it, and eventually by wind and currents it comes ashore. That's what fouls the rocks and beaches, that's what you step in, that's what seamen call "tanker shit."

On the *Seatiger,* however, in the Meddy, we were preparing to do more than butterworth. The tanks were in execrable shape and had to be further cleaned by hand. It's a job everybody hates. The sailors hate it because it's noxious and dangerous and hot, groveling work; and the captain hates it because, like painting or fish-oiling the decks, it can't be done effectively on regular watches. All hands turn to on overtime and that's expensive. The insides of the tanks had rusted, and the butterworth streams had knocked sheets of oxidized scale soaked with gasoline from the walls and stringers to the tank floors. All that had to be scooped up and brought out by hand.

First of all we rigged windsails which were long tubes of white canvas with outspread wings at the top. They were hoisted high over the open tank tops and trimmed to the wind so the air funneled down them and ventilated the tanks, blowing out the dangerous fumes. The men were then sent down the long spidery ladders into the belly of the ship. The experience was biblical. The only light was the blazing round hole of sunlight from the tank top far overhead and the pathetic lights on cords lowered through the butterworth holes. Each of us had a flashlight and a scoop and a bucket. As each bucket was filled it was hoisted to the deck and an empty one sent down. There were ribs and bones of rusted steel in the leviathan cavity of the ship, and we clambered over them and between them in the sweaty half-light scooping up the odoriferous decay and sending it into the open air.

The windsail airing had been insufficient and the fumes were so strong that we frequently became giddy and high, giggling and dancing and tossing buckets at each other. When that happened, the mate brought us up because after the euphoria and eurythmics comes asphyxiation and even death. One man tripped out so far he dropped from the ladder before he could get up and we left him, later, in a hospital in Port Said with a broken arm. That's when I became able-bodied against my will.

Cleaning tanks was mandatory overtime, but working in such dangerous gas was illegal. The mate, however, was frequently drunk, and when he took the gas-level readings from his meter, he may have made a mistake. Or else the captain had him send us down regardless of conditions to try to get the job done while we were still in quiet Mediterranean seas. It would have mortified him to have to slow down and come in late to Egypt.

Two men remained on deck with the bosun. They did the hardest though the least distasteful work. One man pulled up the heavy, full buckets and the other lugged them to the rail and dumped them into the sea. Because Scotty, the bosun, and I were on very friendly terms, he gave me, after a couple of days in the tanks, the job of hoisting the buckets. That pleased me because in those days I suffered from physical vanity, and I knew that, like muscling those valves around, hauling up those buckets from the very bowels of the *Tiger* would help make my arms and shoulders tremendously powerful. But after a while, the captain, pacing and overseeing operations from his bridge, caught me enjoying my exercise, and he said to the mate, "Tell the bosun all Kentfield wants is to develop his physique. This ship's not a gymnasium. Tell him to put him back in the tanks."

(One afternoon, months later, at the grand old Casino Palace Hotel in Port Said—balconies, balustrades, terraces, potted palms, jasmine, Moorish tiles, tall cool drinks in the shade in the heat of the day, Arab women in black making holes in the sunlight, goats bleating, piastres clinking, red fezzes nodding, shockingly-beautiful French-Egyptian women with jet eyes and diamond earrings stepping in and out of taxicabs—I was drinking with the mate—hierarchy had broken down by then—and he told me what the captain had said. He told me, he said, because he liked me and didn't want me to think *he* had been picking on me. I never felt that Parker picked on me. I felt sorry for him and he knew it, but he was very difficult to get along with sometimes because he was frequently hungover during the day and irritable in the extreme. I remember once on our way from Gibraltar to South America after the Persian Gulf shuttle was completed and another one from Venezuela was scheduled, we were painting the foredeck [Captain Dantzler's Arabs, you remember, had mucked up the last deck job]. Using a long-handled roller, I was painting just below the bridge, and to make the job less monotonous, I was painting in abstract patterns à la the New York School, Franz Kline, black-on-white, black-on-deck. As long as I covered the area, it seemed to me, it didn't make any difference how I did it—I used to cut the grass at home in the same way and my father never objected—but Parker, watching me from the bridge and having already revealed his inner self in drunken confidence, didn't understand. "Kentfield, stop playing around and get to work." Feeling inadequate and paranoid because of his drinking, he felt I did not fully appreciate his authority, and he was right. I ignored him, pretending I didn't hear. I made a few more strokes, broad swatches in fairly exotic directions, and he became incensed, screaming and shouting so many threats and reprisals at me that I was forced to conventionalize my technique to pacify him.

Perhaps the captain was the one who really objected. The mate hated him but he was bound to him because the captain used his drinking to grind him to the deck though the captain would never fire him because he needed him as receptacle for his petulant and peculiarly feminine rages. The captain was a moody man—I suspect he was a Cancer—and could, sometimes, as I will illustrate shortly, be almost nice.)

At Port Said we brought aboard fresh stores—lettuces, onions, tomatoes, melons, grapes, dates, figs—all the rich produce of the Nile delta. Fresh milk and eggs for the steward to serve as long as he could make them last. There were no stores available at Mina' al Ahmadi and when we had eaten all the fresh eggs and drunk all the fresh milk we switched back to dried and powdered. We even got some of those huge red-and-yellow Nile mangoes which are so sweet and succulent, so sensuous and female, Arab men have an improper name for them.

We also rigged the Suez light and readied the special Suez davits on the well deck for the Suez boat. The Suez light was a powerful headlight that was rigged on the prow so that ships passing through the canal at night could see where they were going. Our Suez boat was the same treacherous skiff that had sunk with me in Arthur Kill. We had hauled it out, and during the voyage, Scotty, the bosun, had caulked it and covered its bottom with canvas which he soaked with many coats of red paint. It was an unusual-looking craft with its red canvas bottom, but it didn't leak. Unlike the Panama, the Suez has no locks and until 1951 when the Farouk bypass south of El Qantara was completed, it was a one-way ditch. Ships went through, usually, in convoys starting from either end (it's well over a hundred miles long), and at one point or another, one convoy had to pull aside and tie up to the desert out of the way. The *fellah,* who accompanied the ship through the canal and slept on the forepeak, used the Suez boat to take the mooring lines ashore. Often the ships pulled aside at the lake at Ismailia or in one of the Bitter Lakes. One trip we were anchored in Great Bitter Lake waiting for the northbound convoy. It was a bright hot day and several of us off-watch and the messboys decided to go swimming. We put a ladder overside from the well deck and stripped down. Then somebody remembered that the Red Sea and the Gulf of Suez seethed with sharks. The captain and the canal pilot, a pink, shiny-faced Britisher (the British still controlled the Suez Canal Company then) were watching us from the boat deck. One of us asked the pilot if there were any sharks in the lake, and he laughed and replied, eyeing our young bare-ass bodies, "Only some of my colleagues with . . . aa . . special tastes." Some canal pilots did long stretches, too.

Into the summer and through the fall and winter we made many passages through the Suez, and it was strange to be on a huge steel ship traversing the empty desert like a camel. One trip we broke down in Port Said.

(We had broken down before, once in the Mediterranean in the Sicilian Channel and had made an unscheduled repair stop at Palermo which delighted me because the radio operator, who had become my close friend, and I took a taxi up the mountain behind the city to Monreale. It was almost too fortuitous to be real. Of all the splendid churches of the Norman kingdom of Sicily of the 12th century, Monreale was my particular favorite. It was a silent sunny afternoon overlooking La Conca d'Oro, the rich valley of the Golden Shell. The war had not damaged the cathedral, the cloister gardens full of sweet scents and the litany of bees were deserted, the mosaic walls of gold and multicolored glass glowed softly and luxuriantly in the cool interior, the saints lined up along the sides, the colossal Christ in Majesty filled the half-dome of the apse with a background of gold, an elaborate inlaid halo like a spoked crown, long dark hair, enormous Byzantine eyes looked down without expression—not love, nor pity, nor censure. Outside in the *campagna* below the ancient walls, a young woman sang and hung up clothes on low branches of the olive trees. Bright oranges shone like gems from dark green foliage. It was altogether too much. My thanks to the Elliott Company for their rotten engines. I have a funny story about Palermo, but I'll save it for the next chapter, the sex chapter.)

We were broken down in Port Said for two weeks. The main motor had really conked out. The chief and his engineers couldn't fix it so new parts and an Elliott man had to be flown from the States. Since Port Said was not a port of loading or discharge, the captain was not legally bound to put out a draw, and he chose not to. "I don't want all those drunks over there getting into trouble. This crew's enough trouble as it is without their going over there and getting drunk and rolled by all them filthy Arabs. It's for their own good." That's what he said to the radio operator. All he said to the crew's representatives was, "No draw!"

Since no one had any money, no one went ashore except me. A.b.'s also stood gangway watches on the *Seatiger* and I had, as usual, chosen the midnight-to-eight. I borrowed some money from George Webber, the chief engineer, a good soul who always had whiskey and cash.

As the voyage had progressed from the Mersey to Gibraltar, Gibraltar to the Canal, Suez to Aden, Aden to the Gulf and back, the radio operator, the chief, and I formed a secret society roughly called the Society for the Discussion of Ignorance and Barbarism on the Tiger. It met in the chief's room which was aft. Most tankers including T-2's house the engine officers in the main house on the stern where the messrooms and the crew's quarters are. The midship house contains the master's and the mates' and the radio operator's quarters. They are separated by half a ship. The captain seldom came aft except to meals, remaining alone on top of his center castle, pacing the parapet of his private bridge. Conversations in the radio operator's room would have been overheard, but discussions in the chief's room were quite safe. The society was secret, too, because the chief didn't want his engineers to know that he sometimes invited a sailor into his rooms, I didn't want my shipmates to know that I was palsie with an officer—the radio operator was all right because anybody might be friendly with Sparks who commanded no one and was given orders by no one except the captain. We had some fine sessions, the three of us, though we were fairly snobbish in our talk of personalities. Seamen's stories are traditionally called yarns, but more often they are plain gossip. We gossiped about the chief steward who was a fair, efficient, but solitary and unlikeable old fellow who wore spectacles on the end of his nose and looked like a Jewish Ben Franklin, and who was, from time to time, when the crew was generally disgruntled, victim of cruel and unjust anti-Semitic accusations—stewards, of course, are traditionally prime targets of a crew's discontent and, indeed, many an unscrupulous steward has, by cheating on stores, making deals with the captain and with chandlers, or buying inferior goods at excessive prices to the company, filled his own pockets at the expense of the crew's well-being; but not the steward of the *Seatiger*.

We gossiped about the marathon drinking of the mate and Harry Suleri, and made fun of the unbelievably profound ignorance of Smitty the Alabama cracker. Smitty was my contribution for ridicule because for a blessedly short while I was on his watch. He had been an a.b. in the fo'c'sle, but when the third mate—who appears in "Dancer's Cricket" as Mr. Henke —left the ship, Smitty, who claimed to have junior officer's papers but who was no more fitted to command a watch than the messboy, was raised up by the master from the fo'c'sle to the bridge where he forthwith demanded that his former fo'c'slemates call him Mr. Smith. Smitty was a saver, a rare bird. He never went ashore, for, not only did he not care to spend his money on frivolity, but also he feared, truly and genuinely feared the touch of foreign soil and the contamination of strangers. He was worse than Kenneth Patchen ever was when Patchen, in the old days, used to go about Europe with disinfectant cream smeared on his lips. Smitty was not just xenophobic, he was anti anything that he felt threatened his fundamentalist version of human existence. He shunned the Jewish steward for Jews had murdered Christ, and he deplored the Arabs of the crew and the Egyptians, calling them heathens and worshippers of Baal though I'm sure he had no notion at all of who Baal might be. On night watches on the wheel I made some mild attempts to discuss religion with him attempting to mollify some of his violent prejudices, but he always countered with talk about sin and corruption and with hilariously outrageous misquotes from the Old and the New Testaments. One night, during one of these hopeless discussions, his tone changed and he approached me in the dark and said,

"You know, Cal, you're a smart fellow, tell me," he giggled diffidently, "I've always wondered, what is Jerusalem?"

In "Near the Line" I put one of Smitty's bizarre Bible stories, touched up a bit by me, into Harry's mouth:

"Never trust anybody that's little and dark," he said. "No dark little people of any kind." He explained that all Italians were Jews disguised as Italians and were not to be trusted. "Listen . . . you ever hear of the Lost Tribe of Is*reel*? Well, twelve thousand years ago there was the biggest fight ever fought amongst the Christians and the Jews, and it was led by a Christian name of Armand Gideon, and all the Jews was killed or taken prisoner by Armand Gideon except for onc wandering Jew name of Roamus, and his uncle, Remus, and they wandered all around until they come to It'ly and that's how come . . . how come all Eye'ties are Jews in disguise—because they don't want it spread around that they're the lost tribe, see, because when they got going again, calling themselves *Roamins,* see, they started to toss Christians to the hungry lions . . . Don't believe me . . . believe the Bible."

We, the secret society, drank the chief's whiskey and discussed art, literature, politics, science, and world affairs, but most of the conversation focused upon our master and we indulged in a good deal of malicious laughter at his expense, but we all suffered from time to time from his pernicious eccentricities, the chief and the radio operator more than I because they had more direct dealings with him; and our sessions were a way of exorcising him.

Though he refused to give out a general draw, the captain filled his own pockets with money, went ashore, booked some rooms at the Eastern Exchange Hotel. I saw him in the bar there, getting plastered. We were tied up across the canal by the salt basins near Port Fuad. It was fiercely hot out of the prevailing north wind that blows year round and pushes the fellucas up the Nile against the current. And it had been a long trip from dreary Liverpool. When I came back aboard, I passed the word around that the captain was sloshing it up at the Eastern Exchange. He came back the next day for a couple of hours, and Charlie Goodwin, who felt he could handle the captain when others failed, went to his cabin to plead the crew's cause, but he came back cussing and frustrated. The master went back to the Eastern Exchange and stayed drunk for several days. We made up a delegation and visited the consul to try and persuade him to influence the captain, but consuls always try to do as little as possible for the people they represent. The captain did finally issue a draw, but his reason for changing his mind was venal and unscrupulous. The waterfront merchants, sitting in front of their shops with their hassocks and handbags and stuffed baby alligators and elephant-foot footstools and inlaid mother-of-pearl trays and striped shirts and Spanish fly and pornographic books and "Scotch" whiskey, had been wagging their fezzes in concern and frustration. There was, after all, a whole shipful of customers drawing lush American wages, and one man alone keeping them aboard. A delegation of merchants visited the captain at his rooms in the Eastern Exchange and made him a deal. If he would issue money to his men, he would receive a kickback from everything they bought from certain shops. I learned this later from the radio operator who was the one man on the ship most privy to the master's affairs. The rest of the crew never found out.

On another occasion, however, in Liverpool, at the end of our first voyage (our shuttle, except for one discharge at Heysham in Lancashire and one at Port-de-Bouc in Provence, was to be from the Persian Gulf to Bromborough in the Mersey near Birkenhead and across the river from Liverpool) the captain took a room at the Adelphi, the huge elegant Victorian hotel at No. 3, Ranelagh Place at one end of Lime Street. Nearly every wealthy or well-known traveler who has been compelled to stop over in Liverpool has taken advantage of the Adelphi. Joseph Conrad did; but Captain Dantzler was not Captain Korzeniowski. He moved into the Adelphi, planted himself with a satchel-full of money at the American-style bar and proceeded to consume as much, and as swiftly as he could, of the 86-proof produce of Scotland.

The normal turnaround at Bromborough was about three days depending upon the traffic and the weather—heavy cold solid fogs are common in the Mersey and in Liverpool Bay. The second night the master was back in the Adelphi bar with his money and his Scotch. Even though he was captain of his ship and dressed respectably and was a guest at the hotel, he still stuck out roughly in the starched, understated clientele of the Adelphi. By the third night most of the crew had spent their money in the bars and dance halls, on movies and the girls of Lime Street or in the small family-style "parties" such as the get-togethers at 24 Canning Street described in the next chapter. Some men had bought new clothes, shoes, books, radios, and, of course, whiskey. St. John's Market in Great Charlotte Street notwithstanding, Liverpool was not a notable shopping town, but it was the best we had and seamen can always find something to spend their money on. Very few of us were savers. Also, by that third night, the captain at his station at the American bar, was saturated. Other members of the crew were seeking each other out in the various popular resorts trying to borrow money. Some desperate sailor dropped into the Adelphi to try to pry some cash from the master and found him in a deeply sentimental mood. He not only bought the sailor a drink, he pulled out his wad and peeled off what the sailor asked for, taking care to note, however, the man's name and the amount. He wasn't giving money away. I've forgotten who that first sailor was, it was neither Bob Ferrara, my watchmate, nor Charlie Goodwin because they were with me. Whoever he was, he went racing up and down Lime Street passing the word to his cash-starved shipmates. By the time the word reached us and we made our way to Ranelagh Place, the quiet bar had been turned into a raucous public house with the suddenly popular master buying drinks and passing out pounds and fivers to a noisy staggering horny-handed lot. When I asked him for money, he called me Cal. "Sure, Cal," he said, "how much you want?"

None of us could believe what we were witnessing, his change of character or his charity, and, as we discovered later in

Egypt, we certainly couldn't count on it. The Adelphi barman, who was a tall, silver-haired man in his fifties dressed immaculately in white jacket with mother-of-pearl buttons and cufflinks, black tie and cummerbund like an officer of a Colonial regiment attending a cocktail party, and who was accustomed to serving dry martinis, Pimm's cups, and Dubonneys to ladies and gentlemen, performed his heavy task of making the seamen's drinks with an expression of intense pain, unconcealed. As the months passed, each time we put into the Mersey, the captain took up his residence at the Adelphi and others of the crew also went there. Those periodic visitations were trying times for the barman. In fact, after the *Seatiger* finally paid off in Hoboken, I took my substantial accumulated pay—more money than I had ever had at one time—and bought a passage on the *American Builder* right back to Liverpool preparing to tour England and Europe on a bicycle. I put up at the Adelphi, went into the bar, and there was the barman. He blanched when he saw me. "Oh no!" he exclaimed, "you're not back. That terrible ship, it's not back." Not to worry, I assured him. "*I'm* back," I said, "for a day or two, but the ship's long gone."

"Thank you," he said with genuine relief and gratitude. "Thank you."

Without breakdowns or delays in the canal, and with good weather, each trip from the Mersey to the Gulf and back took about a month and a half. Members of the crew deserted in England, in Egypt, in Sicily, anyplace where the ship put in long enough to get a foot ashore except the Persian Gulf. Though this relentless turnover of men deepened the captain's paranoia —he considered each illness or resignation to be a personal desertion—he was not solely to blame. The chief engineer was an excellent superior and well-liked, but his men quit too. There were, of course, almost no qualified American seamen in those ports to fill the gaps so the captain took whomever he could find. We had Arabs with prayer rugs in the engine room, Egyptians, Italians, Germans, and, of course, Scotsmen and Englishmen. They came and went, and, as I said, when we paid off in the States, Charlie Goodwin and I were the only remaining members of the original deck crew.

All along its shuttle route, the ship became notorious. The English harbor pilots knew us, the canal pilots and the waterfront citizens of Port Said knew us, the dockworkers in the Persian Gulf and seamen of other ships, even the sheik of Kuwait knew us, so did the consulates. Because—though from no specific source or personality—the ship generated violence spontaneously, wherever it turned up there was bound to be trouble even if it was only an oiler gone berserk on "canal juice" and trying to "escape" by leaping into the canal. We pulled him from the taffrail and, under captain's orders, took him forcibly to the infirmary where the master handcuffed him to a bunk. And the entire ship, officers, crew, and all, was nearly outlawed from the Mersey after an incident that alerted port officials to the potential perils of our presence. Petroleum carriers of all types are likely to be dangerous in crowded harbors either from leakage, collision, or fire. (Permanent warning signs, NO SMOKING NO OPEN LIGHTS NO VISITORS, are posted on all tankers and the crew lights cigarettes only in the houses, never on deck and even the maintenance tools such as chipping hammers are made of bronze instead of steel to prevent sparks when the cargo is a volatile one though regular tools are safe with dirty cargoes which are extemely difficult to ignite.) One trip in early winter we fetched up loaded on the Mersey bar in a fog as firm and cold as ice.

(I had come aboard in Arthur Kill almost, but not quite, schooner-rigged which means naked, not bare naked, but without gear. And what work clothes I did have, I had to throw away after my baptismal dunking in the font of black paint. I bought new clothes from the slop chest, and in Newcastle I equipped myself with foul-weather gear. In the olden days a sailor's outfit was provided by the waterfront crimps—which is how Brooks Brothers started on South Street in Manhattan—from money advanced by the ship owners, but nowadays every man provides his own clothes and a well-stocked slop chest should give him everything he needs; but all slop chests are not well stocked. Slop or slops comes from an Old English and Icelandic expression meaning a loose jacket or wide-legged pants thence, in the seventeenth century, cheap ready-made clothes. I still had rubber boots from the *Paul Revere,* but I bought oilskins and warm clothes even though I knew we were heading for the Persian Gulf because winter was bound to come, and the North Sea and the Irish Sea are hoary and cold in those months with short days and long nights. At a surplus store I found a huge, padded, wool-lined canvas coat with toggles and a hood, left over from the war. And it became "the coat." It was too big to fit into any sea bag, and it was too big and authoritative to be owned by any one man. It became the property of every sailor on every watch. Encrusted with salt and rigid with sea water, it stood on its own in the messroom on winter nights like an apartment or a willing mistress, and one man after another, as he came and went to the icy bow for lookout, inhabited it. When I payed off the *Seatiger,* "the coat" remained, and it may still be there, confronting the seas with the *Globe Explorer.*)

The captain, who had become more irritable and uptight with every trip, was determined to get off the ship and on his stool at the Adelphi bar, fog or no fog; but he was refused permission to enter the river until the weather cleared up. It had been a traumatic voyage, the violent incidents of which are described in "Dancer's Cricket." He became abusive to the port official on the radio and threatened to come in with or without permission which would have been madness since you couldn't see your hand in front of your face and the Mersey channel in clear sunlight is tricky enough. Of course, he didn't dare take the risk; but when the fog did lift after nearly two days, and we were finally tied up to the buoys at Bromborough, he took the first launch ashore leaving the ship in charge of the mate. Almost the entire crew went ashore, too. A T-2 carries two pumpmen who correspond roughly to the deck engineer of a freighter. The pumpman's position is slightly special. He has his own room and some authority like the bosun has though he is not an officer. The first pumpman on the *Seatiger* was a splendidly crusty character like my uncle Tom about whom I once wrote a perfectly true story and who sat around in the living room chewing tobacco and spitting into a brass spittoon. The first pumpman was fat and pockmarked and went around deck like a farmer around the barnyard in undershirt and bib overalls. Though he was raunchy and obscene, he was also the kind of man who would never undress in front of his wife and would go to bed with his hat on. He knew all there was to know about pumps; and he was easy as could be to work with because, though he toiled and sweated in the infernal depths of the pumproom, he never lost his cool and he never criticized. He laid intricate and flamboyant curses upon the rotten machinery but never upon the sailor who assisted him. (During loading, discharging, and butterworthing, a sailor, usually the ordinary of the watch or whoever was available, stuck with the pumpman to turn valves for him or accompany him down the rusty ladders to the pumproom, his rattling, wheezing, steaming wet kingdom beneath the sea.)

The second pumpman was a German engineer who was high-handed with his shipmates whom he clearly considered his inferiors. A vindictive chess player, he let it be known that he was employed on our miserable bucket as pumpman solely because of the sordid economic state the world ashore was in. He was so tense I don't know how he ever slept. He showed brief signs of coming apart the first trip through the Red Sea, but he held himself aloof and together until that fifth Merseyside discharge. The first pumpman went to see a distant English cousin in Chester that night after the fog lifted, arranging for the second pumpman to stand a double watch so he could visit longer (trading and switching and doubling watches was common practice). The entire steward's department went ashore after supper, the mate drank himself into a stupor in his room, and the German, who had always eschewed strong drink and evinced scorn at the untidy escapades of his shipmates, was left with the responsibility of discharging cargo. Pumping out is a simpler process than filling up, but some rudimentary care must be taken to keep the operation smooth and even so the ship stays level. Either the censorious German had been drinking secretly or he finally cracked his puritanical shell and ran amok, but as the gangway watchman said later, "I don't know what the hell he was doing, but I saw him running up and down the deck laughing and turning valves like crazy."

When daylight came, someone on shore pointed out to the dockmaster that all was not right on the *Seatiger*. It looked like it was rolling over in the stream. The dockmaster brought down the agent who went out to the ship which had, by then, developed a ten- or twelve-degree list. One mooring line had snapped and a couple of the others were so slack the ship was beginning to twist in the current. The mate had awakened, pulled himself together, and gone ashore leaving the incompetent Smitty in charge. The German had disappeared and was never heard from again. Captain Dantzler was found and prized off his bar stool and told the news that his ship was commencing to capsize. He lurched back aboard and excoriated Smitty and the mate when the mate showed up. Fortunately, the first pumpman's cousin had not been home and he had returned. Without a word he got into his old overalls and started to bring things back to an even keel. The port authorities told the master to finish with his cargo, gather his crew, and get the hell out.

We lost Harry Suleri that trip, too. He was my watchmate along with Bob Ferrara after Charlie was promoted to day work. Harry was a huge blustering Estonian who began straight and true and capable, but who was finally beaten by the Red Sea, by the maddening relentless waves of the northeast monsoon piling up slow sultry implacable seas along the coast of Arabia, by booze, and by a testy Egyptian half his size who punctured his bravado, split his lip, and permanently humiliated him. After that fight which took place in the street in Port Said, Harry stayed drunk almost all the time. When the ship got underway and there was nothing more to drink, he guzzled shaving lotion which made him so sick he threw up in the wash basin. The fo'c'sle reeked of vomit and Aqua-Velva.

The master used his drunkenness as a tool for blackmail to compel him to bathe Little Harold, the master's ill-tempered poodle. The master threatened to log Harry two-for-one if he refused. I used Harry's Herculean body and some of his style to house the character of Whitey (though, in fact, Harry was not at all the predatory, pernicious schemer that Whitey was) in the story "Near the Line." And I turned the agent of his humiliation from an Egyptian to a shark and an innocent boy called The Rock. And I had Harry-Whitey transferred at sea to a black ship of death in nighttime equatorial seas off the coast of Brazil though, in truth, it was the Egyptian, himself, who was put aboard the *Liberté* just then inbound for New York on a winter cruise. The Egyptian had complained of severe abdominal pains. He claimed he had an ulcer and perhaps he had one. I saw him later on in Brooklyn. He'd had a lovely trip, he said, on the *Liberté* and he felt fine. He had escaped not just the *Seatiger* but wretched Egypt as well. He had American seaman's papers, a union permit, and was in top shape. Harry, like the unsteady German, vanished into the Liverpudlian jungle.

I should point out that the *Seatiger* under the suzerainty of David Dantzler was not one of your usual merchant ships. Hundreds of vessels did and do traverse the seas regularly without incident, peacefully and on time. I have worked on some. But as Conrad said when someone asked him what he remembered most about all his years at sea, "I remember an unutterable boredom." Unfortunately, working on well-run straight-forward ships is a dull proposition sometimes. The last time I went to sea as a sailor was on the *J.H. MacGaregill,* and I became so bored after a couple of months that I quit forever.

Though the bizarre vibrations that pervaded daily life on the *Seatiger* were often hostile and sinister, we never knew where they were going to lead us though day after routine day went by without incident, days of chipping, redleading, "slushing" down the rigging, washing down in the morning, tending boilers, baking bread, playing cards, reading books, telling stories, drinking coffee, painting bulkheads, washing clothes, sweating, steering, eating, watching the sea, reading the stars, plotting a course, sleeping and smoking. We were an eccentric assemblage sailing those seas, but we all had our jobs to do, and we were a community, an uneasy community confronting an uneasy world whenever we touched shore. By the time we passed through the canal for the last time, the Egyptians had abrogated their treaty with Britain, there was fighting and killing in Ismailia and violence in the streets of Port Said, nighttime raids by Moslem Brotherhood terrorists against British civilians, and British warships in the harbor. Inexperienced British-navy sailors bumbled through the *fellaheen* work in the canal, and not long after we carried our last cargo into the Mediterranean, the canal was closed for a while. Charlie Goodwin never got his suit.

The story of Charlie's suit is threaded into the narrative of *All Men Are Mariners,* and rather than attempt to extract it, I'll retell the story briefly here. During the disabled weeks in Port Said while we were waiting for the Elliott man and engine parts and for the captain to crack loose and let some money flow, we were tied up next to another disabled ship, the *Roma,* a troop-carrier converted by an Italian company—Lauro Lines owned by an Italian profiteer who had been mayor of Naples or Genoa—into a passenger ship and filled with tourists and emigrants to Australia. It was its maiden voyage in its new clothes. Big neon letters on each side of the boat deck spelled out the ship's name except that on the port side, the side next to the *Seatiger,* the name-sign had burned out so what we saw were the starboard letters in reverse, AMOЯ. There was partying every night in first class, music and dancing. The master of the *Roma* had met our master at the Eastern Exchange Hotel and invited him aboard for a gala. Colored lights, merry people moving past the broad windows of the saloon while we, a dark, penniless, horny, thirsty shipful of sea-weary seamen scarcely fifty feet away watching our captain laughing with the ladies and holding up the bar. (The ironies of our lives. Four years later, after my English wife and I had spent our honeymoon in the Canary Islands and returned to the Spanish peninsula, to Seville, for her permanent visa, the only ship we could book out of Gibraltar for New York was the *Roma*. They had fixed the name-sign and repaired the engine, but the "stateroom" we had must once have been a paint locker. There were no portholes, no ventilation. The two of us could not dress or undress at the same time. My wife was pregnant again and seasick. It was a miserable trip and *I* held up the bar.)

As my off-watch was daytime and I had money borrowed from the chief, I went ashore and became acquainted with a young Egyptian named Sayed Osman and some of his friends. In a few days we had become, as my mother would say, thick as thieves. My shipmates, after they were able to draw money, were pestered and cheated ruthlessly, particularly the detested Englishmen—who were, of course, also drawing glittering American wages—by the harbor boys and peddlers, noxious *paparazzi,* not taking pictures, but buzzing around selling every imaginable kind of junk. Port Said had a well-deserved reputation for evil and trickery in the past, and most of the crew were apprehensive about venturing very far from the downtown international quarter, but I spent most of my time in the Greek-Egyptian district surrounding the main mosque, and after Sayed lent me his bicycle, I moved freely about the city, even through the Arab quarter, unmolested. I realized later that many of my Egyptian friends were militants of the Moslem Brotherhood, an organization now generally outlawed throughout Islam, but I enjoyed my innocent freedom and security. I was experiencing "real life" in Port Said even though I found it to be a disappointingly lifeless town.

After his conversion by the harbor merchants, the captain allowed us to draw up to twenty Egyptian pounds at a time. Since I had observed that Sayed and all of his friends were very smartly dressed indeed—they talked about and admired each other's clothes more than they talked about sex and politics and sport or admired their girl friends or their wives who were never in the streets except to bring them their dinners at the café where they hung out. Sayed was not married though he was engaged. He lived with his mother and sister in a small apartment where he took me on a Mussulman holiday for a special meal of kid and thrushes that he had bought that morning in the market. His affianced was there too. Though none of the women could speak English or even French, they smiled a great deal and were shyly gracious as they served us, the men. Since only worldly Mohammedans drink wine or spirits, we drank iced mango juice and coffee and ate honey cakes and melon for dessert.

Sayed and his friends also bathed a lot. Frequently during a somnolent afternoon in the café Sayed would take leave of me and the game-players, the coffee drinkers and Coke drinkers, and other friends who were just watching the passing inhabitants in the street and listening to the radio broadcasting the chiaroscuro voice of Mohammed Mahmoud Ahab—the most popular singer in the country at the time, the Egyptian Sinatra—saying he was going home to bathe. An hour later he would return glistening and spotless in fresh togs and fresh scents. The others did the same. I also observed that the native quarter of the city seemed to be populated almost entirely by tailors. I decided to spend some of my money on some new clothes. I had never had clothes made just for me, and the notion seemed to embody the ultimate in extravagance and luxury. Hell, what was I sweating in the Red Sea for anyway? Sayed took me next door to the café to the brothers Sambouskani who were not the kind of tailors who ran up the usual sleazy quick suit for the passing sailor. There were plenty of those down on the waterfront. The brothers Sambouskani took great pride and care in their work. First they made me some shirts in beautiful subtle stripes from fine Egyptian cotton cloth that I was still wearing nearly ten years later. They also made me a *galabieh,* the long muumuu-like garment commonly worn by North African men, and, finally a suit. I picked out the material, a heavy striped flannel of superb English wool. The price was £15. It was designed to my specifications, and it was not sewn, it was built. The brothers Sambouskani were armorers. The suit had double vents and wide cuffs and, inside, in embroidered half-inch, bright blue letters on white satin, it said: CALVIN KENTFIELD. It was finished the day before we left for the Persian Gulf. I showed it to Bob and he ordered one. Sayed, who supported his mother and sister catch-as-catch-can, became the tailors' agent, and the price went up to £20. Bob was measured the day we left and his suit was ready when we came back from the Gulf two weeks later. We did not customarily stop at Port Said on the way back, but Sayed and others could come aboard from launches as the ship moved slowly through the harbor toward the lighthouse. When Charlie saw Bob's suit, he wanted one too. Sayed, who had found himself a new business, did the measuring himself, on board. He was also taking orders from men on other ships. There was a down payment and everybody had to trust everybody else which, given Port Said's reputation for venality and corruption established in 1859, was remarkable indeed. But Sayed was my friend and I trusted him. Other crewmen on the *Tiger* bought suits from other tailors, but they were expensive, hurried, makeshift jobs, not the Sambouskani product. Until it perished by fire in 1969, my Egyptian suit was recognized by all who knew it as one of the wonders of the ancient world.

Charlie's suit was promised for the next voyage, but it wasn't ready. Sayed said he needed additional measurements, but it would be ready when we returned from Mina' al Ahmadi. He also needed more money, he said. Charlie had already paid half, £10, and I told him to give Sayed five more. On the return trip, the jacket was nearly ready. It was cut and basted. Sayed brought it aboard and Charlie tried it on. He was pleased. It was a good blue wool gabardine, very smart, just what he wanted. Sayed said the whole thing would be ready when we came back from Liverpool, but it wasn't. Charlie's natural good nature and forbearance was beginning to corrode. "When you come back through," Sayed said. "That's what you said last time," Charlie said. He felt he was being taken, but there was nothing he could do. On the way back, on our last passage through the Suez, a cold wind blew down from the sea. It was January. We were nearly through the harbor, heading for DeLesseps statue at the end of the breakwater, when Sayed appeared. He had a long scarf wound around his neck and chin like a French student. He didn't say a word. His launch pulled alongside the well deck and he handed up a brown-paper parcel. Charlie handed down the final payment, and that was the last we ever saw of Sayed. His launch fell behind and the *Seatiger,* passing the Father of the Canal, began to move with the open sea. But it wasn't Charlie's suit. It was brown and made for a man twice his size. Perhaps it was a mistake, perhaps it was a swindle, I'll never know. I gave an explanation in the novel, but it was pure conjecture and contrivance for the purposes of fiction.

The final discharge of Kuwait crude, before we departed the Eastern Hemisphere, was made at Port-de-Bouc in the south of France. To get there we passed very near Crete, moving into a winter storm that raged purple and green and wine-dark, a Homerical storm with the island of Minos looming like a fortress in the bright horizonal space beneath the clouds. The next day, storm abated, the sea still rose roughly, blue-black, a cold blue; and the only waterspout I have ever seen spun along its edge, a sea tornado. The air was crisp, clear, and the sky was a fabric of swiftly sailing clouds and brilliant flashes of winter sunlight. A perfect rainbow arched across the heavens, and one end of it, for a moment, actually fell on the *Tiger.* I had never seen a waterspout before nor had I ever bathed in the end of a rainbow. I felt I was witnessing not Nature, but Art, that I was being included in an ancient painting illustrating the prodigies of Creation. The sun, as it came and went, sending out singular scimitar rays, seemed to have a face.

And that wasn't all. Not for nothing has the Mediterranean been called the cradle of Western civilization and myth. The captain, perhaps inspired by the fabulous meteorological display or perhaps to save time, decided to cut through the Strait of Messina, that tricky, treacherous, crooked neck of water between Italy and Sicily that brought Ulysses such sorrow. With Scylla, the rock (Ulysses encountered a many-headed man-eating monster there), on one side, and Charybdis, the sucking whirling currents on the other, it was a bold move, bolder, of course, for Ulysses than for Captain Dantzler even though the captain, who was an indifferent, not to say inadequate navigator himself, had to depend upon the piloting talents of the mate to get him through. When he was sober, the mate knew well what he was up to, and with Etna towering, snow-white, behind us in the glazed blue sky, he took his fixes on the lighthouses of Scilla and Punta del Faro and steered us through the heavy currents into the Tyrrhenian Sea. That night we passed through the Liparis, the caper islands, with Vulcanello glowing, indeed, like Hephaestus's forge on the southern horizon and Stromboli spitting fire to the north. The fine storm-cleared weather prevailed all the way to Provence though the seas stayed high and the mistral put ice in the air and forced the waves against us.

We left, empty, from France, put in for fuel and stores at Gibraltar and headed out through the Canaries for Venezuela. We made two shuttles from Puerto la Cruz (from the docks the *John Ringling* had brought the steel beams for) to Montevideo, then returned to the Hudson. Articles were broken. We all got paid. The girl I had left had flown to Brazil to get married. I had been gone just a month under a year.

Recreation: Inhabitable Islands

All men are mariners, and all women islands to be inhabited.
—*Phoenician saying*

The Phoenicians were intrepid and enterprising sailors, but we don't know what they may or may not have said since almost no examples of their wit or wisdom have survived to amuse or instruct us. It's not likely, however, that they ever said anything like the saying above. I made that up so I'd have a title for my second novel which was supposed to have been called *The Small Rain,* but I had to change it after I found that a lady in the forties had published a novel with the same title drawn from the tender despair of that verse that has been romantically ascribed to Richard I, Lion-heart, written while he was prize captive of the Emperor (Henry VI), but which is, by more sober scholarship, acknowledged to be anonymous.

Western wind, when wilt thou blow,
The small rain down can rain?
Christ, that my love were in my arms,
And I in my bed again.

It's lonely at sea unless you're homosexual and lucky enough to find another fellow of like persuasion. Most seamen, these days, are not. They masturbate a good deal for sexual exercise. Mary, a shoreside girlfriend of mine in those days, asked me straight out one time if seamen jacked themselves off. Had she asked the question today, I would have given her a straightforward answer because our attitudes have changed, but I dissembled then. I told her that no man ever came up in the dark to relieve a watchman on the bow or the flying bridge without making some sound, singing or calling out or showing a light. It was an unspoken rule not because of the fright or startle factor alone in the black night next to the hissing sea, but because the watchman might be engaged in private sensual fantasy. Dark fo'c'sleheads in tropical nights were ritualistically anointed with the seed of dreaming sailors. So were the bunks in the Red Sea. We bought those terrible pornographic books in Egypt and read them in our fo'c'sles. They were the most ugly and sadistic pornographic books I have ever encountered. I adore clever and wholesome pornography such as the old classics, *Fanny Hill* and *The Perfumed Garden,* but the Egyptian pornography, however stimulating, was political. It was always proper British women—good Lord! how the Egyptians, with good reason, despised their pedestrian middle-class overlords, the colonial British—always British women who were forced to perform un-British and unnatural acts upon the huge triumphant bodies of Egyptian males. Revenge pornography, it was, cruel and, therefore, repellent.

There was a very pretty Arab boy about fourteen who, like the stores and the peddlers and the changey-for-changey lad, the gilly-gilly boy (give him a watch and he'll change it into a baby chicken, give him some piasters and, gilly-gilly, you get your watch back), came aboard each trip at Port Said and who offered to do anything he was asked. He would shine your shoes and perform fellation simultaneously if you wanted him to though none of us as far as I know felt inclined to take advantage of such vulnerable youth. I had not hesitated, however, at an earlier time to take repeated advantage of an azure-eyed, mocha-toned girl of fifteen named Conchita at No. 9, Trocadero in Havana. I gave her to my protagonist, one of my alter egos, in *The Alchemist's Voyage,* calling her, symbolically, Amata. I was in love, then, with love, with sensual love (my love-affair with love was never spiritual), and medievally sentimental. I could raise tears, then, to the strains of "Greensleeves" or "Brigg Fair"—*Unto Brigg Fair I did repair/ For love was my object there/ For love I was inclined.*

We always treated the Arab boy well, giving him homemade pecan rolls and horsecock and American cheese and an occasional piaster for doing nothing. Those were hard times in Egypt. The British, Farouk and his friends, and foreigners owned everything and the *fellaheen* starved. A boy had to get along as best he could.

While I'm talking about homosexual practices, the radio operator had occasion to visit another Orion ship (Orion was the company, sometimes called Colonial, that owned the *Seatiger,* the Goulandrises, a Greek family, controlled the company that named all its many ships Sea-something—*Seawave, Sealion,* etc.) at Mina' al Ahmadi where he was glancing through the deck log and found an account for a complaint that a messboy had made to the captain. The messboy had been drinking with the steward in the steward's room and had passed out briefly. When he awoke he found "the steward massaging my penis with his mouth." The radio operator told that to the captain who thought it was very funny. Well, as I said, that kind of thing is rare. Buggering exists. Dave, my watchmate on the *John Ringling,* a handsome young fellow whom I used as the physical model for Ira Garrett in *The Alchemist's Voyage* and whose history I usurped as well, once was violated in a C-2's shower by a strong anxious bosun, but such instances were not common because ships were seldom that long away from shoreside relief. There were, of course, some seamen who did not act out of necessity or circumstance, but who acted out of preference but I've known many more such folk ashore than at sea. Most seamen preferred girls to sailors and spent a great deal of money pursuing them. I'll tell you my funny Palermo story.

The *Seatiger,* as you know if you've read this far, broke down in Sicily. After I had seen Monreale and the *capella palatina* and the incredible beehive-domed early churches including the church of St. John the Hermit, I was ready and eager to couple-up in the flesh. Every whorehouse in Palermo had a waiting line of twenty or thirty men—homelife in that city must have been miserable. So the radio operator and I, after having played loose and cultural, stationed ourselves in a café in the better part of town, knowing something would undoubtedly occur. Before long we were propositioned by a young man who not only had a sister but a sister's sister and a friend. All he needed was money, and we had plenty of that. We gave him a bunch of it and he disappeared for a while then came back with three girls one of whom was quite lovely. He took her himself and absconded leaving the sister's sister and the friend with us. Neither of them were as beautiful as the sister, but we really didn't care. In the sack, in the dark, it doesn't make that much difference. Except the girl that I took home didn't turn out the light, she turned on the radio. She spoke no English and I had not yet learned any Italian, but conversation wasn't the purpose anyway. We drank some wine and smiled at each other and listened to the music on the radio, but then the music stopped and some kind of play came on. I couldn't understand it and paid no attention. We took off our clothes and began to make love. She was very easy and so was I, we both wanted to make it last. I did my best educated insertion, and she gasped and cried out until I couldn't hold back any longer and I had to let everything go, flat out. Still she cried in ecstasy and breathless excitement, so I figured I should get it up again with that little trick I had learned of making it stiffen up inside from slack to huge by subtle pressure. She responded and I came again, but she was still gasping. I rolled off and still she gasped. Puzzled, I lit a cigarette and sat up on the edge of the bed, but she still lay there oohing and ahhing. Then I realized that all the time I thought I was being so strong and good and clever, she'd been listening to the radio. It was some kind of soap opera, some kind of serial, *una òpera sapona,* some *Maria*

Marleno, or *Helena Trento,* or *Mamma Perkinsi,* or *Giovanni's Altra Moglie.* Male arrogance, Jesus! If you don't have a sense of humor it can lay you low. But I gained an insight during that pleasurable, comical session, an insight into the power of fiction. I was putting out everything I had, sharing my adaptation of reality with the girl, but whoever had devised the script, whoever had written the drama, the soapy fantasy, had beat me hands down.

Many seamen these days have wives, children, tract homes, and station wagons; and when I went to sea with Standard Oil, New Jersey, on the *Esso Gettysburg* after only a couple of years absence during which I had married and instigated a child, I presented myself at the hiring office wearing Frisko jeans, boots, and a denim shirt, my usual sailor's slops; and the port captain said to me, "You don't look like one of *our* people." (Frisko jeans, or black jeans as opposed to blue jeans, were tough cotton-twill West Coast pants worn by sailors and longshoremen and made by Can't-Bust-'Em. They had flared cuffs in the nautical tradition of bell-bottoms and, like the original button-fly Levis which ranch and woods men preferred, they were hip-hugging and nearly indestructible. They washed out to a pale soft gray and lasted and lasted. My last pair never did wear out. Like my Port Said flannel suit, they burnt up when the house burned down. They were worn with a white cap called a "Lundberg Stetson" named after Harry Lundberg—or Harry Lunchbox as old survivors refer to him—who was the champion of seamen's rights on the West Coast, founder of the Sailors' Union of the Pacific (S.U.P.), and, along with his close friend—until they fell out and became enemies over a girl, some say, or over political philosophy—Harry Bridges, leader of the monumental general strike in San Francisco in 1934. The Lundberg Stetson was a standard commodity on all A.F. of L. ships, that is, S.U.P. and S.I.U., but not the N.M.U. which was a C.I.O. union, the Congress of Industrial Organizations, and therefore "commonist" attainted though they are all together now, rich and reactionary. The slop chests of A.F. of L. ships were also stocked with denim dungarees on the East and

Gulf Coasts and Frisko jeans on the West. Denim, by the way, the traditional sailors' cloth, comes from Nîmes in the south of France, *serge de Nîmes,* the cloth of Nîmes, *serge* being a development from the Latin name for the Chinese, Seres, "the silk people.")

"No," the Esso port captain repeated, "You don't look like one of *our* people." Esso operated a company union, a community of seamen whose jobs were totally within the company's purview and who, as soon as the gangway nuzzled the dock, poured forth resplendent, as if they had never heard of a ship or the sea, in tweed jackets and gabardine slacks, loafers, stretch socks, and wide-winged sport shirts, joining their wives waiting in Impalas and Capris. In such a short time, seagoing had become blue-collar, hard-hat respectable. As my friend, the former radio operator or Sparks (now called electronics officer) of the *Seatiger,* who lives in what used to be called Levittown, Pennsylvania, says they sit around at coffeetime "talking about cholesterol and property taxes instead of broads." Some homesteaders, if they are not married, have permanent girl friends abroad, and some, like Stopper in my story, "The Big Surprise" (or like Alec Guinness in that fine, funny film, *Captain's Paradise*), have one at home and one overseas; but Stopper, as ships got faster and he got older, found the pace rather trying so he tried to give one away to his friend the mate, Harley Asgard:

"Look, Harley, I'm pushing forty, see, and I'm just a . . . radio man, see. I got no place to go, I can't go up unless I get on one of them big liners with all that phoney brass and uniform stuff, see, and I can't make no more money than I make right now, and, like I say, I'm not getting any younger, I mean there's ten days between Ella and Eunice, and, man, I tell you it's too soon . . . and Ella, she wants a new mixer, she wants a new stove, she wants a new pink washing machine, she wants a color T.V., and the kids—my boy's about ready for college and my girl's coming up to the formal stage, and I'm just not man enough to take care of them and the ones on the other side, too, that's the God's truth . . . Now look, Harley, Eunice is a wonderful girl, she's not beautiful, but she's . . . attractive, and I *know* she'd take to you like that. I'm not married to her though she looks to me for support, and I know she would look to you for the same, and . . . I mean, Jesus, that's what a man's for, isn't it? And the kids are both just little, they don't hardly know who their daddy is yet . . . and, Harley, *you* could marry her, she'd like that . . . No no no, Harley, *you* take *Eunice.*

Before the blessed change in sexual attitudes which has come about in a newer, easier generation, the seaman had no choice but to purchase the release and affection he required. "Nice" girls wouldn't go with him (except in rare, fortunate, instances such as Beverly of Rouen), and, except for Charlie Goodwin who fell in love with every women he touched, he didn't want them to. There wasn't time for games and acquaintances, for families and dinners and shows and cautious approaches. He needed to get straight to the core of the matter, but there was seldom sex without some kind of love. That may sound mawkish, but believe it or not, some love was always there. Jacking-off at sea was O.K. when that was all there was, but that sweet conjunction with a woman's body extends a man's limits, he becomes more of a man than merely a man, more than an aggregation of muscle and hair and a handy plunger. There's tenderness and wonder and pleasure there as well, and women often don't realize how *much* pleasure a man derives from *her* pleasure. But this is not a marriage manual.

Of the forty-two members of the crew of the *John Ringling,* I don't think more than four or five were married, not even the captain. Engineers were more likely to be husbands and providers than deck sailors or mates. Sailors were less responsible, freer, more experimental types, readier types, tell-me-what-you-have-in-mind-and-we'll-give-it-a-go types. As Mr. Solly (short for Solomon), a rather pontifical character in many of my stories, said to an old sailor and a young one in "The Great Wondering Goony Bird," " 'Common as air and free as a bird, because it seems to me that seamen and birds have a lot in common, like you take that man-o'-war up there—' he raised his chin in a quick gesture toward the frigate bird that still lounged in the upper air—'or you take a bird like the Great White Pellycan or the Great Wondering Albatross, they go hither and yon without a thought for home nor rest . . . like us, I mean.' "

With all our shuffling back and forth along the Spanish Main, we encountered many Venezuelan girls, none, as I said, with baskets on their heads, but often desirable, often available, and often more than pretty, for, occasionally, a conmixture of contesting bloods, of Carib, Arawak, Spanish, African, French, Irish produced a *mestiza* of startling exotic beauty, a thrilling creature to behold. In the world of the States, in the dim forties when I was young, though I was not unattractive, I was also not altogether irresistible to women and I had to work and play games and spend more money, often, than I earned to achieve my ultimate desire. But in Venezuela, I found out immediately that my money went a lot farther. Once I had the touch of it, I expended most of my free time and substance ashore wrapped around a smooth brown body with soft lips and breasts and slick thighs and a furry garden since there was precious little else to do on the Venezuelan mainland except swim and drink. (There was a country bullfight one day in La Guaira which I used to advantage in *The Alchemist's Voyage,* and there were movies in Spanish.) There were no Monreales, no Carthaginian ruins (I forgot to say that when the *Seatiger* broke down in the Sicilian Channel, we put in briefly at Tunis before proceeding to Palermo in an unsuccessful attempt to repair the engine, and I had hopes of visiting Carthage, home of Dido), there was really nothing to do in Venezuela but swim and drink and fuck. At La Guaira and Puerto la Cruz, Cumanà, and other places I, having stood my gangway watch from midnight to morning, went ashore in the afternoon when the girls were not busy and were lazy, with no rush or tension in the establishments, and spent several languid hours in sexual exercise and siesta. I was usually the only customer, and nobody was in a hurry. Tall rum drinks, sunshine and birdsong, distant music, and sweet cunt. That's what Ray had told me about back in cold Iowa.

I didn't mention it before but the *Paul Revere,* within its regular occupation of bauxite gathering, also made one trip with general cargo along the Venezuelan coast, and one cargo we carried was two native girls. The bosun and his roommate, the deck maintenance, smuggled them aboard in the night at Cumanà, past me reading, probably, Dostoevsky—I wasn't reading *War and Peace* because I read that later on my honeymoon in the Canary Islands, but it would have been something long, sea voyages are perfect for reading really long, involved books; maybe it was *Buddenbrooks,* the only novel of Mann's I could ever finish. Whatever it was, I managed to be so entangled in the language that I couldn't possibly see the girls come aboard. They stayed in the bosun's room sleeping with the bosun and the deck maintenance and certain other selected members of the crew none of whom, of course, not even Whitey the Rat, letting the intelligence of their presence reach topside. But somehow, the second mate found out. He may have heard girlish laughter, I don't know, but he knocked on the bosun's door. Of course, he could not enter because that would have been a violation of nautical etiquette (only the master may enter a seaman's fo'c'sle without permission and then only on official inspection tours and accompanied by a representative witness from the crew; a man may not sit on another man's bunk without an invitation, for a man's bunk is as private as his coffin, and even if a visitor *is* invited to sit down—and on a Liberty there was only room for one chair in a fo'c'sle so if you were entertaining, your guests *had* to sit on the bunks—it was as rude to sit on the pillow as it was, back in Iowa, to visit somebody at dinnertime and watch them eat).

"Bosun!" the second mate called through the door, "Do you have women in there: I'm going to report this topside."

He was a blond fellow with a heavy face, a busybody and a homosexual, I mean, we've all done things unusual and been attracted to many people, love is not restrictive, but he, the second mate, really despised women. He was offended by their pendulous flesh and their smell, their habits and all that. He threatened to tell the captain and have them thrown off preferably, I'm sure, directly into the Cariaco Trench. And he threatened to insist that the captain log the bosun and his roommate. Unfortunate captain: he was the man, you remember, who had to contend with the gale and a cracking ship in the Bay of Biscay and with the bosun's revolt in Paramaribo. He was generally sympathetic to his men and disliked trouble, but one of the girls (they'd been having a fine old time—good meals sneaked in from the galley, rum and Coca-Cola, a free passage to Maracaibo, affection, money) heard the threat the second mate made outside the bosun's door, and her English was strong enough that she understood. The bosun's room was right next to the saloon mess. Picture this, then. A ship at sea, a contained functioning society of men, only men. A certain propriety—officers were officers, crew was crew, they ate in different places, they kept to their own domains, the crew's mess-room was noisy, talkative, profane, even a bit rowdy; the officers' was sedate with conversation following the quiet master's lead. Suddenly, into the officers' dinner sprang a naked tigress of a woman screaming Venezuelan obscenities. The poor captain had no idea there was any such foreign creature aboard, but right in the middle of his Swiss steak and mashed potatoes, a naked angry woman. Though several of us who had finished our lunches (dinner in the merchant marine—breakfast, dinner, and supper) were outside the saloon mess and heard the commotion, I couldn't see the master's face, but I didn't have to. The poor man, what could he do? The screaming woman picked up a sugar bowl preparing to brain the second mate, but one of the engineers leapt up and restrained her. I saw that much from the passageway. The girls, who hadn't donned a stitch since they came aboard, were required to dress and were put ashore at Puerto Cabello, but I don't think the bosun was logged that time either. Well, no, he must have been; the captain couldn't have very well let that go by after the "mutiny" in Paramaribo. One time on the *Seatiger* a girl came aboard in the south of France, but I'll come to that bit last.

In the Mediterranean, on the second voyage from the Persian Gulf to the Mersey, we were told by Scotty, the bosun on the *Seatiger,* that we were going to paint the stack. Everyone knew I was an artist of sorts since I frequently made sketches and painted pictures on deck in full view of everyone. (I was arrested in Port Said, in fact, for making a drawing of the Casino Palace Hotel which was right next to the army barracks, and the suspicious police couldn't see the difference; it was Sayed who talked me free, that's how we became acquainted.) I was invariably detailed to do the "artistic" work, the "cutting in," for instance. (For some traditional reason, the ship's deck color—usually red or black—along inside and outside passageways or anyplace where the decks and the houses meet, comes up about four inches onto the white bulkhead. All the walls aboard a ship are called bulkheads, even the elegantly paneled walls of the grand ballroom of the *Queen Elizabeth* would be called bulkheads by the sailors. Creating that straight-line trim at the base of the bulkhead was called "cutting in.") Well, I cut in, and I stenciled and drew numbers on the tank tops and the fire stations and I was always the one sent overside in a bosun's chair to paint the draft numbers and freshen the letters of the ship's name. But the big art job was repainting the company insignia on the stack. Orion's sign, not surprisingly, was a star. But a stack is a huge thing, like a billboard, in fact, that's what it is, it's outdoor advertising. To paint it, a stage or a bosun's chair must be rigged. A painting stage needn't be explained, they're common on land and sea, but a bosun's chair is a little wooden seat fitted in a rope sling and attached to a long gantline. The gantline is run through a block on a mast or a king post or wherever it's needed so the man in the chair can be raised to working position. Sometimes he's hoisted aloft by the deck winch, but that wasn't possible in the matter of the stack. Scotty rigged the chair from a block hooked on the rim of the stack, and I pulled myself up by hand. There is a moment aloft when you use one hand to swing a loop of the rope under your body to form the special knot that will allow you, by twisting it, to descend a little at a time, a moment during which you are holding yourself in the air with the strength of one hand by "marrying" the two parts of the line in your fist. (Squeezing, holding, or seizing two lines together in a tight embrace is "marrying" them. Though shipboard names include many cats, dogs, rats, and hogs, they also include many sexual and scatological terms of which marry is certainly the most respectable. There are snatch blocks, cunt splices, and shit boards as well as any number of cocks and jacks.) Once the movable knot is formed, you release the lines, your body weight (180 pounds in my case) in a short downward jerk, tightens the knot. When I let go and my body dropped, my left thumb somehow got caught in the cinching turn of manila, and when I managed to extricate it, the thumbnail was a bloody howling mess. I've checked and inquired from time to time, but no other sailor of my acquaintance has ever admitted to catching his thumb in the knot of a bosun's chair. I admit it now, and I put it on record as possibly the only such gratuitous aleatory event that ever occurred at sea.

With a swollen throbbing thumb, there was little work I could do between Gibraltar and the Mersey, and Captain Dantzler, more as punishment, I think, than cure, sent me to the doctor in Liverpool. Charlie and another sailor, Paul, went with me because we planned to have some drinks and find some action when the doctor was through with me. They waited outside the consulting room and heard me screaming. The doctor, who was retained by the company's agent, was Norwegian and sadistic. He didn't tell me what he was going to do. He injected a token drop of Novocain into my bony thumb, then he took a little sharp-nosed pair of scissors and shoved one point underneath my thumbnail and cut it right down the middle snipping off first one half of the nail and then the other. My screams brought the nurse, who was too late, but who gave the doctor a dark look and gave me sympathy and a huge bandage like a wad of cotton candy which I carried aloft through the bars and streets of Liverpool like a torch. Everytime I dropped my arm, the pain became hideous. We were drinking Scotch in a pub near the market in Great Charlotte Street, and the whiskey helped dull the pain. Paul said, "I know a place, if I can find it, in Canning Street, I think, where we can have a party."

"Let's go," Charlie said.

"I can't go with this thing," I said.

"Hell, Cal," Charlie said, "you don't fuck with your thumb."

We had some more whiskey, drinking until the pub closed at three. (Three in the afternoon. English licensing laws were, and are, pretty strange.) Then we did some shopping. I bought some watercolors and some books. Then we went to a movie, and when we came out the pubs were open again. We drank some more, and finally, toting our purchases, went looking for the place in Canning Street. Canning Street was up the hill from Liverpool cathedral which was a nineteenth-century fake-Gothic structure like Grace Cathedral in San Francisco and St. John the Divine in New York. It was begun in 1904, but it still wasn't finished.

After some searching, Paul found the place in Canning Street, an unassuming row house in an innocuous middle-class neighborhood. On the way we had come across Bob Ferrara who came along. It turned out well, a gratifying respite from the crowded, competitive, impersonal gin mills and dance palaises of Lime Street. Besides the lady of the house, an older woman with a vast swelling bosom, a long purple velvet gown, jet necklace, and, drooping perpetually from her lower lip, a lighted fag that littered her plush shelf with ashes, there was also her husband, a common English Pa with receding hair, eyeglasses from the National Health, and Clement-Attlee moustache; and there were four girls, just exactly enough. Each of us sailors contributed five pounds—toward expenses—which we casually tucked into a tumbler on the hall table. The roll shades were pulled down, the draperies drawn behind the aspidistra that stood in the bay window. With the girls snuggling on our laps we lounged on the chesterfield and the overstuffed chairs that were protected from sweaty hands and hair oil by crochetted antimacassars while Pa and his wife served Worthington and Irish and potato chips. The wireless broadcast dance music from the Light Programme, and we danced on the carpet in the cozy room. A large framed chromo of "Shoeing the Bay Mare" hung over the chesterfield. A coal fire burned in the grate, for it had been a raw summer now going into fall with daily rain and mist from the Irish Sea. Only a few signs revealed that seafarers were entertained in that parlor—a cocktail tray made from the layered wings of jungle butterflies and commonly available in several tropical ports in Africa and the Indies; a monkey that chattered and squeaked on one girl's shoulder as she danced; and the generous quantities of Irish which had likely crossed from Dublin in Yankee lockers and found its way from Queen's Dock to Canning Street unobserved by His Majesty's Inland Revenue. From time to time there were knocks on the front street door, but the party was complete, and the callers were quietly turned away. Paul brought out some Egyptian grass—*cannabis* was rare and *very* wicked back then, the devil's tool—but the lady with ashes on her breast pointed out the impropriety of smoking anything other than the likes of Players or Luckies or Craven A's. The place had been under surveillance recently; that's why the curtains were drawn. Pa got squiffy on the ale and spirits that tasted of bog and peat smoke, and he began to sing some of the old songs, then he did a music-hall turn amongst us dancers, amongst the girls, the monkey, and the sailors. He was a sketch and a caution was Pa.

One by one, as the evening passed, we sorted out our partnerships and climbed the hall stairs to the bedrooms. The girl that took me up was just getting over the flu, and she sniffled frequently, but she was warm and comfortable under the mound of covers; and I was a kind of invalid, too. I had to keep my thumb in the air, but being tall and being on top, I was able to prop my elbow on her pillow and manage the night's activities satisfactorily. Many months later, when I came back on my own to Liverpool, I sought out No. 24, Canning Street past the cathedral and the Anglican cemetery, and the girl I had spent that night with answered the door with a tissue to her nose, still sniffling from the Liverpool climate; but if she recognized me, she didn't show it. She kept the chain on the door and said, no no, go away. "No one's here anymore," she said. "Go away!"

When I was apprenticed in London,
I went to see my dear,
The candles were all burning,
The moon shone bright and clear,
I knocked upon her window
To ease her of her pain,
She rose to let me in
Then she barred the door again.

I like your well behaviour,
And this I often say,
I cannot live contented, love,
Whilst you are far away.
The roads, they are so muddy,
We cannot gang about,
So roll me in your arms, love,
And blow the candles out.

If you should prove successful, love,
Pray name it after me,
Kiss it sweet and dress it neat
And daff it on your knee.
When my three years are ended,
My time it will be out,
And I will double my indebtedness
By blowing the candles out.

Blow the Candles Out
English folk song

On its single call in the south of France, the *Seatiger* put in at Port-du-Bouc just before midnight on a Saturday, and by the time the work was done and Charlie and Bob and I had showered and shaved and got into our shoreside clothes, it was nearly one o'clock, an odd time to go ashore, but it wasn't Liverpool, it was a new country, and we were eager. Charlie, a day worker, had nothing to do on Sunday, and Bob and I had traded off our watches so we were all free until Monday morning at eight o'clock. Port-du-Bouc was a tiny place in low flat countryside with marshes, ponds, and canals—Bouches-du-

Rhône, east of the Camargue, south of Arles, Van Gogh country. We found one café open where we drank brandy with some other shipmates until it closed and the others went back to the ship. Since I could stumble rudely through a little French, I was leader. I found out there was a village up the road where we could find girls and a hotel to rest our heads. All three of us were stuffed like scarecrows with francs the captain had issued on the way into port. We each bought a bottle of cognac and began a search for a taxi. We were laughing and singing more from high spirits—being off the decks and under the trees—than from spirits though the brandy helped. The biggest building in the town was the Hôtel de Ville and Sûreté. I went up the front steps and pounded on the door. It was three in the morning. "Hulloa!" I called, trying to sound Gallic. *"Personne ici? Un taxi! S'il vous plâit, un taxi!"* Why I thought we could engage a taxi at the City Hall or the police station, I can't say, but apparently it seemed feasible at the time. "Hulloa!" I shouted, banging on the big front door. Bob and Charlie were laughing and leaping up and down in the street which was dead empty and dead silent except for the echoes of my shouts. *"Un taxi!"*

A shuttered window on the second floor of the Sûreté swung open, and a figure in cap and light pajama top leaned out and said something, angrily. *"Un taxi, s'il vous plâit,"* I called up to him. There was a sharp crack in the winter air, and I withdrew quickly down the front steps. "You know what, Cal, you know what?" Charlie said. "That was a shot." "You're fuckin' A that was a shot," I said. The shutters of the Sûreté slammed shut as we began jogging, if not actually running up the middle of the street.

"We might as well go back and wait till morning," Bob said.

"Back to the ship? Hell no," I said.

"I'm sick of the fuckin' ship," Charlie said.

"Besides, it *is* morning."

"Let's walk to that town," Charlie said. "Cal, what's it called, what's it called." Charlie frequently repeated himself when he was excited.

"Easter," I said, "or Eastray."

"Sure," Bob said, "let's walk it, there might be something on the way."

"It's only a couple of miles," I said as if I knew.

"Shit, yes," Charlie said. "Shit yes, let's walk to Easter."

There was only one road, and within a few hundred yards we were out of the village and engulfed in a moonless, overcast night, silent as a grave, full of the smell of dank grass and brackish water. We were lightly dressed, and the night was cold, penetrating. We pulled on our brandy bottles to warm, at least, our insides; we talked, we made plans, we speculated upon whether the ship was really going to Venezuela, I said I knew all about Venezuela, we conjectured upon what we would find ahead of us, up the road and in the years ahead, we slogged on and on.

"How far'd you say that Easter was?" Charlie said.

"I thought the *garçon* said a couple of miles. If we see somebody we'll ask them."

"*See* somebody! *Shit!*" Bob exclaimed. "Nobody's been to Easter since Christmas. I can't even see the road."

As the early morning deepened, white mist thickened over the lowlands and the canal alongside the road. And when one of us stumbled onto the shoulder, the grass crackled with frost. We were chilled to the core, brandy notwithstanding. A shadowy form came up from behind, a dim figure on a bike, and vanished like a ghost before I could hail it.

"I say, Cal, old cock," Charlie said, turning Limey, "would you say we're on the proper road to Easter?"

"Cor blymey, 'ow should *I* know."

"You know wut she said to me?" Bob said, "You cawn't sty hall night, sir, but you can feel me on the stoop."

"I thought she said," I said, "it's all right, ducks, but I think you've got me scarf caught."

"That's wut she said when I stood 'er on 'er 'ead against the bleedin' Lime Street wall."

"What was that song," Charlie said, "the old geezer sang in

Canning Street where the cunt with the monkey took us both to bed?"

"Charlie, old cock," Bob said, "you never told us you fucked that monkey."

"I'm Burlington Bertie," I sang. "I rise at ten thirty, I walk about town like a toff. I stroll down the Strand with me glove in me 'and, and I stroll back again with it off."

"Hey Cal, hey Cal," Charlie said. "There's a light up there, there's a light up there."

And so, indeed, there was. It emerged from the mist by the side of the road. "Cor blymey!" I exclaimed as a lighted window drew abeam. "A bloody bakery, a ruddy *boulangerie.*"

It seemed to be an odd place for a bakery because in the thick morning air we could see no other habitation, but a *boulangerie* it surely was. There were shelves of *baguettes, brioche, croissants* blurrily visible through the misted window glass beyond the sign saying *Fermé*. The door was locked, but there was a bicycle leaning against one wall inside; and, as the three of us, like three poor little match girls, peered into the warm interior, a man in a white apron emerged from a door behind the counter carrying another tray of warm loaves. We tapped on the door, the baker gave a start then came to open it, but he didn't let us in. "How far is Easter?" I asked in what I meant to be French.

"Je ne comprend pas," the baker said.

"Parlez-vous anglais?"

"Non!"

"Easter," Charlie said.

"Eas*tray*," I tried.

"Je ne comprend pas. J'ai fermé."

Bob, ever resourceful when cold and hungry, took a swallow from his brandy, offered the bottle to the baker, and pointed to the shelves. The baker almost smiled. He put down a good belt of cognac, then stepped back and gathered up three *croissants*, handed them to us and closed the door in our faces.

We had long since finished our bottles by the time we

reached Easter which turned out to be the village of Istres. It was first daylight though there had been no dawn. The lights of the village hotel still burned in the gray morning, and the bar was still open, warm and welcome. The *patron* behind the bar could not believe his eyes. Three American sailors emerging on foot from the fog.

"Formidable!" he exclaimed over and over as he poured us cognac and coffee, hot coffee, *"C'est formidable."*

American seamen almost never came to Istres. They, as our shipmates subsequently did, went the other way, taking the long ride to the vile caves, the scrofulous warrens of sex and corruption in Marseilles. We, on the other hand, had walked fifteen kilometers into the wholesome country.

"Formidable," the proprietor said. He was clearly the kind of homosexual who feels solicitous toward young men whether they be of his persuasion or not. He tried to accommodate us in every way. He had the sleepy hirsute chambermaid prepare three rooms for us upstairs when I told him what we wanted; and while we drank and warmed up, he sent out a runner to find three girls, and he refused to take money for any of our drinks. All he could do was shake his head and say *Formidable*.

I don't know what the other fellows did, but stretched out naked in those smooth white sheets (it was a spotless, simple country-village hotel with high ceilings, plastered brick walls, tiled floors, a washstand, and huge wardrobe with mirrors trimmed toward the bed) next to that naked black-haired girl, I couldn't do a thing. We'd worked till midnight, hiked till dawn, and drunk flagons of brandy. Though I tried and the girl tried, regardless of how ready and impatient I had been when we had left the ship, I just couldn't firm up. The girl began to cry because I stayed soft and couldn't keep my eyes open. She thought it was her fault. She spoke a little English. She said, "You not like me." I tried to assure her that I did, and, in fact, I did. She was young and pretty and quite sweet. That wasn't the problem. Trying to reassure her, I put my arm around her and fell asleep with her weeping on my chest. I slept until lunchtime, awakened upright and starving, and went into her, as the British say, straightaway. Before I had a chance, even, to withdraw, Charlie burst into the room. He was still high, ebullient. He slapped my ass and said, "Come on, come on, pull out old cock, soup's on. We're going to eat and take a little trip. I got us a cab. We're going to—I'll tell you later."

The three of us and the three girls had a long slow Provençal midday meal in the plain dining room. The fog had gone, the day was cool but sunny and bright, the way I wanted the south of France to be. We had soup and artichokes—which the girls had to show us how to eat—fish and lamb, canned vegetables and compote, and lots of sharp red wine. I've forgotten how much it all came to, but we gladly paid.

Over the strenuous objections of the girls of Istres—Bob's girl tried to pull him from the back seat—the cab driver took us several miles away to a farm outside Martigues, another village on the Étang de Berre. The farm was a walled compound with chickens, pigs, goats, a vegetable garden, and a two-story provincial country house with tiled roof and thick walls, a cobbled courtyard, a large bar and dining room with a dancefloor, and lots of other rooms besides. Once again the numbers worked out. There were three of us and three girls—older and obviously more professional than the Easter girls. There was also a toothless, grizzled old man, and a middle-aged couple who were the proprietors. It was late Sunday afternoon when we arrived. The only customers were two French sailors whose navy wages couldn't compete with our rolls of francs and who soon departed. I had four five-thousand-franc notes which I kept secreted in a small card case containing my seaman's document. I also had nine or ten one-thousand-franc notes which I kept in a wad in my pants pocket.

Here, again, we were a welcome phenomenon. American sailors almost never visited that pastoral retreat. We were taken in like family. We drank cognac at the bar, talked to the girls, listened to phonograph records, to Edith Piaf, Charles Trenet, Yves Montand, Germaine Montero. By that time, with the sun going down, sinking over the western horizon into the

Camargue, the horn was really on us. The old man had a projection room where he showed some funny, jerky old porno flicks—fat-bottomed ladies in hose and garters stradling reclining moustachioed soldiers of the Third Empire with their pants pulled down. Using our thousand-franc notes like tickets, we took one or another of the girls to a room upstairs, were either sucked or screwed, came back down, drank some cognac, gave the old man a ticket, watched a movie and came out ready to go again, gave another girl a ticket and went upstairs. Round after round this went on until their dinner time. Since we showed no inclination to leave, we were invited to dinner. We all—the girls, the old man, we sailors, the *patron* and his wife—sat around a huge oak table in the family kitchen, ate white bread and *potage,* roast chicken, goat's cheese, fruit and nuts, all with jugs of local wine. Coffee, brandy, and cigarettes after dinner. The girls asked us if we wanted to spend the night, and I, delivering the consensus, said, Sure, but we had to be at the ship by eight in the morning. The girls said not to worry. Again I don't know what my companions did, but the girl in whose room and bed I slept and I screwed some more before going to sleep and once again when she woke me in the morning. She drew me a bath, washed me tenderly, and lent me a razor and a toothbrush. When I was dressed, I went downstairs where I was joined by Bob and Charlie at the big table set with *croissants* and jam and hot café au lait. It was six o'clock. We had a couple of shots of brandy with our coffee, kissed the girls good-bye, and emerged, warm inside and happily wrung out and drained of juice, into the frosty, foggy countryside where, outside the farmhouse gate, a taxi, already paid for, awaited us. In Port-du-Bouc, before going back aboard, we stopped at a café for a bottle of brandy apiece. All my thousand-franc notes were spent. When I looked in my wallet, one of the five-thousand-franc notes was missing. Lots of girls would have taken them all.

We couldn't discharge that Monday because the mistral began to blow so fiercely that we were compelled to move the ship to deep water until the wind dropped. Somehow a girl had got aboard, and Scotty and the third assistant engineer had locked her in the engineer's room and were renting out the key for 500 francs. What you paid the girl was between you and her. Charlie, Bob, and I had already taken more sexual exercise in the last twenty-four hours than we would customarily take in a fortnight, but working on deck that afternoon, each of us knew what the others were thinking.

"Cal, are you going to?"

"I don't know, Charlie. Are you?"

"I was thinking about it."

"So was I."

"You guys are a couple of sex fiends," Bob said.

"You never know, Bob, we might never get another chance. We might sink between here and Venezuela."

"I don't know if Scotty will let me. He's got the key."

Scotty, who was in his forties, had a kind of fatherly crush on me. He figured me for a higher type than the others. He scolded me when he found me reading a dirty book. "I never though *ye'd* be reading that filthy trash, lad," he said, deeply disappointed in me. And when, at coffeetime, I asked him for the key to the girl, he looked hurt, but he gave it to me without charge. But a few minutes later when I was stripped and exposed, perched on the edge of the bunk with the girl kneeling on a pillow working on me, French style, Scotty walked in to see how I was doing. There were two other sailors with him. Nowadays I wouldn't be embarrassed, but I was mortified then, for a moment anyway.

"Come on you guys," I said, "get out of here."

Scotty just stood there looking at us, fascinated, while the others giggled. They'd all been drinking, of course, since Saturday; in fact, Scotty was even then clutching a bottle of brandy in his fist. "I thought ye might like a wee dram, lad," he said in an accent thick as Shetland wool.

"Knock it off, Scotty," I said, accepting the bottle and taking a swallow. "You and your wee drams." I laughed and handed the bottle to the girl who also took a swallow. "You just want to watch the show, you wee creep."

The girl handed the bottle back to me, I took another swallow and passed it on to Scotty who said I was the last one because we were shifting back to the dock in half an hour. They left then, and I, having slackened off, lay back on the bunk. After spending all those tickets in Martigues, I admit I was fairly well, to risk a pun, petered out. But the girl climbed on me and shook me and cajoled me and rolled around on me until she got something out of me, enough so I could say I got my money's worth. Afterwards, I lay in the engineer's bunk while the girl bent over me and washed me thoroughly and gracefully with warm water and Palmolive. She was younger than the women of Martigues, and slighter. Her breasts were small, her hips slim, skinny in fact, and she had a little cat face and curly hair. In her ears were little gold rings. I laid my hand where her buttocks curved as she lathered me, and I felt myself start to fill up again in her hands. She looked at me, and I smiled and shook my head. It was too late, that was the last one. I had to get back on deck before the captain caught on. She rinsed and dried me, and I told her she might as well get dressed because there wouldn't be anybody else now. I stood up and pulled on my shorts and dungarees. On the pillow lay a gold chain with a cross on it. It must have come off her neck. I picked it up and was about to hand it to her then changed my mind and dropped it in my pocket. She was dressing and didn't see me. I put on my socks and boots and, finally, my shirt, feeling guilty but unwilling to give up the chain. I gave her a thousand francs, more than she was asking, and stepped quickly into the passageway. I don't know if she ever missed it, it wasn't worth much, a confirmation cross. And I had a use for the chain.

For more than a year in my wanderings, I had been wearing a silver chain around my neck with a small scallop shell attached in much the way young people these days wear ankhs and peace medallions except that I wore the shell under my shirt next to my skin like a dog tag or a charm. All through the Middle Ages, people wandered over Europe making pilgrimages to many places. To protect themselves from brigands and the armies of warring princes, to proclaim their poverty and peaceful intentions, they wore a scallop shell, usually in their caps or in some way attached to their persons. Iconographically, the shell was assigned to the apostle James, the Great, brother of John, son of Zebedee.

> And Jesus, walking by the sea of Galilee, saw two brethren, Simon called Peter, and Andrew his brother, casting a net into the sea: for they were fishers.
>
> And he saith unto them, Follow me, and I will make you fishers of men.
>
> And they straightway left their nets and followed him.
>
> And going from hence, he saw other two brethren, James the son of Zebedee, and John his brother, in a ship with Zebedee their father, mending their nets; and he called them.
>
> And they immediately left the ship and their father, and followed him.
>
> Matthew 4: 18–22

James, supposedly, was buried at Compostela in the north of Spain, and from the ninth century onward the shrine at Santiago de Compostela was the destination of thousands and thousands of pilgrims displaying the scallop, the coquille St.-Jacques, until the shell came to mean "I am a pilgrim, and I come in peace." Whatever the pilgrimage, whatever the search. Sir Walter Raleigh began his poem, *The Passionate Man's Pilgrimage:* "Give me my scallop-shell of quiet."

What I was searching for, I don't know—love, knowledge, understanding, fortune, beauty, excitement, entertainment—everything, I suppose; but I broke my chain while working one day on the *Seatiger*'s deck. I needed another so I stole the French girl's. I took off the cross and hooked on my tiny shell, restoring my rights to peaceful pilgrimage. Those rights were the core and central theme of my novel, *All Men Are Mariners,* the pleasures they gave and the disasters they brought. This story from the book of how that chain was acquired you will recognize now as mostly romantic fiction, still, though it strays from the facts for the sake of depicting characters, contains some truth. Tom and Ulla—the girl to whom he, eleutheromaniac that he has always been, has fallen captive, has fallen in love with against his will—are in bed together, and he is explaining how he came by the pilgrim amulet.

"The shell came from Florida on the beach of Captiva. The chain came from a girl . . . and you must promise that you won't be angry."

"Of *course* I won't be angry. What girl?"

"I have no idea. She was a prostitute on the island of Margarita, which is just off the north coast of Venezuela. Ships seldom go there, but we did. We couldn't dock because of our draft, but we anchored out and the girl slipped aboard from one of the fishing boats. We hid her in the bosun's room. It was only for the space of a watch that we were there, but a few of us in the deck gang—the sailors—who knew about her took turns at odd times during the afternoon. The bosun slipped us the key and we went one by one to his room. She just stayed there on his bunk, naked as we are, and men went in and came out and passed along the key.

"She was dark-skinned as Sheba, and this chain she wore with a cross around her neck. Well, the other guys, they just screwed her, as was right and proper and what she expected—just, you know, as the limeys say, 'W'ip it in, w'ip it out, wipe it off—' "

"Men are terrible people."

"I know we are, but we can't help it. I went in at coffee time . . . Only I didn't just screw her like the rest, I made love to her. She was gorgeous lying in that sunny tropical cell with the bright chain against her black flesh . . . so I made love to her as I would to you, and though she tried to resist me—to keep calm and feel nothing—she simply couldn't—"

"Oh, Tommy, darling, *Yndling Tommelfinger,* you are so *arrogant*. You think there is no woman in the whole world who could *possibly*—I *adore* your pride and arrogance."

"Then don't interrupt, because in a minute the girl came beautifully, luxuriantly. It was really spectacular."

"And she fell so *madly* in love with you—"

Tom laughed. "Oh *no!*" he exclaimed. "She was *furious.* I had intruded upon herself. 'Oh what you do to me, sailor, what you do to me,' she cried, really furious because, suddenly, she was languid and drowsy and wanted to sleep and there was no time; there was money to be made and I had destroyed her willingness to accept the others. There was already somebody tapping on the door. *Oh,* she was mad.

"I put my dungarees back on and sat down on the edge of the bunk to tie my shoes and she beat my back with her fist in a slow sultry way like the beating of tropical surf upon the shore, and she demanded three times what the others had paid . . ."

"And the chain?"

"Yes, the chain . . . I saw the chain had come loose . . . and lay beside her wild black hair . . . I laid my hand over it, thinking that when she had recovered and opened her eyes, I would give it to her; but my hand closed over it and my lips sealed tight and, when I reached for my dungarees, I let the chain slip from my fist into my pocket."

"You *stole* it."

"Yes . . .I stole it. I don't know why. I didn't know then and I don't know now, but here it is around my neck. I took off the cross and put on the shell and here—"

He felt Ulla's fingers in the chain . . . twisting it. He felt it cutting in the back of his neck before the links parted. He saw her raise her arm high and caught the glint of the soft silver thing as it passed through the shaft of moonlight in the middle of the room, and he heard the delicate click as it fell on the balcony.

"I don't want you to wear it. I don't want you to wear it."

"Why not? She meant nothing to me, that girl. I don't know why I wanted the chain, I— She meant nothing to me, and that was a long time ago—"

"I know, I know. She meant nothing to you." Her eyes flashed with anger and distress. *"Oh!"* she cried. "This . . . this *Pillegrim shit!* . . . You will go from me to another like a bee to a flower, meaning no harm. Oh my dear, I am a *Pillegrim* and I come in peace. You will go and never come back, and I will be left old and alone when you go . . . passing on your way with your filthy little shell."

Well, that *was* a long time ago. The world has changed and so have I. The chain's long been broken and has disappeared; but the shell still lodges in the cap of my mind. More's the pity, perhaps, but that's the way I was, and, well, that's the way it is.

The Last Ship

The last ship I worked on was the *J.H. MacGaregill,* a T-2 tanker named after a former chairman of the board of Standard Oil of California, and operated by Standard Oil's maritime division, Chevron Shipping Company. At that time the home port was Richmond on San Francisco Bay where the last, and now defunct, American whaling industry flourished by capturing the migrating California gray whales off the Farallones, but the California grays were threatened with extinction and shortly after I left the sea, whaling in America became a thing of the past. From my house in Sausalito, I could watch the whalers struggle into the bay with the big dead grays lashed to their sides. They hunted, as the Russians and the Japanese do, with harpoon cannons loaded to explode in the beast's head so the whale never had a chance. I could also watch the Standard Oil tankers pass by heading in and out of the Golden Gate. Though the *MacGaregill*'s run included Hawaii and Wake Island, thirty pacific days across the earth's vastest ocean, it never signed foreign articles. It was a local vessel and half-union—half Sailors' Union of the Pacific (S.U.P.) which meant that if you were a union man and wanted to accept Chevron's working conditions, you could ship on it. The chief mate was a thorough company man, an uncommunicative, authority-bound, heavy-faced functionary of, perhaps, fifty-five, a man who expected, whatever the word he uttered, to be obeyed. He was a ready type for caricature with his severe facial features, and I drew many laughable images of him in ship's chalk on the dry bulkheads of the shelter deck.

In 1959, the year my father died, we carried fuel oil out to Wake, but we also carried some general cargo—some machinery and some household packages for Navy wives—that was stowed in the forepeak (all T-2 tankers have a dry cargo hold forward that can be worked by a single boom, and we, the sailors, against all union regulations worked that cargo because the mate told us to. When we got back to Honolulu, it was a Sunday. Everything was closed, but we managed haircuts from some Japanese lady barbers who opened up for sailors, and we obliged some shipowners to unlock their doors by tapping on the glass. I bought some tiny muumuus for Kate, my tiny daughter. Then we found some Polynesian fishermen down on the dock who had just come in with octopuses. We also found a man who would open up his bar and sell us illegal beer. We bought a couple of six-packs and a Sunday paper, and we spent the long sunny afternoon on the fishermen's dock reading the news and the funnies and drinking beer and talking to the fishermen who were cleaning their octopuses by turning the heads inside out and rinsing them in clear water. All this while—a long easy afternoon after a long empty voyage over an empty ocean (the size of the Pacific is a wondrous thing, but it's a boring ocean with remote boundaries and crossing it takes forever)—the mate was visiting with his son who was, I discovered, an executive employee of Standard Oil in the Islands. The father was an authority on his ship, the son an entirely different kind of man, a different authority ashore. I was back aboard when the mate returned, driven home by his offspring and his daughter-in-law; and I know as well as I know my own chest when I scratch it that they were putting the old man back aboard with pleasure. He had been an embarrassment. I saw their faces. The young fellow—what? thirty-two? thirty-five? He'd been *embarrassed* by his crusty father's visit. (My own father, one time, when I was nearly grown, when a freight train ran off the track and he had to go out and help the repair crew, took me with him, and for the first time I saw my father as an employee, for there were Rock Island bosses there calling him by his last name, swearing at him, and ordering him around; and he knew I had never seen this before and *he* was embarrassed.)

The mate's son was button-down collar with a manufactured, Barbie-doll, hair-spray wife. They were putting old Dad back aboard after a Sunday sojourn with the grandkids. Well I saw them return him in his son's T-Bird, and he saw me see them, and he understood that I understood. Back in Richmond he raged against me because I had skipped a dead, unnecessary watch and gone home to Sausalito to see my wife and Jason, my new baby son, and my mother who, mistakenly, had come west after my father died to venture into a world that was no more her own than the mate's was to his son's. We fought, my wife and I, and I went back to the ship. The mate was at the dockshed on Richmond Long Wharf. He saw me come aboard. I was quite drunk and he knew it, and the next day he called me before him, and he said "Kentfield, you were drunk last night when you came aboard for your watch." And I said, "Nosir, I was just tired," but he shook his head, so I said, "O.K., sir, if that's the way you want it, I was drunk." That pleased him. "It's appearances that count," he said, laying a word of wisdom on me. He didn't log me, he just wanted to show me who was boss. Not his son. Not the button-down world.

Not long after that he discovered that because of a new policy of the company he had worked for for twenty years, Standard Oil, all of his and his wife's purchases on their Chevron credit card, such as tires, oil, and gasoline would be deducted from his salary. Some shiny-eyed, deodorized, passionless, Brylcreme android—maybe even his own synthetic son—or some printed-circuit humanoid machine buried under the main office wouldn't even allow him the dignity of settling his own tick. They deducted first, got theirs first, and he got his after.

The insult was too much for him and he fell into a sorry rage. He was too old to quit, too long devoted to his employer to protest. He could only beat his fist on the desk of his little room. I had come to call him, to tell him, in accordance with custom, the time, to signal the change of the watch; but he was talking to himself, cursing aloud. I wouldn't stay to have his rage turn upon me or to witness his pathetic impotence and frustration. "Mate," I said, "it's twenty to," and left.

I also left the sea that trip after standing for four straight hours on Christmas day, 1959, in a heavy vertical, relentless, windless rain in Puget Sound, just standing while the pumps pumped, while the oil—black gold, they called it in the early days—coursed from ship to shore, and the rain poured over me as if I were a stone. But it wasn't the rain. The rain produces its own ambiance, its own introspection. Standing there with the rain pouring from the end of my nose and my ears through my collar and my drawers, flowing over my boots, I, tending the valves and listening to the pumps, I came slowly to the realization that not only was I bored but that I was no longer pursuing the Possessor of All Secrets, the Father of All Gods and of the World, I was standing in the cold rain serving Standard Oil, a false god if ever there was one; so when I got back to Frisco, I quit.

Bolinas, 1972

Appendix

"A Place for Lovers in the Summertime" (see page 8) was originally published in *The New Yorker*. This story is hardly fiction at all, only a couple of names are changed. Everything else is true. *The New Yorker* pays outrageously well (in the olden days I used to get a minimum of twenty cents a word with a stipulation in my contract that they reserved the right to pay more if they wanted to) and the proceeds from this story, my first in that magazine, sustained me in Sicily after my *Seatiger* pay ran out; and, after my Danish lady went back to her husband, *All Men Are Mariners* got me to England where I met Veronica, the girl I subsequently married and divorced after five years and two children.

Some time ago, at the end of my second year at college, I found myself with neither a job for the summer nor the prospect of one. As June wore on and I was still around the house, my mother decided something must be done. "If you won't find something, I will," she said.

She thought, and then she went to the telephone. The operator was busy. While my mother waited with the receiver at her ear, she told me she had seen Fern Evans on the street the other day and that *her* oldest boy, Billy, had a job on a dredge on the Mississippi, and that she'd thought at the time that was just the place for me. She hadn't said anything to me, she went on, thinking that perhaps I would get up a little gumption and look around. Fern Evans hadn't asked her about me, and it was a good thing. She would have been ashamed to say I did nothing but lie around and read, and not even make an effort. "If that dredge is still here, I don't see why in the world you can't have a job on it," she said. "It's the government engineers that run it, and we pay our taxes, Lord knows, as well as Fern Evans or anybody else. It's healthy, and all you'd need is a pair of pants."

One of the ladies of my mother's bridge club was the wife of the chief engineer on the dredge *Rock Island,* and it was her number that my mother gave when the operator finally answered. I was sitting with a Coca-Cola in one hand and in the other the Keokuk Public Library's copy of *The Theatre Guild Anthology*. I tried to read, but with my leisure being seriously attacked, and in my hearing, I found it impossible to concentrate on *Strange Interlude*. Of the conversation between my mother and the wife of the chief engineer, I remember chiefly the words "Of course, he couldn't do the *hardest* work. He's not very strong, you know."

I was nineteen at the time, six feet two, weighed one hundred and eighty, and was strong as a horse, but my mother could not forget the times when, as a child, I had been held above a steaming teakettle with a towel over my head to inhale the vapors that were supposed to cure my bronchitis. It was manly and proper to resent this, and later that afternoon, when I drove down to the other end of town to keep the appointment the chief engineer's wife had made for me with the captain of the dredge, I determined, whatever the consequences, to refute it. I might be lazy and good-for-nothing, but I was not weak, I could work, and work hard, if I wanted to.

In the dim parlor of a small frame house which, like its owner, had settled a little, I met Captain Elmer. His wife had admitted me and then had left me alone with the captain among the sparse, new, and scarcely visible furniture.

The shades were more than halfway lowered and the lace curtains were drawn against the sun that would otherwise fade the carpet. The captain's wife busied herself in the kitchen, but there were photographs of her all around the parlor. From chromium frames she peered at me, smiling, with her cheek tilted against her clasped hands, or, sober, with her eyes raised, her lips slightly parted. She held blossoms, books, cigarettes. She was reproduced in sepia and in plain black-and-white. Now and then, she was tinted. I remembered my mother mentioning that the captain had been married recently.

Patently at his ease, he sat in a new rose-colored overstuffed chair with his stocking feet on a matching hassock, equally overstuffed. He was about forty, very large, taciturn, and nearly inaudible. I thought then that it was the quiet parlor and his happiness that made him speak so low, almost reverently, but I observed on later days that he spoke the same in broad sunlight and in times of trial.

"I hear you're not very strong," was the first thing he said. I warmly assured him this was not so, and said that I could work, and work hard, if I wanted to.

"You're a college boy," he went on. "That's what they say. You know how to use a typewriter?" He waggled his blunt fingers in the dusky air as if he were playing a piano.

I answered that I did, but that I was not very good at it. "I need a clerk that knows how to use a typewriter," he said. "You can have that job if you want it."

I felt at once betrayed and rescued (I had not really wanted to work hard that summer), but it must have been the betrayal that showed in my face, for the captain added—sympathetically, I thought—"It's the only job I've got left."

I did not hesitate long. I told him I'd take it, though I spoke with little enthusiasm.

"We go upriver tomorrow afternoon," he said. "We go straight to Foxtown first of all and deepen up the channel—no stops between. We're tied up at the dam now. You can board there."

A few other details brought the interview to an end. Before I could leave, however, the captain's wife, looking exactly like her pictures, came in bearing a round Miller High Life tray with a bottle of Miller High Life on it for the captain and a Coca-Cola for me. She then retired, with some remark about women interrupting men's business, and the captain and I drank our separate refreshments in darkness and in absolute silence.

All during my childhood, I had played and hiked and hunted along the low bluffs and among the islands of the Mississippi, discovering in the willow thickets fragments of boats, and the haunts of river tramps and of lovers in the summertime. I had watched kites and eagles soar, or perch alone in the tall sycamore trees. I had swum off the spits of sand, away from the current, and I had thought there could exist no fuller life than, in the middle of summer, to be drifting easily along in a boat on the river's current.

There were only a few stern-wheelers left, and I knew them all by sight, the *Red Wing* and the *Bluebird* among them. From the bluffs, I had seen them struggle against the current or slip downstream, effortless as clouds, caught sometimes by a cloud's shadow. And the *Rock Island* itself, cumbrous dredge, had always been familiar. It wintered often at Keokuk, when the river froze, and sometimes at the first break of ice in the spring it would be out working; other years it was not ready until early summer to creep along and clear the channel for the boats—for the *Red Wing* and the *Bluebird*.

As I drove home from the captain's house, I took out all the old dreams and pleasures and polished them up as bright as a binnacle, until they looked as good as they ever had. They shone even brighter the next day, when I went down to the dredge. Everything was ready for departure. The stores were aboard, and a number of narrow barges, each loaded with a large section of pipe, had been made up into a tow. Wherever we stopped to dredge a channel, the barges were to be secured end to end, like a pontoon bridge, and the sections of pipe joined across them. The dredge would scoop the mud, and sand, and gravel from the river bed, and the pipeline would pour it out wherever it was to be deposited. Many of the crew were needed to tend the line—to watch it, keep it secure and right with the currents, and, should it happen to be crosswise of the channel, break it, separate the barges, and, with motor launches, push them out of the way of approaching boats. Those men had the hardest jobs and the best ones. Before long, I learned to envy them.

I was prepared to work but not to be bored. Each morning, in my office, on the top deck, I took out a batch of files and made a mark on each crew member's chart to indicate that he had worked the day before. Sometimes I wrote a letter for the captain or the pilot. Most of the day, I had nothing at all to do. I had thought to lie out on deck in the afternoons and watch the passing shores, but the steel deck was too hot, and except for the square cast by the wheelhouse there was no shade on it. The river was very wide where we were, and the shore was merely a line of low willows or a distant rise of hills.

We were soon far from familiar country, so even the pleasure of recognizing landmarks was denied me, except once, in the late afternoon of the third day, when we passed close by a town I had known the summer before. I had come there frequently because of a girl named Alice. At the north edge of the town, the river makes a deep bend around the lonely bluff she and I used to ascend to watch the barges pass—or, if the stream was empty, the red-winged blackbirds flash and teeter in the willow trees—or to lie in the heavy grass and pretend to be in love.

Unfortunately, I had little to read. I was to be away too long to take *The Theatre Guild Anthology* or any other books from the Public Library with me, so I had gone quickly over my mother's collection of books. She never read, herself, but she had a strong feeling for the aesthetics of bookcases and liked to see the shelves full. She visited auctions and sellouts, and bought books, apparently by the pound. For fifty cents, she could get enough to pack two average shelves.

In my hurried examination, I had passed over such titles as *Dalmatia For The Dalmatians, Gems of Poesy,* and a complete set of *John L. Stoddard's Lectures,* and had taken volumes of Blasco Ibanez, because of what I hoped would be their salacious content. I lent one, *Blood and Sand,* to Captain Elmer and never saw it again. The other, *The Temptress,* I made a stab at reading, but failed. Finally, I threw it into the river.

I wrote long and fanciful letters to friends, though I was unable to mail them. One time, as we were raised through some locks, *Look* magazine came to take our picture, but the photographers stayed less than a day. After the excitement of their visit faded, I took to wandering away from my office and drifting around the dredge, observing its operation or looking over the shoulders of poker players in the crew's messroom below. One day, unluckily, the captain happened to be watching the same game. "Clerk," he said to me, "are you on duty?"

I answered that I was, and he sent me back to my office. From then on, there was nothing to do but sleep in my chair.

With genuine excitement, therefore, I welcomed our arrival at Foxtown, though it was not much of a place. It lay on a marshy point of osier and mud nearly detached from the solid land on its own side of the river and obscured from the opposite shore by a puzzle of islands that bent and confused the flow of the current. The islands created false and hazardous passes and sent the river, in its one true channel, narrowly and swiftly around the point of the town and almost into the people's doors.

Like so many others up and down the Mississippi, the town had declined—or, rather, collapsed—at the end of the substantial river commerce, many years back. Coal boats and oil barges still went by, but they had no cause to stop, and the showboats, which, until I was thirteen or fourteen, had knocked around the upper Mississippi like aging acrobats, were no longer on the river. The nearest paved road was six miles away, the nearest railway ten. Yet even such a place was a welcome change to me.

We broke tow a mile or so downstream from the town. By

nightfall, the barges had been made fast together so that the pipeline stretched from the dredge, in the middle of the river, to the nearest uninhabited island. Then the vessel shuddered and, like a mole, began to gouge out the channel while its floodlights played upon the water and the willows along the shore, upon long-necked birds, and upon the men tending the line.

For a time, I watched the bottom of the river pour out of the end of the pipe.

By the time I went to bed, the refuse sand had already piled up between the island's oak and aspen trees. By morning, inlets had been filled, islets obliterated. Refugee birds circled and squawked in confusion at their sudden dislocation.

Slowly, following the channel, the vessel and the line of barges, spewing havoc on the way, moved upward toward the town. The next night, after supper, most of the *Rock Island's* crew, for the first time, took one of the work launches to Foxtown, and I went with them. Only the men who had to tend the pipeline remained behind. We debarked at a ruined steamboat landing at the foot of the only street. On one side of the landing stood a blacksmith's shop converted into a garage. Most of its occupants were Model A's and old Plymouths whose bodies had been cut down and made into farm trucks. On the other side, a two-story brick hotel that had a decaying frame veranda and appeared unprepared to accommodate visitors leaned precariously toward the riverbank, which had been eaten away by years of high water. The river front, with its worn pilings and the trash scattered along it, was an unattractive place, gray even in summer.

Nearly the whole town had gathered at the landing to observe our arrival.

They were solemn people and they did not speak, but turned and watched us walk up the street in a tight knot as if we knew where we were going. We split in two, the older men turning toward the only tavern, the younger—mostly high school boys, some of whom I knew—going on ahead toward the sound of a juke box coming from what proved to be the Epworth League recreation room.

I went neither way. I was too old and too sophisticated for the Epworth League, too young—and I think, perhaps, too proud—for the company of the tavern. For some minutes, I stood alone in the dusty street; then I walked around the town. I saw the Methodist church, and the hardware, feed, and grocery store. I peered in the window of the Western Union office at the lady sitting alone there. The few houses along the street were old and widely spaced, and had chicken coops and pigeon cotes in back. Chained in the yards were watchdogs that barked and growled at my approach. There was nothing else to see. To pass the time, I had a Coca-Cola at the Epworth League and, later, a beer at the tavern, remaining at each place only long enough to drain the bottle. The people down at the landing could see me whenever I was in the street. For a long time, they sat on the running boards of their cars or stood in small groups, the men separated from the women, and watched me.

By dark, I was back at the landing. The bugs were out and most of the people had gone home; a few lingered, talking, uneasy about the strangers who had gone so directly, so unashamedly, to the tavern. Some children played listlessly in the mud along the bank of the river until their mothers called them. Eventually, the lingerers went away. Two couples, holding hands—hoping, I imagine, that the landing would be deserted—arrived from the Epworth League. When they saw, by the spark of my cigarette, that I was there, they moved to one side, talking in whispers, looking at the *Rock Island's* lights downstream. There was no other place for them to go.

Thus it was, every evening for over a week. It became my lot to stand apart on the landing, to watch the lovers and listen to the conversation of the others. The townspeople took no notice of me, so concerned were they with what they felt was the outrage against them. So many strange men in the town, filling the tavern, brought anxiety to their minds. "And the young ones!" I heard them exclaim. "Not even out of high school!" (Indeed, some of the boys took advantage of being away from home to move from the Epworth League to the tavern, and drink for the first time in their lives.)

And as the dredge progressed upstream toward the town, the twilight crowd at the landing grew. People came from the bottom farms and from other towns. They watched with interest and apprehension the vessel's upward and shoreward approach.

All day and all night the sand and water poured from the mouth of the pipe, filling everything, covering everything, like a flood. The land it covered was uninhabited and useless; nevertheless, the complaints of the people became louder, more open, more frequent. The fishing was being ruined, they said, the birds were being driven away, and the character of the town was being damaged by the drinkers in the tavern. The Democrats were blamed, the government was discredited. Still the people came and watched the dredge and met old friends they had not visited for months.

In the semidarkness of those summer evenings, I stood back and heard them wonder if the destruction would stop when it reached the landing and the street. I knew it would not. When the boat came close, there would be nowhere else to spill the sand, and I knew the town would not even be considered. I had seen the plans, and I had heard Captain Elmer and the pilot talking. I knew that they had checked their orders to make sure there was no mistake. The orders had been verified. The channel had to be dug, and the refuse had to be dumped somewhere.

I said nothing, for it was not my place to, but I thought, "it is a dreary spot. Let them bury it."

It was near the turn of the month into July, and the nights had grown hot. The dredge, groaning, thumping, squealing in its labor, lay, with its lights, like another town not half a mile away. The townspeople had at last taken action. The dredge's crew were forbidden by the chief of police to come ashore. Thus restricted, they lined the outside passageways of the boat, standing with their elbows on the rail, and watched the town. And the town still watched the dredge, uncertain of the extent of its danger or the intention of its enemy.

On the thirtieth of June, which was a Saturday, the dredge lay just below the town and many people from the country around stayed the night to see what was going to happen.

I went to bed early, and awoke early on the morning of the first of July, on Sunday. After breakfast, I ascended to my office on the top deck, took my customary turn around the wheelhouse, and encountered the captain and the pilot conferring over a roll of plans. I did not approach them. The captain was even less audible than usual, but I could hear the pilot clearly. I heard him say, "There can't be any mistake now. I've checked and rechecked until the office is tired hearing from me. They can't change the plans, because there's no place else to spill it."

They stood for some minutes in silence. I looked toward the town and found we were so near I could almost see into the second-story windows of the hotel. During the night the dredge had crept forward, and the mouth of the pipeline was now trained like a howitzer on the landing and the street. The landing, which had been crowded the night before, was empty. Many cars were still parked near it, but no one was in sight.

It seemed to me then, in the clarity of that silent morning, that the river front looked even drabber than before, the mudbank by the landing more noxious, and I thought again, "Bury it." But even as I thought, I wondered where the couples that held hands on the landing would go when the landing was buried. And I remembered the summer before—the grass on the hill, the speech and actions of love—and I wondered where I would go when the landing was gone. Where could I go to stand apart, alone, to listen in the summer twilight, an embarrassment to lovers, unnoticed by the rest?

In an hour, the sand began to pour from the pipeline. The noise brought people from their houses, from the church—brought them together in a crowd, shocked and angry. A few stones were thrown at the boat. The name of President Roosevelt was shouted bitterly, as was that of the United States Army's Corps of Engineers, whose emblem was so vaingloriously displayed on our stack. Frantically, automobiles were driven away from the area around the landing.

All that day and the next, to make a channel for the *Red Wing* and the *Bluebird,* the river bed was piled up on the bank. Frequently the pipe was moved back and forth like a hose watering a lawn. For a quarter of a mile on either side of the landing, the refuse was spread; the landing itself went first.

And the townspeople watched, cursed, and drew back as the line of spill advanced into the street.

During the night of July 2, the job was finished. On the morning of the third day, the vessel rested. The sudden cessation of the boat's vibration and noise woke me. I lay awake, uncertain whether I wished to view the destruction. When the sun was up, I went out to look. Before me was a great beach of sand, which filled the spaces between the big trees above the river and lay in a wide, smooth bank for half a mile. It buttressed the sagging walls of the smithy and the hotel.

It covered the rubble and the wasted pilings, the trash and the dirt. All that was mud and mud-colored before had been interred. As the sun grew in strength, it blazed and bleached and dried until the sandy park was bright with newness, freshness, and resurrection.

Even as I watched, the people began to gather. The children, first to understand the nature of the change, leaped from dune to dune. They slid from the roof of the smithy down the sand. They built forts and castles. The older boys swam where there had been no good place to swim. Gradually, the adults realized their good fortune. They brought out shovels and picks and wheelbarrows, and trimmed the largest mound, which filled the end of the street. They shifted it about, spread it evenly. In the spring, when the water rose, a levee would be there to keep the river from their doors.

By noon, the top sand was dry and nearly white, and although it was a weekday, picnics were preparing in kitchens. President Roosevelt was, I think, praised. That night, the crew was invited back to town. An ice-cream social prepared by the Ladies' Aid was held for us on the sand, with tables and chairs from the Sunday-school room.

We made tow the following evening, the Fourth of July, and left in a blaze of fireworks. At the tavern, before our departure, a second celebration was given for the captain, who was as surprised as anyone else by what he had done. He was honored, after some discussion (and some competition from President Roosevelt), by having the park named after him.

An enormous crowd saw us off. They lined the banks when the sparkler-and-pinwheel display was over, and many sat on the roof of the hotel waving to us as we struggled clumsily and slowly upstream. I knew that we on the dredge would discuss the event as we went from job to job that summer. In the mess-room, or during the evening, we would turn it over and over, adding and changing until it became a fable. It would help to pass the time.

I stood on the top deck as we departed, and looked back for a long while at the fires in the sand, the rockets in the sky. Soon, I realized, the grass would begin to grow on the dunes and there would be, among the farther trees, places for lovers in the summertime.

•

"Mortality" (see page 65) was first published in *The New Yorker.* The character, me, from the tugboat was originally called "the intruder," but the editors thought that was too heavy-handed and spooky so they changed it to "the tugboatman." In those days I remembered everything I heard as if any word might be the secret to the riddle of the world, so the story is not really mine but belongs to the young man, whose name I never knew, who tells it.

Inside Barataria Bay, behind the slim protection of Grand Isle, an enormous floating derrick, one of the largest in the world, lay at anchor awaiting orders and deserted except for a skeleton crew. It was called *Number Four,* and it had been made to build platforms in the sea. Beyond the measured signal of the lighthouse marking the pass between Grand Isle and Grande Terre, a circuit of hysterical lights, jumping erratically from horizon to horizon, marked the calm, dark face of the Mexican Gulf. These were oil rigs built on platforms that

Number Four, or others, had made. The wild lights said to shipping, "Keep away!"

On its own, the derrick could not move; it had to be towed from place to place, location to location, by a tugboat. Such a boat, called the *R. Thomas,* was tied up alongside, standing by. One man aboard it was awake. Though the crew of the derrick and the crew of the tug knew they were different kinds of men and did not usually mix, there was no law against it, and the tugboatman stepped from the breathing gunwale of his boat, crossed the deck of the derrick, and went into the kitchen, where powerful chicory coffee called Black Annie was always brewing in an urn. His presence, as he drew a cup and sat down, interrupted the conversation of two men seated at the table. It was late in the watch, around four.

"That was my second brother who was in the Navy," the younger man was saying. The other broke in to greet the tugboatman.

"What say, Hoss?"

"What say, Hoss?" the tugboatman returned, as the man who had been talking nodded and went on talking. He was a man of thirty, with strong shoulders and a small new mustache that reminded him, when he looked at himself in the mirror, of Errol Flynn's. He had no reason to be awake except that he could not sleep. Though the summer night was cool, he was barefoot and wore only the blue-and-red-striped under-shorts he had worn in bed. He was one of the roughnecks, standing by, and had no work to do in the morning. "The one you're thinking of is my older brother, who was lost at Iwo Jima," he said to the other man, who was the night engineer. "He was a Marine. He was the oldest in our family. The one who was in the Navy was twenty-seven months older than me, and a bigger man, too, but it's just like we was saying a minute ago, it don't have a thing to do with how big you are. He just couldn't take the rolling and the rocking."

"Amen," said the engineer.

"They put him on a minesweeper and sent him out for four months, and he was sick every day of the four. When he left home, he outweighed me twenty pounds, but when he come back I bet he didn't tip a hundred and twenty-five. He asked them couldn't they assign him something else, put him in the Army or something, but they couldn't even hear him. They was about to send him out again, but he wasn't about to go, so he just left and come home."

There was no animation in the young man's voice, few tonal changes, little variation in his stress on words; a quiet voice, respecting the hour; a calm voice, respecting the slumber of the vast, trembling marshes and the bay. His back was to the light, which came from a milky fixture over the stove, but he could not see the face of the tugboatman, opposite him at the table. A revolving caster holding salt and pepper, mustard, mayonnaise, ketchup, pickles, toothpicks, and paper napkins came down from the ceiling like a chandelier and hung between their faces.

"They're supposed to let you off, you know. They're not supposed to keep you there when you're subject to that kind of seasickness." The engineer spoke in a high, soft, childlike voice, and he rolled his wide eyes when he talked. He sat at the end of the table, completing the triangle, and he could, therefore, see the faces of the other two without difficulty.

The young man went on. "They are, I know they are, but they wouldn't leave him off, so he left and come home. Mother said, though, he had to go back. So he went back and they put him in the brig for a while, then they took him out and put him on some other boat. This time he got wounded, a red-hot piece of steel went clean through his arm—" He laid his bare arm across the table and pointed to the inside of the elbow. "Clean through there."

"That's a mighty bad place," said the engineer.

"He was in the hospital for thirty-three days, then it healed up except it did something inside to the nerves or something, so it was stiff and numb like it was asleep all the time. But the Navy doctors said that would go away, and pretty soon it did, because he was judged well enough for duty again. So they sent him back and he got so sick he could only lay on his belly on the deck and moan and pray he'd die. He'd gained some weight back in the hospital but he lost it all again, and when he come off that time he said he wasn't going back again if they hung him, so he come home."

"I'd think so," said the engineer. "They're supposed to let you off when you got that kind of seasickness."

"But Mother said he couldn't stay, because he had to face up to his duty, and he allowed, and so did I, how she was right. They'd come git him anyway, so what could he do? He said they wouldn't do a thing for him but torment him, but Mother, who had a blood disease that ran on and on and sometimes got better and sometimes worse, she was having a spell of badness that second time he come home, and he didn't want to upset her, so he went back and finally they had it all out there in Norfolk and he come out with an undesirable discharge. That's not the same as dishonorable, it's just, you know, undesirable."

"Undesirable," said the engineer. "That's not the same as dishonorable, by a long shot. They oughtn't to of kept him on. They're sup—"

"He was mighty glad to git anything—anything to git out. By the time he come home he was all right and the war was about over anyway, so he come on at the plant with me. It wasn't very long though, his arm began to stiffen up and he couldn't do the job. He went to Old Doctor with it, and Old Doctor said it was the wound all right. Something had been done to the nerve or something, in there. Old Doctor said it might go away and come back again or it might not never come back, but it didn't go away at all. It got worser and crept all long his arm until he couldn't use it for anything at all. That's when I had that Guff station on Ninth and Delachayze, you remember that Guff station, that little bitty one, or wasn't you around town then when I had it?"

"Sure I was around," the engineer said. "I remember you having that Guff station, only what I don't see is why you ever left it. And for roughnecking, anyway, climbing all over them jackets and platforms, that's purilous work. I mean, you make a little more—"

"Shhh, you make a damn sight more. You can't make nothing at the filling station unless you stay open all night, and you stay open all night, you got to have some hep. Long as I had my brother it was fine, but he got so bad he had to quit and go to bed. I had to let the station go. I couldn't afford to hire nobody. Roughnecking ain't bad—"

"Long as you got a strong back and a thick skull." The engineer smiled.

"That's right, that's me, strong back and thick skull," the young man said. "If the good Lord'd wanted me to be rich I guess he'd of left me a little more room upstairs. Take my brother, he was a bigger man than me, but he had what it took up there, besides." He tapped his head with his fingertip.

"Well, as I recall, your Daddy had a parful noodle of his own."

"My Daddy was one of the smartest men you're likely to come across, it's pityful to see him like he is now."

The smile had not left the engineer's face. "Where do you reckon you come from, then? I mean, you must of cropped up out of something long forgot. What do they call that, a turnup?"

"Throwback," said the tugboatman.

"Throwback. You must be a throwback to something long forgot."

"Mother always claimed I was the family exception. She said she was sorry her and my Daddy couldn't of passed the brains around a little more even. My sister and brothers got the biggest share. Shhh, it was a shame to see my brother filling up cars and all, and it hurt his pride, too, I could tell, working for his dumb little brother. He had to quit altogether pretty soon, he couldn't hardly move one whole side of him."

"Why didn't he go to the hospital?" the engineer questioned.

"They took him to the hospital and started giving him some kind of stuff, but pretty quick and he was back. The hospital bills were too big and the doctors said there wasn't a thing they could do for him there they couldn't do in his own home. They told us he had something called mlultiplul sker—"

"Multiple sclerosis," said the tugboatman.

"That's what Old Doctor said it was. It got all over him. They couldn't do a thing but leave him lay and pump him full of costly medicine. The Navy wouldn't do a *Damn* thing, wouldn't give him no pension, nothing, and my Daddy was having to pay all the bills. You know that fella that's been running for governor last three or four times and can't never make it, you know who I mean, Morton or Marvin, I know him well, he's a friend of my Daddy's."

"I know who you mean," said the engineer. "But I'm like you, I can't recall his name."

"Well, you know who I mean. He and that Senator Whatsisname, I never did know his right name, my Daddy knew him when he was sheriff, we used to call him Heartache, among and between the bunch of us—"

"Always had a grievance, I know who you mean," said the engineer.

"Mal da Cur we used to call him, his real name was MacSomething. It don't make no difference. The two of them heard about my brother and come to see him and my Daddy. They said they'd go up to Washington, D.C., and do something about my brother's pension, because it stood to reason my Daddy couldn't go on paying bills like that. My Daddy's retired and I knew he couldn't afford it. He didn't want them to go, said he could take care of his own boy, but my brother told them he sure would appreciate it if they would do something, since Daddy spent so much money on Mother's funeral. She always said she wanted a plain box and not have nobody do any bothering, so she never would save up for a casket, and of course she never needed to save up for a plot, because Daddy's got the family ground."

"Whereabouts is that?" the engineer asked. "Seems I never did know where your folks are buried."

"You know that cimitery way back in the trees? Well, you

know that shell road that cuts off at La Rose from the Golden Medda Road, going toward Houma? Well, it's off that road back in the trees. You know it?"

"I believe," said the engineer.

"You know where I'm talking about?" The young man leaned a little to one side to look around the caster into the tugboatman's face.

The tugboatman replied that he was not familiar with that part of the state, and the young man turned again to the engineer. "All my Daddy's people are planted there, and Mother, now. Just about everybody in there's kin. It's a pretty place if you like cimiteries. I never took to them too hot, though Mother did. I guess that's the difference between being young and being old, I guess when you get old you start thinking about cimiteries. She always said she wouldn't need a silk-satin casket when she'd have such a fine peaceful spot to lay in, and she meant it, too. Me and my brother and my married sister tried to tell my Daddy it would be a wrong to go against her wishes, but he said she never really meant it that way, and even if she did he wasn't going to lay Mother in no pine box. He had to have the best. So he got a big Philipyne mahogany thing with silver handles, all stitched up thick and pillowy on the inside, you've seen them, what do they call it?"

"Quilted," said the tugboatman.

"I believe. That cost my Daddy more than he could rightly afford, though he never said what he paid for it. It was the least he could do, he said, for all the years Mother had put up with him. Senator Heartache and Morton or Marvin—maybe it's Madison, can't never remember—they went up to Washington, D.C., and talked to some men they knew up there and, by golly, they got it done. They said it was the only way to get justice done. I used to think every man was entitled to justice and got it by rights, but I don't know. I believe they're right, because I think Brother could of wrote and wrote until he was too purralyzed to move, and not a *Damn* thing would of been done. But they went up there, and they did it, and they put it in the papers and all." He leaned aside again to look at the tugboatman. "Ain't that what you say? If you want justice done, you got to know somebody who can do it, some friend of your people, or some friend of a friend, some good buddy who knows who you are. Ain't that what you say? I mean for justice."

The tugboatman answered, with a little laugh, "You don't ask for justice any more, you ask for mercy."

"Amen!" said the engineer. "How much did he get?"

"They come through with all the back pension payments," the young man said. "Four thousand in the first, I think, and two thousand five hundred in the second, and then he kept getting regular four hundred each and every month to take care of him. I know my Daddy was spending that much and more right along, because it got to the place they was having to shoot him full of dope every hour and that's costly, but they said it was the only way to keep the pain down, and he was suffering then. Maybe you've talked to dope fiends? If you have, you know they'll tell you how much it costs them when they've got to have it. Twenty-five, thirty dollars a day, and you can figure what it would take to put a shot in every hour. But the way his muscles knotted up, you should of seen them, it was pityful. His feet would all draw up like a claw? And his hands and body all over would just draw up. It was like you had Charley horses all over your body. The stuff they give him hepped to ease away the pain. He was thin, he was down to nothing? Toward the last, there, he was like a skellyton. His fingernails, you know that part right around your fingernails—" He held out his hands, indicating the cuticle on his thick, callused fingers. One finger, the tugboatman noticed, was missing. "That part there drew all away, and his fingernails was just like you set them, there, like something you'd picked up and set on the end of your fingers, like little cellaloid chips. He was rotten away. You could smell him as soon as you come into the room. He couldn't move, toward the end there, he couldn't move but for his eyes, he could move his eyeballs. My Daddy made him a blackboard with all the letters of the alphabit on it, and when he wanted to say something, one of us would hold the blackboard up and point to the letters one at a time, and when we come to the letter he wanted he would roll up his eyeballs, and we'd write it down and go on to the next one. He was breathing so slow you could hardly know he was alive. I timed him. He took seven breaths one minute, then five breaths the next, then seven the next, then five the next. We had a old woman there to take care of him after Mother died. She was a registered nurse, I guess she used to be, she lives there in town, been taking care of people around there for years. She warshed him and kept his bed clean and give him his shots and wrenched off his face to keep him cool. I spent a lot of time with him then. I was home on crutches around the house, after I got my foot smashed up, you know, that time I fell off the engine."

"I well remember the time you fell off the engine, boy. You're lucky you didn't get more than your foot smashed."

"Well this old girl wanted to put a cover over his face, but I said I didn't believe he was dead. She took his heartbeat and listened, and she said she couldn't hear a sign of life in him, but I got me a rag, and I soaked it in cold water, and I wiped his face with it, and then I did it again and pretty soon he went kind of AHHH, kind of choked, you know and . . . drug in? But he didn't last long. If it was me, I would of found something to put him out of his misery. Seven years he suffered."

"I heard of a man up toward Layfayette lasted ten years, but suffering, you just can't think the suffering, you can't know," said the engineer.

"Well, there's a man right there in Golden Medda, I don't know if he's got multiplul skerosis or not, but he's turning to stone, he's turning to *Stone,*" the young man said. "That old boy knew my brother, too, and he used to come up to the house when he was just starting to turn and could still get around. And he was scared. He'd look at my brother, and I could tell that old boy was scared. He got written up not so long ago and I think the state's taking care of him now. Wasn't nobody knew about him for a long time."

"I've heard of that man," said the engineer. "They say you get that disease when you get to be about thirty-two or so, you start to turn to stone."

"My Daddy knows him. He goes up there to see him sometimes in memory of my brother, well, he used to, he don't no more, he ain't able."

"How old is your Daddy? He don't seem so like an old man to me."

"I don't know exactly how old my Daddy is, he's over sixty-five, but his trouble is cancer of the lung."

"No, *is* that right? I never knew your Daddy ever had a day of sickness in his life. Of course it's been a few years since I seen much of your Daddy, I mean to talk to. There was a time when I was a boy, your Daddy was a young man grown, of course, him and me was pretty good buddies, before he ever married your mother. I always looked up to your Daddy as a boy, though I never knew him to have a day of sickness."

"Shhh, wasn't but ten years ago he had a kidney removed."

"No! *Is* that right?"

"That stood to do him some good, but this other one—he went up there to the clinic there in New Oryans and had a round with the doctors. They told him he could have it operated on, but it was a pretty big price they wanted, so he said he'd have to think about it, and he come home. We sat down and talked it up one side and down the other, me and my married sister, that was just the other year, can't remember exactly, just before my married sister had her little girl. We sat down and talked about it, but it didn't seem to me how he should spend all that money on another operation. I mean, like I say, the last one stood to do him good, but this one would just leave him with one lung, and he's already got one lung. He could have the bad part of the one cut out, but he couldn't use what was left. He allowed how that was right, and I believe, don't you?"

"I believe," said the engineer, nodding. "I believe."

"I mean if he's got one anyway, ain't that what you say?" The young man addressed the tugboatman again.

"I've heard it said that each and every one of us carries inside us the thing that will kill us," the tugboatman replied.

"I mean, he had one good lung anyway," the young man went on. "And Old Doctor come up on the sly to me and my married sister and told us my Daddy didn't have but a very short time to live anyway, though he ain't dead yet. But me and my married sister didn't breathe a word to him. We just let him on. He was all hopped up about the baby coming, figuring it was going to be a boy. And it was late. Old Doctor kept saying it was coming tomorrow, and then tomorrow. Well, tomorrow never comes, and that baby child almost didn't, and when it did, it never had no Daddy. I bet you knew my sister's hubby, little guy they called Frank who was a diver, did most all the work for this company, little fella like a piece of rope, best diver they ever had."

"Little fella," said the engineer. "Like a piece of rope, could but hardly see him if he turned sidewise. I remember him, did a lot of work for this company, didn't he? I've been with this company nearly to four years, I can't recall a better diver. I didn't know he married your sister though. What happened to him? Frank, that was his name, Frank."

"He got killed."

"No!"

"One time there just outside the Chafalaya he was down and a seismograph outfit started dropping charges and they dropped one too close and concussion got him. They didn't know we had a diver down, and by the time we raised them on the radio it was too late. We didn't know they was anywhere around, I guess you'd call it a acci-dent, they come up out of nowhere."

"They're nothing but a smart-pants bunch of kids you know, them jologists," said the engineer. "They come down here from college with nothing but education and not a ounce of sense or caution. They come down here wild and reckless and hop in a fast speedboat full of explosive and take off. Then there ain't nobody safe. I almost wish the government never let them drill out here. You know what they're doing? They got Derrick Six down there at Southwest Pass building a drilling platform right smack in the middle of the ship channel. The main ship channel to New Oryans and they're planting a drilling rig smack in the middle. Sooner or later, with things like that, somebody's going to get it."

"Frank sure got it," the young man said.

"They don't realize how few and far between good divers are."

"I guess nobody could of hepped it. It was a acci-dent."

"I remember that little fella, like a piece of rope, didn't throw a shadow but one way," said the engineer. "I never knew he joined your family, though. You sure couldn't of found a better one. He was all heart and core, though taken ounce for ounce I guess there wasn't much to kill."

"Taken ounce for ounce," said the tugboatman, "there's not much to anybody. I don't suppose he had to be a diver, nobody made him, he took up the thing that killed him of his own free will."

The young man nodded. "That's what my sister said. Nobody made him be a diver, she said, and my Daddy said the same, but he took it as a great hardship when my sister passed away under the ether. They had to open her up to get the baby, and I said, and my Daddy allowed how he believed it was all for the best that the little bitty orphan thing never come alive."

"He didn't have no insurance, then?" asked the engineer.

"Frank? No. He had some, but it run out, and when he went back to take his physical to renew it, he had a cold and they wouldn't pass him, so meantime he went on diving and got clobbered. But my Daddy took it as a burden when my sister died. I mean, the little baby, you can't find it in your heart to grieve much about something that never was alive. In fact, between us here, I think my Daddy never bore it no grudge for being dead, I think he thought it served it right for killing off my sister, particularly since it was a girl. Sis and my Daddy were close."

"She was older than you, wasn't she? It seems to me, if I recall, you was the baby of that family."

"There was just Arlington Junior, after my Daddy, and Arthur, and Althea and me, we was twins, only she was a girl and I was a boy, and she was a hundred and seventy-two seconds older than me and a lot smarter. Arlington Junior was lost at Iwo Jima and Art was in the Navy. By the time I come up, I already lost my trigger finger, so they wouldn't take me." He showed his finger stub around the table in the galley light, which was beginning to be mixed with the light of dawn. "I didn't care none. There's nobody left now but me and my Daddy. I never had no wife nor no baby children, though I done my share, you understand, of working at it, but I never stuck. My Daddy said to me once, maybe a hundred times since I fell off that engine, if I didn't stop rough-necking, I'd just go on losing piece by piece. First it's your finger, then it's your leg, he said, though I got nothing left but a little limp that don't bother at all. Then your eye, then your toe, piece by piece, he said, but I allow my Daddy don't always know what he's talking about, specially now."

"He beginning to feel it now, is he?" asked the engineer.

"Shhh, it's a shame. He wonders in his mind, sometimes, talks to Mother. Sometimes he talks just as plain as you or me, only instead of real words he says sort of duck talk, 'qualk slootin, ketalkin gook,' stuff like that, just like he was saying real American, only . . ."

The dawn light had grown until the electric light was no longer needed. The young man rose, tugged at his shorts, then switched off the light. The room dimmed and cooled slightly with the blue daylight. After drawing another cup of coffee from the urn, the young man stood by the table looking down at the tugboatman. "I don't guess you know my Daddy, do you? You acquainted around Houma?"

"I been there many a time, though I wouldn't say I was acquainted. I don't know your Daddy."

"You're new on the *R. Thomas*, are you?" asked the engineer.

"On that boat, I'm new," answered the tugboatman, "but I've been working for this company, here and around, for, oh, long time."

"You put me in mind of somebody I used to know," said the young man, "though I can't rightly remember his name. You ever spend any time over around Lake Charles or Cameron, Cameron Parish?"

"Well, I've been over there," said the tugboatman, "but not recently."

"You sure look like this fella I used to know, though I just can't pick up his name."

"I think I know who you mean," said the engineer. "Only I'm like you, I can't recall his name."

"Well, it don't make no difference, you ain't him." The young man swallowed his coffee, set the cup on the table, and stepped to the kitchen door. Then he stepped through, after a moment's pause, onto the deck, and remained, clearly visible in the doorway, facing the Gulf and the rising sun.

"It's a shame," said the engineer, keeping his seat and talking out to him. "I'll sure hate to see your Daddy go."

"He's the same as gone now, keeps hanging on."

"I used to look up to your Daddy when I was a boy."

"Here come the shrimpers," said the young man, yawning and stretching his arms. Beyond him, the head of a long, long string of small white shrimp boats passed from the Gulf into the bay, going home past the derrick like a migration of birds. Beyond, still farther, the oil rigs sitting on tables in the waters of the Gulf no longer flashed demented lights but rose in the gray-blue sea like cool and thoughtful monuments.

"I never knew he had it so bad, he always looked strong as a mule to me," said the engineer.

"Shhh, he's had it for a *Long* time. Old Doctor says he might of had it from the day he was borned."

"*Is* that right?"

"I'll be the only one left," the young man said. "Maybe I'll get me a wife, though, and start us all up again before I get too old."

"Sure makes a man think," said the engineer, shaking his head. "You can't exactly call it a punishment. I mean, you're not old enough when you're a baby child to of *done* anything. I guess you can't exactly call it a punishment."

"Maybe I'll go shrimping," the young man said. He stepped toward the washroom, vanishing from the kitchen doorway. But to the eyes of the tugboatman his image seemed to linger.

"I don't know exactly what you would call it," said the engineer.

The tugboatman stared long into the lingering image of the young man as the white caravan of shrimpers passed the framing doorway, moving across the bay like camels crossing the face of the desert, and after a moment of deep thought, into the tugboatman's eyes came a look that clearly said, "I could tell you if I wanted to."

•

"Dancer's Cricket" (see page 91) was published in *Harper's Bazaar,* an unlikely place. The story delighted the late editor-in-chief, Mrs. Snow. When I first submitted the story, it was rejected by the girls in fiction, even though I was quite close to them all, as being inappropriate for a women's magazine of ultra-high fashion. But subsequently—I think because they knew I was broke—they asked for it back. It's a true story, of course, about the only fiction being the captain's name. It truly describes him. He was, indeed, his own Jonah.

The *Tiger*, an aging tanker whose home—if such a vagrant ship could be said to have a home—was Texas, shuttled for months and months fetching and carrying black oil from the Persian Gulf to England. Liverpool, the port of discharge, was the only port the crew, who had signed a year's articles, could go ashore in, and then only for a few hours. Each round trip took forty-two days.

After three such voyages winter came to the north, but the *Tiger*'s men fortunately gained a respite from both the weather and the sooty jungles of Liverpool when the vessel paused in Suez for stores and fuel, and George Dancer, master of the *Tiger*, received orders to discharge his fourth cargo in the South of France at Berre.

It was cold when the *Tiger* arrived there, but the sun shone and the air was clean and blue. Though it was only for one trip, this change lifted Captain Dancer's spirits. He authorized the purchase, as part of the ship's stores, of sixty-four bottles of ordinary wine—three cases of red and three of white—for the Christmas feast which would take place, according to rough calculations, off the southern coast of Arabia during the return voyage from Kuwait.

Out of his own commodious pocket he bought a case of Three-Star Martell for his officers' celebration. He had never done anything like that before and everyone who heard about it was amazed.

He also procured as a personal companion, for he had none aboard the *Tiger*, a small black poodle which he came to call Little Harold or Little Hubert, depending upon which name came first into his head. It was an adolescent when he bought it, and in subsequent weeks he trained it up in his own image.

He taught it to growl at sailors when they came onto the bridge, to snap at them if they made a sudden move, to play rough and earnestly with the will to win. He did not teach it, but it learned from him to trust no kindness from the hand of man, to follow a plate of food and snap at the hand that set it before him, to sleep with its black eyes open.

Soon it became its master's shadow and followed him like a shadow everywhere. That was what the captain wanted it to do, but sometimes, the poodle did not follow him but rather dogged his tracks. He could never swing around and pick it up in his arms and rub it against him like another pet or reach down and stroke its unclipped fur. He knew it would snap at him or even bite him, as indeed it did once, or worse yet, desert him.

When the master was on the bridge so was Little Harold, but he stayed off in a corner, curled up with his chin on his paws, waiting and watching and, if the weather was hot, panting with his pink little tongue stuck part way out, his shaggy black whiskers forked out along his paws, and looking for all the world like the Devil's messenger.

After thirty-six hours in the South of France, the *Tiger* sailed for the Persian Gulf again. Port Said was chilly when the vessel passed through and the Egyptians wore scarves, but the Red Sea was warm and became warmer almost by the hour as the ship moved south. In sight of Daedalus, the lighted shoal called Abul el Kizan, the *Tiger* broke down for several hours in the middle of the night, imperiling itself and other vessels on the busy track. When the ship was underway again, the captain called in the chief engineer and requested he make five more revolutions per hour in order to regain some of the time lost. The chief engineer warned that the extra strain would probably cause trouble, but the captain, certain that his fellow officer was out to discredit him, insisted, and the chief, who was a peaceful man, obeyed.

Five hundred miles farther on, in the still latitudes where the winds meet off the coast of the Sudan, the vessel broke down again. The chief did not say, "I told you so," but when he called the bridge to say he had stopped for repairs, the captain shouted into the telephone that he didn't see how anybody as stupid as he was could get to be even a tourist or a garbage man, let alone a chief.

Through a heavy twilight and a torpid night and on through the next morning while the sun blazed, the vessel drifted dead in the water. There was not a trace of a natural breeze and the men went about their work or lay in their cots on the poop deck wound around like mummies in sweat and stifling air. Some swore they would get off the *Tiger* even if they had to jump off in Egypt, and Goodwin, one of the sailors, said he would never, never sail a tanker again or make another trip with any man whatsoever whose name began with "D."

Some days later just inside the Persian Gulf a sandstorm struck across the narrow water though it was not the time of year for sandstorms. Billows of pink sand rolled across the Gulf as if it were not water at all but just another desert, scattering enormous green and yellow grasshoppers, crickets, and frantic birds and covering the blinded *Tiger* with dust until it looked as if its job was to plow the desert rather than to ply the sea.

Enough additional hours were lost creeping through the sand fog for the *Tiger* to certainly lose its berth in Mena al Ahmedi, the oil dock in the Kuwait sheikdom.

"There's a Joaner on this ship," the master said in his usual half-joking, half-threatening way. "I've felt it for a time now. Somebody's hexing me." To Captain Dancer "me" meant, of course, the *Tiger*.

It was just his way of talking, speaking of a Jonah, for it made him feel salty and in the old tradition to hark back to ancient sailors' fears. He had been a sailor himself, having come up in his work from the bottom and, like most sailors, he believed in luck and in the bad luck, for instance, that whistling on a vessel brings. It was just his way of talking, but he began to keep an eye out for an evildoer.

At Mena al Ahmedi the captain was forced to anchor out for thirty-eight hours in the tranquil shark-infested roads watching other ships go in ahead of him to load. He could lose his charter if that kind of thing kept up.

When he finally did get in to dock he had more trouble. Mr. Henke, the third mate and junior officer, visited the oil company's doctor and returned with a letter in duplicate saying, in effect, he was a nervous wreck.

He presented Captain Dancer with this letter, which was addressed to the master of the *S.S. Tiger* and which explained that Mr. Henke was of a disposition unsuited to such confinement as pertained to a tanker on a year's articles and with a long run.

It recommended that he be relieved of his position at the next port of discharge, sent to a hospital for a thorough mental and physical examination, and returned, if necessary, to America at the company's expense. Mr. Henke kept the duplicate.

Captain Dancer read the letter, glancing suspiciously from time to time at Mr. Henke. When he came to the end, he grunted and asked sarcastically what kind of lies Mr. Henke had told the doctor.

"I don't lie," Mr. Henke said, drawing himself up and quivering a little to bear out the doctor's diagnosis. "I told him the God's truth."

"Such as," the captain demanded.

"All right, since you ask me, I'll just tell you." Mr. Henke hooked his thumbs cockily into his trouser pockets and thrust his face forward until the two black moles on his forehead were right under the captain's nose. He was much shorter than Captain Dancer and, of course, much younger. He was scarcely twenty-five.

He said that ever since the trip began in Texas he, the captain, had done nothing but torment him and play jokes on him and give him extra work to do that he knew he couldn't do because it was his first trip on the bridge and then jump on him because he naturally made mistakes. He had told the doctor, he said, he got so rattled with the captain standing over him all the time that he made all kinds of stupid mistakes he wouldn't of made if the captain had just gone ahead and left him alone.

Then Mr. Henke repeated about a dozen specific grievances he had listed for the doctor, not the least of which was the captain's habit, which Mr. Henke said was downright deliberate, of coming up and turning on the chartroom radio as loud as it would go and picking up some program like crazy Arab music or that Radio Moscow program with the woman reading the same speech over and over all day long, then *him* running off down to his room where *he* couldn't hear it and blowing up if it wasn't still on when he come back. "That *one thing* is enough to drive *anybody* out of their feeble mind," Mr. Henke exclaimed. By that time he was red in the face and shaking violently and not because he thought he should.

They were in the captain's office. Without another word to his officer, Captain Dancer snatched up his wide gray Stetson, which he wore all over the world though he did not come from the West, and crammed it upon his head so hard the felt tipped over his ears. He strode out of his office and along the catwalk.

The little third mate, watching him go, danced with pleasure and agitation, crying, "Look at 'im go, look at 'im go, look at 'im go!"

With the letter clutched angrily in his hand, the captain marched straight up to the doctor's office which was in the company's infirmary just off the dock. There he caused a great deal of excitement. That particular doctor had given the captain trouble before by siding, as he usually did, with the men, and supporting their vaguest illnesses.

"He's no more nervous than I am," the Captain shouted, and the doctor replied that he was doing Captain Dancer a favor by allowing the man to make the trip back. Then the captain accused the doctor of taking a bribe, and the doctor ordered the captain out of his office.

Captain Dancer marched straight back to the *Tiger* still crushing the letter in his fist and muttering, "We'll see, we'll see."

It was not the company's money that worried him most, nor was it the sizable inconvenience of engaging a new mate in Liverpool, nor even Mr. Henke's impertinence. It was, rather, the personal insult of a man's contriving to leave his command.

It had happened before, many a time. Men he had been fond of, good men, had left him and he could not understand why. Jim Day, his radio operator, who was in a position to say things no one else dared to, told him once what the trouble was as he saw it. "You assume a man is dishonest by nature," he had said. "You take him for your enemy before you know him, and you make an enemy out of him because you force him to abandon his dignity to deal with you."

The captain had looked at him with his piercing, but uncomprehending, ratlike eyes and said, "My men have got to live with me; I don't have to live with them."

Sooner or later every living creature turned away from him. His wife had left him not so long before, his two adolescent sons away in school took his money but never came around where he was. On the second trip through the Suez Canal two little land birds of the indiscriminate breed called "sailors' friends" had hopped aboard and stayed. The captain had fed them because he liked to be kind to what he called "poor creatures." Many a hot afternoon he had sat in his underwear on the boat deck spying on the sailors at work on the deck below, and sprinkled meal for the two birds that hopped and pecked around his feet. He didn't have Little Harold then.

The birds lived around the midship house and played and quarreled constantly. If the captain closed his eyes, the rustling of the sea sounded like poplar leaves and he could imagine the birds teetering and darting in the tops of the trees as birds had done when he was a child. But even they, the sailors' friends, had left him. They had disappeared one day from the midship house and turned up back aft by the crew's quarters. They never came back, and he claimed they had been kidnapped.

Less than nine hours after it had tied up at the dock, the *Tiger,* turgid with oil and a little down at the head, got underway again for the twenty-one day voyage back to Liverpool; twenty-one days, that is, with good weather and good luck. It was five days to Christmas.

The very first night out the tanker hit a freak storm. There came a tremendous flood of rain and a wild wind that swooped around the vessel and scooped up the sea quickly building high scrolled waves and jumbling them in every direction. Being poorly loaded, the *Tiger* rammed each towering sea like a man dumbly beating his head against a wall. Shortly, the rain stopped, the clouds moved away revealing hard bright stars overhead, but neither the wind nor the waves abated.

Captain Dancer kept watch in the wheelhouse, with the second mate on the wing of the bridge, while the poor helmsman struggled with the wheel which was taking three turns right and left just to keep to any kind of course at all.

"Oh keep to the course, can't you?" the captain said in despair to the helmsman.

"I can't Cap'n" the helmsman answered irritable. "She steers like a block of concrete."

The captain grunted and braced himself against the bulkhead by the porthole and stared out with a black look at the equally black and aggressive sea. Aloud he repeated, "Shame, shame," like an old lady, and closed his eyes each time the vessel's head rushed stupidly at a tall hard wave. "Oh shame on him," he said.

Each time the *Tiger* pitched, the pencil on the bellbook desk rolled, and on one particularly large sea, it hopped the ledge of the desk and dropped to the floor.

"Stoopid, stoopid," the captain muttered, referring to whichever officer it had been that had finished loading his ship and left it in such a condition. Then he began to pace. Accidentally he stepped on the pencil. He reached down automatically and picked it up and put it back on the desk where it began to roll again.

"Did you top off this oilcan?" the captain shouted out to the second mate. The wind was too strong for the officer to hear, but the man on the wheel volunteered the information that it had been Mr. Henke.

"Wouldn't you know it," the master said.

The pencil hopped off the desk again, and again the master picked it up. He returned to his post by the porthole and the pencil hopped off again and rolled across the floor to his feet. In sudden wrath he seized the pencil, held it up before his eyes, and shook it violently. "You little bastard," he said threateningly with his lips tense and his eyes squinted almost shut. "That third mate brought you in here; he's no good and neither are you."

When the chief mate relieved the second mate at four o'clock the sleepless captain was still on the bridge though the wind had stopped and the swells were smoothing away. The instant the captain caught sight of the mate he lashed out at him.

"How come you didn't notice she was down at the head?" he asked.

"How come *you* didn't?" the mate snapped back. He was always irritable just after being awakened at three-forty in the morning, and that morning the erratic pitching of the *Tiger* had so disturbed his sleep he was irascible enough to say things he wouldn't ordinarily have said. "*I* had nothing to do with it. Henke topped off, not me."

"Makes no difference, you know how stoopid he is, you should of kept an eye out, it's your job—"

"Cap'n, I didn't want to bring this up, but if you'll just think back, you'll remember I stood right here when we were leaving and told you we were down at the head and you said, no. And I made the suggestion that we ought to anchor and even her off because we might hit some rough weather but you wouldn't take the time—"

"It's your job," the captain said.

" 'We can do it in the Red before we hit any weather,' you said."

"It's your job."

"And it's *your* ship, you've said so often enough."

"Well I never heard any mate talk to his master like that before."

"You're not quite dead yet, Cap'n; you've got a *lot* of things to hear before you die."

"You'd better apologize."

"All right, I apologize. I'm sorry. I *am* sorry. I shouldn't have spoken like that but, Cap'n, every once in a while you get on a man's nerves."

The quartermaster, Goodwin, heard the whole argument, for it took place directly in front of him, and he could hardly wait until breakfast time to warn the deck gang about it. He knew what the result of the argument would be because he knew the captain's habits. Bright and early in the morning the captain would be out on deck in a frenzy, turning everything upside down.

He would have his gloves on and his most mistrustful face, and by casting aside the work the mate had ordered, and changing men from job to job, and standing over them making remarks while they tried to work, he could, after an hour or so, inject such disorder into a day's operations that it would seem to the sailors, as it had seemed so often before, that their very tools took on his nature and conspired against them. As tempers tautened, ropes would snarl and part, hammer heads fly off their handles, paint cans tumble down steps, and winches jam.

The captain did not need an argument to set him off, nor did he need to set foot on the deck to disturb the peace. Boredom would set him going, or anger within himself, or suspicion. Some days he would pretend to be taking the sun or reading a book in a chair in the open air, but he was watching everyone he could, and the men who were forced to work in the open felt his eyes on them. It made them begin to suspect themselves, and to feel guilty just walking the decks; and it made them pick at each other for little reasons or for no reason at all.

"This ship's no home," Goodwin frequently remarked, "it's a penitentiary."

Goodwin was wrong about the next day, however. The rainstorm, like the sandstorm, brought some birds and insects with it and washed some flying fish aboard. The fish lay strewn about the decks next morning, wide-eyed and gasping in the quiet daylight. The birds ate the insects and flew back to greener islands, and the Arab cook, Halim, gathered the fish, slit them, stuffed them with salt, and hung them up like Chinese kites to dry.

By the time the *Tiger* turned out of the Persian Gulf into the Gulf of Oman, the only living alien creature left from the storm was a cricket that had begun to sing as soon as the sea had quieted and the sun came up.

It had lodged itself during the tempest in some crevice of the bridge, and after the wind and rain, the dawn was so still the sailor standing lookout on the bow could hear the singing. It sounded very near to him, and he began to look forward to Christmas.

It sounded so good to Captain Dancer, he forgot all about

the storm and his trouble with the mate. He figured if a cricket could bring good luck to a household, it could bring it to a ship. After he had slept some, he awoke in the afternoon with the decision that the smartest thing he could do would be to capture the cricket and keep it safely in his room where it could go ahead and bring about, unmolested, such luck as it chose.

"The best thing for a Joaner," he said to himself, "is a cricket."

He looked around his office and found a little box, then he went to the bridge to trace down the insect. Its chirping, he found, came from the port wing, but he could not locate its hiding place exactly because each time he approached too near to it, the noise stopped.

All that day, at odd times when he happened to be on the bridge and heard the cricket, he went out to hunt it down, ignoring the smart remarks of the mates, the radio operator, and even the sailors at the wheel.

At nightfall when he gave up trying to find it, he decided the next best thing to do would be to feed it. From breakfast the next morning he brought a saucer of scrambled eggs and tucked it up in the beams in the overhead of the port wing, well out of the dog's reach. Mr. Henke was on watch, and as soon as the captain stepped into the chartroom he fed the eggs to Little Harold.

The next day the captain put out more eggs which vanished in the same way, and the third day, the day before Christmas, Captain Dancer, who had been going about in very high spirits and cracking jokes and talking about his Christmas party, put out the eggs again and retired as usual to examine the charts.

He sang to himself as he stepped off the days to go to Aden and calculated the speed from the noon the previous day to Ras al Hadd which had come abeam at dawn.

"Boy, oh boy," he exclaimed. The speed had been very good indeed. Of course there was a following breeze and a favorable current, and since the chief mate had shifted around the cargo, the *Tiger* sat better in the water. It had averaged a good fourteen knots. "Boy, oh boy," the captain chuckled to himself, "the greyhound of Oman."

"Cap'n, Cap'n, come here quick if you want to see something," Mr. Henke called as he crossed the wheelhouse to the chartroom door. The master looked sourly at him, but he hurried to the port wing when Mr. Henke added, "It's your cricket."

The third mate followed the captain who found Little Harold out on the wing of the bridge, stalking the cricket which had come out of its hiding place. Each time the cricket hopped, Little Harold sprang after it until he had it cornered. The captain, looking in dismay from one creature to another, was unable to decide whether to let the dog alone and lose his luck or save his luck and maybe lose his only friend. His instant's hesitation was too long. Little Harold yapped, pounced upon the cricket, and ate it.

"There goes your cricket," Mr. Henke said, spluttering into laughter. "And in nothing but one gulp."

"*You* set him on it," the captain said still bewildered. "You been a thorn in my side ever since you come on here."

"How could I? I didn't know where it was any more than you did. I looked out and there they were, just like you saw them."

"You ain't getting paid to play with my dog."

"I wasn't playing with your dog."

"You're supposed to be tending to business, not playing with my dog. If you're so nervous, you better stay away from my dog, he'll take a . . . piece out of you."

Mr. Henke shrugged his shoulders, turned on his heel and retired to the opposite wing of the bridge.

"Wouldn't you, Little Harold?" said the captain. "Yes, you would." He reached out his hand but the poodle backed away, lay down, and rolled its eyes upward toward its master. It began a whine that changed to a growl as the hand drew nearer. "Wouldn't you?" soothed the captain, slowly withdrawing his hand. "Poor Little Hubert."

For several minutes the master paced the wing of the bridge

from the wheelhouse door to the very tip, approaching the railing with the pathetic demeanor of an insect which, having long labored its way by instinct along an undeviating track, finds itself at length frustrated by an enormous stone. Each time, his eyes, like feelers, explored the sea. He turned, paced again, and again felt out the ocean with his gaze. Finally he said, "Come on, Little Harold," and he went below with his fuzzy black shadow of a dog scampering along behind him.

That evening, Christmas Eve, Mr. Henke, before he left his room to resume his watch, looked in his desk drawer for some matches and discovered that his copy of the letter describing him as a nervous wreck was gone.

The next day was more like Midsummer day than Christmas. At noon the islands of Korya Morya had just passed astern, the temperature touched eighty-six, and the wind, unseasonably, remained a mewing kitten breeze that tagged along behind the *Tiger*.

It seemed that all the fish in the ocean had come to feed and sun there, for the weedy sea was like a meadow. Whales and spotted blackfish rolled in the sun, dolphins split the waves, and banks of tiny white fowl flew up at the ship's approach and fell again, like a shower of paper, farther on. The clear air was riddled with the greedy cries of terns and wheeling gulls who saw a feast in all the fishes.

For months the *Tiger*'s steward had prepared for Christmas dinner. On Thanksgiving he had slyly mixed in slices of duck with slices of turkey to make the store of turkey do for Christmas. In Provence he had ordered nuts and apples; in Egypt, melons and oranges; and in England, each trip, he had added to his store of sweets. The tables were laid with white cloths even for the unlicensed crew, and from half past eleven to half past twelve the feast was spread.

Half of the red and half of the white wine were put out together. Besides turkey and cranberry sauce, there were baked ham with raisin sauce, mashed potatoes, sweet potatoes, broccoli, succotash, coleslaw, hot rolls, corn bread, pumpkin pie, hot mince pie with brandy, hot raisin pie with brandy, melon and coffee. Relishes of celery, olives, and pickles, and a tomato juice cocktail preceded the turkey.

Everyone ate and drank too much. At five o'clock the rest of the wine was served with a supper of lamb chops, and after sunset, when the shore had crept nearer and crouched like a sooty leopard in the moonlight, Captain Dancer, although he did not feel like having a party, invited all his officers except those on watch into the midship saloon. With a marlinspike he pried open the case of brandy and, brushing off clinging excelsior, handed each guest a bottle. He took a bottle for himself, opened it, and poured drinks all around; then he raised his glass and said, sourly, "Some Christmas." After that he took his bottle and the case and he sat down by himself in a corner.

Jim Day, the radio operator, carried down his record player from the radio shack and put on a long-playing record of Christmas carols. The men sat around quietly, somewhat leadenly, sipping their brandies and listening to the boys' chorus.

The high voices hurt Little Harold's ears and his occasional howls, mixed with *Adeste Fideles, O Little Town of Bethlehem,* and *Silent Night,* drifted across the water to the Moslem shore.

"Black little devil," said Mr. Henke on the bridge. "Listen to him howl." In spite of Christmas the junior officer had eaten little, but since he had lost his letter he had been drinking considerably on his own. He spoke in frantic whispers to Ferguson, his helmsman. "He means to keep me on here like a prisoner. Just *listen* to him howl."

Ferguson, who was keeping a sorry course, sang softly with the music for a while, then he said, "Let him howl. What can you do about him? What can any of us?"

"Do you make it out?" Mr. Henke asked. "He hates me, he says I'm more harm that good to him, but he won't let me off. Do you make it out?"

"I know this for sure," answered the melancholy Ferguson, "this is no happy ship. Even back aft there, for weeks now he's had everybody so jumpy they're just waiting for the gong to tear each other apart, Christmas or no Christmas, yet they all like each other. You take the deck gang, *we* all like each other, yet still—I don't know, when this year's up I'm going to get me a happy ship."

He gave the wheel a turn to bring the vessel back to the course he had drifted from. "You wait and see, before this night's over there's going to be a lot go on that wouldn't on a happy ship."

It was not long before Ferguson's prediction came true. Goodwin came into the saloon leading Tango the Englishman, who was bleeding from cuts in his head, saying that Tango had fallen down a ladder and would somebody please bandage him up.

Hopping out of his chair, the captain cried, "What's going on back there?"

"Nothing's going on," Goodwin said, and Captain Dancer said it was a shame that men couldn't even behave themselves on Christmas. He hustled the two men out the door and around the corner of the passageway into the hospital. He poured some alcohol on Tango's wounds, which were not severe, and carelessly wrapped some gauze around his head, then he hurried out the door and locked the two sailors in saying, "I suppose you think I didn't invent that trick about the ladder."

When he passed the saloon he poked his head in the door to make sure his guests had not slipped off to form a party of their own, then he rushed out into the moonlight, flailing his shadowy arms, and flew aft along the catwalk to get to the bottom of the trouble. That took him longer than he had expected, and when he returned to the saloon he found Tango and Goodwin, who had climbed out the hospital porthole, drinking his brandy with his officers.

"You got no call to lock us up, we didn't do anything," Goodwin said immediately.

"I ought to lock you all up, you're nothing but a bunch of troublemakers," the master shouted. "What are you doing in my saloon? I don't want no sailors in my saloon. Get out." As they stepped out the door, he shouted after them, "And you can tell all those drunkards back aft there that I mean what I said just now, and if you don't do what I told you, you'll *all* regret the day you had the bad luck to scent salt water."

Breathing heavily, he dropped into his chair and noticed he had lost two members of his party. His disappointment showed clearly on his face, and Jim Day explained that the mate, who was one of the truants, had said he was tired and had gone to bed.

"Since when does he get so tired," the captain muttered. For a while he sat in silence on the edge of his chair by one of the doors and seemed to be keeping guard.

Since he and his officers had nothing to say to each other, his officers politely ignored him and talked among themselves. Suddenly he jumped up, roughly replaced the record of carols on the player, and turned up the volume to its limit, thus making conversation of any kind impossible. In addition, Little Harold began to howl again and howled continuously. This amused the master, who laughed, but it annoyed his guests.

Fortunately for them, Captain Dancer was restless. After a quarter of an hour and five or six fast brandies, he jumped to his feet again and went out the door to prowl the decks and the bridge. Little Harold went with him and Jim Day dashed to his record player, unplugged it, and carried it out of the room. He came back shortly and found his fellow officers exclaiming against the master's infuriating ways and telling each other all over again their more serious grievances against him. Not a man was there that had not promised himself, after some moment of anger or humiliation provoked by the master, that some day he would pay him back. Each of them, of course, had been strong and intelligent enough to satisfy himself with promises. The chief engineer, in particular, took great pride in his ability to forbear.

Abruptly the discussion ended when William, a fireman of Italian parentage, wandered tearfully into the saloon. The chief engineer gave him a glass of brandy and asked him what the trouble was. William, who was in his pajamas, explained that, as they probably knew, there had been a big fight and after it was over everybody had been sitting around having a good time in the messroom, drinking wine and singing and forgetting their little differences like they should, when the captain roared in saying he wanted to know who had started it. Nobody knew who had started it and nobody cared, but the captain said if somebody didn't come up and tell him who started it, he would take two days' pay from everybody.

And now, William cried, they were all back there fighting worse than ever trying to decide whose fault it was. As he spoke his tears increased, because telling about it reminded him of how disappointed he was that Christmas was spoiled.

The chief asked William what he was doing wandering around and the fireman said he had come up to tell the captain that he had done it.

"Done what?" asked the captain, stepping unexpectedly into the room. "What are you doing in my saloon? I don't want no firemen in my saloon. Get out."

"I came up to say I started the fight," said William.

"You men must think this is a joke," the master said. "Get out of here and tell them back there I give them until noon tomorrow to send me the real instigator."

"But, Cap'n, I—"

"Get out of my saloon! What do you guys think this is, a bar?"

William returned to his part of the ship, and the captain sat down again in his same chair, beginning steadily and earnestly to drink up his bottle. He brooded over his unruly crew and his unfriendly and dissembling officers who, even then, spoke in muted tones among themselves. One by one, as the long evening wore away, the guests departed, and the sodden captain made no move to detain them. He came to the end of his bottle and reached out toward the case for another, but he withdrew his hand when he remembered that bottle, the last one, was for Mr. Henke.

At twenty minutes to twelve the sailor Ferguson stuck his head in the door and reminded the second mate it was twenty minutes to twelve. At that time, near the change of the watch, only three men, besides the captain and the second mate, remained—the chief engineer, the first assistant engineer and the radio operator.

When the second mate took his leave in order to take over the bridge, the captain said to him, "Tell that stoopid Henke to come down here."

A few minutes later the saloon clock struck the eight bells that ended Christmas, and the officers listened while the bells were repeated on the bridge and struck still again, some seconds later, on the deep brass bell on the fo'c'sle head. Everyone felt a little relieved.

"*There* you are," the captain said, as the third mate stepped rather shakily through the door. "Hey, Henke, I hear you're nervous."

Mr. Henke approached the captain and asked did he want to see him about something.

"Can you prove you're nervous?" the captain pursued. "I hear you got a letter to prove how nervous you are. Let me see it."

"Somebody stole it," Mr. Henke said.

"Somebody stole it, is that right?"

The master roared with laughter. When he had calmed down, he said, "Son, you never had no letter, you had a dream."

"I had a letter and you know it, and the consul in Liverpool's going to know it too. He'll get me off of here, and he might get you a little something besides."

Again the master laughed, then in an instant he put on his pinched and vicious look and said, "I got news for you, you're going to *rot* on this *Tiger*."

Mr. Henke turned away.

"Where are you going?" the master demanded.

"I'm going to bed, Cap'n." He started across the room, but Jim Day detained him, shoving a glass of brandy into his hand.

"That's not your brandy," the captain said. "Here." He rose from his chair, staggered, balanced himself, then reached into the pine case and pulled out the last bottle. "Here, this is your brandy," he said, thrusting the bottle in Mr. Henke's direction. "It's your Christmas present."

Mr. Henke said he wouldn't be caught dead taking a Christmas present from him, and he walked out.

The captain called after him, then followed him, still holding out the bottle by its neck.

The three guests remaining in the saloon heard the master bump from one bulkhead to another as he passed along the narrow passageway.

They heard Mr. Henke's door open once and slam, and open and close again. Little Harold followed along but did not get into Mr. Henke's room.

Several minutes passed and Captain Dancer did not return. The officers, who were a little uncertain of their own steps, sat down again and started to finish off the bottle on the table. The first assistant asked why some guys couldn't leave other guys alone, and the chief said he had some influence with the company and would personally lodge a complaint against the master at the end of the voyage, particularly if the master ever dared insult him again.

Several more silent minutes passed, then there was a crash that set Little Harold to barking. Before anyone had a chance to stir himself to see what it was, the master came stumbling and wailing along the passageway to the door of the saloon. He stood there with his head back, his hands over his eyes that poured blood through his fingers and down his arms. All he could say was, "Look what he did to me."

For an instant none of the officers could move, so unexpected was the sight of blood.

"Look what he did to me!" the master piteously cried, still covering his bleeding eyes with his palms.

They crowded around him then, and Jim Day took his elbow and guided him across the saloon and through the opposite door and up the steps to the cabin while the others, now joined by the chief mate who had come out of his room when he heard the noise, hurried into Mr. Henke's room. They found him mostly undressed lying back on his bed clutching a pillow over his face. When they pulled the pillow away and Mr. Henke saw them, he began to struggle. The first assistant ran up to the captain's room for the handcuffs while the other two dragged the junior officer to the shower. They shoved him into it, turned it on, and assailed him with questions: What did you do it with? Where is the weapon?

"You'll never find out," he shouted.

When the first assistant returned with the handcuffs, they turned off the cold water, pulled Mr. Henke dripping from the shower, pushed him down on the tiled floor, and cruelly locked his wrist to the lavatory pipe.

"To lay violent hands upon the master!" the chief engineer exclaimed in anger and disbelief. "To lay violent hands upon the master!"

Up in the captain's room, Jim Day washed and examined and bandaged up the victim's wounds. He gave him a shot of penicillin and a heavy sedative and stayed with him until morning.

Five days passed and Captain Dancer did not emerge from his bedroom. He kept the outside door open, for it was hot, and the sailors working around the bridge could look through the screen door into the dim chamber and see the master flat on his back with both eyes bandaged up blind. Little Harold kept to the room as well.

No one visited them except the steward, who personally brought what little food the master and his dog ate, and of course Jim Day, who tended the wounds. After several days Jim Day was able to remove the bandage from the right eye, allowing the master to see at least that much, but the left eye had been so deeply gouged that he was almost afraid to touch it. He continued the shots of penicillin, which he also gave to Tango for the cuts in his head. He dressed those wounds, too, and put down overtime for it all.

Meanwhile, Mr. Henke had been released by order of the master who made no threats of retribution. The master had called the mate to him and suggested nothing be entered in the logbook for the time being. "Not until my memory comes back," he said.

Mr. Henke, too, claimed to remember nothing. He said he had awakened in wet underwear on his bathroom floor, chained to the drainpipe and, shortly after the mate had come in and taken off the irons, he, Mr. Henke, had discovered some very painful bruises on his throat. He would not venture to say, of course, that that the master had tried to strangle him because, as he said, he didn't remember a thing, but the marks certainly looked like fingermarks to him. There had been no weapon; he guessed he must have used his thumbs. He told everyone how sorry he was, but at night he slept deeply and dreamlessly as he had not done in months.

The master did not sleep at all. The barbiturates he depended upon soon had no more effect than to toss him into a wakeful, spectered slumber. The ship's penicillin, obtained in France, was contained in a saline solution to which, it soon became apparent, the master was violently allergic. He turned red and swelled up and itched miserably, and spots appeared on his face and feet and hands.

Each morning he asked after the condition of Jim Day's other patient, Tango, and inquired if the same affliction had befallen him. Jim Day said no, not yet, and the master said bitterly that he didn't have to worry because it wouldn't.

He asked Jim Day to scout around and find out how much the crew knew about what he called "his trouble." "You know how a ship is," Jim Day answered immediately; "everybody knows everything."

The master also asked if any troublemaker had come up from back aft to confess he had started the fight on Christmas and Jim Day said no, he had seen no one, that everything had been peaceful.

The fifth day after Christmas, the master called in the chief mate and the chief engineer and ordered, in view of New Year's Eve coming up, a general search of all lockers and fo'c'sles aft. Any wine or liquor they found was to be confiscated and thrown overside.

While this was being done, the master stirred himself, bathed and shaved as best he could, then called a general muster of all hands after coffeetime at three-twenty.

It was a cool breezy day in the north end of the Red Sea and the crew gathered on the boat deck with shirts flapping. On bare swollen feet Captain Dancer hobbled onto the bridge and looked down with his one unbandaged eye upon his men, none of whom had seen him in the light of day since Christmas. All puffed up and spotted he was a startling sight, with the white bandage on one eye glaring in the sun.

He said, "There's been some fist fights among you men." This caused a general stir and elicited a few snickers. "You might think it's funny now. I'm talking to you who were mixed up in it. I know who you are and so do you. Maybe you remember I told you to come tell me who started it; well, I haven't been told. Anybody have anything to say?"

Nobody did.

"All right, have it your own way and take your punishment."

Goodwin spoke up and said they had tried to decide who was to blame for everything and they decided that none of them were, but that he didn't care that much about his money so he'd say that he started it.

"That won't do," said the captain. "I want the real instigator." No one else stepped forth. "All right, now, what I want to tell you is that this is going to stop."

His listeners strained to hear, for the wind blew some of his words away and his lips were so swollen he could not speak clearly.

"You men can get along if you want to, you don't have to be —oh I spect you're all mad because I took your liquor. Well go ahead. I should of done it a long time ago. You do something for somebody, you try to do something nice, and it comes back in your face. I authorized that wine to make Christmas cheerful. I knew it was hard being away so long and out in the ocean on Christmas and that's why I did it. Well, I'll never do it again. And I don't want another drop to come on this ship as long as I'm master. You all hear? And I want all this quarreling and fighting and beating each other up to stop. Now it's *going* to stop—you know I can make a lot of trouble for you all."

A gust of wind whipped around the corner of the bridge and threatened to rip off his bandage. He clapped his hand on it and with the other hand, after momentarily releasing the rail that kept him from tottering, he quickly waved his men away.

Thankful to be released, they crowded toward the ladders to the catwalk and the deck, and they broke into discussion even before they were out of the master's hearing. Captain Dancer heard one of the men make an ill-concealed remark to another, saying that in his opinion the best job for him, meaning the master, would be a lighthouse keeper where he would be kept away from human beings.

That night, when the master could not sleep again because of his afflictions, he remembered that remark as he sat on the edge of his bed and looked out his screen door and across the water to Abul el Kizan which was just then coming abeam. He was well acquainted with its flashing light and the stony isolated cluster of knuckles its tower stood upon.

What a terrible thing, he thought, for one man to say about another. What a terrible thing to be compelled to live out there and watch the ships pass by and pass by and have to tend the light that warned them all away from him.

He called Little Harold and the dog came up and lay down several feet from him and kept him distant company. "Poor Little Harold," the master cooed. "Little Harold, there's a Joaner on my ship."

The light in the sea flashed once, twice, three times, and the master repeated to himself that there was a Jonah on his ship, but he could not understand, nor was it likely he would ever understand who it was.

•

All Men Are Mariners, an excerpt from the novel (see page 18), originally published by McGraw-Hill Book Company in 1962. This is the story, with a good many departures from the truth, of my stay in Copenhagen after paying off the *Seatiger* and my falling in love with Aase Hansen, a married lady now divorced. Though I saw her again ten years later when I was in Scandinavia, though we made love and fell in love again, ten years hadn't changed us enough to enable us to put things together. This excerpt, however, only involves the character who was, in real life, the actor, Melvyn Douglas.

You know Nick's father, everybody does. His name is Armand Singer, the baritone, the voice that everybody's mother loves, star of stage, screen, radio, the Metropolitan, La Scala, Rome, Vienna, San Francisco. He was one of the most famous, youngest, and most energetic Don Giovannis in the history of the opera; his Escamillo and Mephistopheles filled the gilded palaces of two continents during the late thirties. He sang Boris in Russian for the first time since Chaliapin. Before the war he rose to national popular fame on a Sunday night radio program that competed with Jack Benny and Charlie McCarthy. After he and Nick's mother were divorced, he remarried and went to Hollywood to make movies. He sang for the services overseas and on the front lines all during the war, traveling thousands and thousands of miles, returning to Hollywood when the war was over. There, during the infamous investigations of 1947 he was named by one of the professional namers who cited his knowledge of Russian (Boris) and mentioned to the investigators that he had seen several Russian novels in Mr. Singer's personal library. He landed on the blacklist. His wife divorced him. He moved back to Manhattan, a marked man.

I saw him there that May of '52 while I was hanging around the island waiting for my passage to London.

I had seen Pete's father the night before, and, although it was seven o'clock in the evening I was still hung-over (Pete's old man lays a heavy hand on the applejack). The day had been soft and warm, almost unbearably suggestive as those days of spring can be in dirty New York, calling up places and people buried deep in the past and the future, arousing restless hungers, some clear and some nameless.

My hunger that evening was no mystery, it was alimentary, if you'll suffer a pun—I don't make many—and I stopped in one of those hamburger paradises on Madison or in the east Forties, I don't remember where because I had been walking up and down the city all afternoon restlessly pacing the avenues, taking the spring like booze, getting drunk again on the air, and by the time my stomach forced me to stop walking and eat, I didn't know exactly where I was, and I didn't care. I chose the paradise because it was there. I sat at the counter and there was Nick's father three stools away. I glanced at the famous face, wondering for an odd moment where I had seen it before, and it looked back at me, old, almost intolerably melancholy. The loneliness that emanated from those idol's eyes, before they brightened with recognition, sent a chill down my spine.

"Tom?" he said in a voice that had thrilled millions. "Is that you? Tom? Tom McKinley?"

"Hello, Mr. Singer, I thought that was you," I said.

"Tom? I thought you were at sea. Well I'll be damned. Come sit by me, boy."

I shifted over the two empty stools. We had a heavenly hamburger together and coffee-divine, and he asked me when I had last seen Nick; and I asked him when *he* had last seen Nick. "I'm going to Copenhagen in a few days, and I'll see him there," I said.

"His mother and I spent our honeymoon in Copenhagen," he said.

"I'm looking forward to going," I said, carefully neglecting to mention my bizarre visit to Covington.

"I'm told it can be a very . . . ah . . . stimulating place for a single young man." He smiled.

"So I've heard."

"I guess Nick's pretty much out of the competition . . . Have you met his wife?"

"Amalie? No. I haven't got there yet."

"I forgot, you're just going, aren't you? Forgive me, I've been pushing pretty hard lately."

He was making his comeback in a satirical musical—called *His Majesty*—that Gorshin and Lutz had contrived from the *Charterhouse of Parma*.

He played the lecherous paranoid King, which had been written up into the main part along with the Duchess, Fabrizio being reduced to a conventional juvenile. It was a great comic part, and both Mr. Singer and the show were smashing successes—but he was on stage almost the entire evening—a very strenuous job for a man his age. He told me to come around the theater some night and catch the show, and I said I would if I could.

And when he had gone to work I had another cup of coffee, which came free from the waiter, who was awed by my familarity with such a famous man.

As I slowly drank my coffee I could not get Mr. Singer's look of melancholy out of my mind and I remembered Nick telling me once that when all the bad times were falling like the curses of Job on his father's head, there had been no one close to him, nobody around. Nick could have been there, but he was not, and he was sorry afterward that he hadn't come when he heard about it, but he told me he was afraid. He didn't know what he was afraid of, perhaps that he loved his father. At that time, he was already becoming enamored of communism and his father's liberalism seemed foolishly idealistic to him, and how could one admit loving a foolish, idealistic old matinee idol.

Those days were over and Nick's father was successful again and busy, two essentials for a theater man, but an evening in spring, whether you're young or old, whether you're going like me or coming back like him, can unbalance the spirit; and when he had picked up my check and said good-bye, he called me Nick. He apologized at once, saying, "I'm sorry, Tom, I *meant* to say Tom, I—I didn't mean to call you Nick."

"That's all right," I said; "people call me everything you can think of."

What's wrong with our world these days, that we are so separate and so far apart, even when we need each other? What's happened to our continuity? What's happened to fathers and sons that they don't even know one from another, that we are let out like seeds to fly on the wind, and wander, detached from our beginnings? I ask these questions, but man, I don't give the answers. We're a pathetic mess of people; we're not tragic, we're just plain pathetic. It was very disappointing for me to find that out.